THE CONVEYANCERS' YEARBOOK 2008

The Conveyancers' Yearbook 2008

Russell Hewitson LLB
Solicitor and Principal Lecturer in Law, Northumbria University
Property Law Consultant with Blackett Hart & Pratt, Solicitors,
Newcastle-upon-Tyne

Shaw & Sons

Shaw's
Since 1750

Published by
Shaw & Sons Limited
Shaway House
21 Bourne Park
Bourne Road
Crayford
Kent DA1 4BZ

www.shaws.co.uk

© Shaw & Sons Limited 2008

Published June 2008

ISBN 978 0 7219 1760 3
ISSN 1462-8201

A CIP catalogue record for this book is available from the
British Library

Printed in Great Britain by
Antony Rowe, Chippenham

CONTENTS

Contents

Contents

Contents

ALPHABETICAL LIST OF CASES

PREFACE

The purpose of this book is to provide conveyancers across all branches of the legal profession and other professionals involved in the property world with a summary of the main changes which have happened over the past year. The book is not intended to be comprehensive and is not a substitute for a textbook, nor for more detailed reading. It merely aims to provide a quick-reference guide to the main and most important changes in conveyancing over that period. As such, it contains a summary of the most important court decisions, ranging over a broad field of conveyancing and landlord and tenant law. The choice of cases is necessarily subjective but it is hoped that those included in the text will be both useful and of interest to the reader.

The past year has seen the introduction of Home Information Packs on which this year's book includes a dedicated section. There is also a section covering the new energy performance requirements.

The remaining sections of the book give a resumé of changes in the areas of statute law, other recent developments, a look at what the future holds; and a reference section at the end of the book which contains a list of new publications, recently published articles and the addresses of some useful websites. Websites are notorious for changing their addresses without notice, but the addresses given were correct at the date of publication.

As always, a special note of thanks is due to my wife Andrea for her support and encouragement during the writing of this book. Finally, this book is dedicated to my daughter, Dominique.

The law is stated as at 1 March 2008, though I have been able, with the publisher's indulgence, to incorporate one or two subsequent changes.

Russell Hewitson
Cleadon Village, Sunderland

THE AUTHOR

Russell Hewitson is a solicitor and Principal Lecturer in Law at the University of Northumbria at Newcastle. He specialises in Conveyancing, Landlord and Tenant Law, and Licensing Law and has lectured extensively on these subjects. He is the author of *Business Tenancies* (Blackstone Press Ltd), *Liquor Licensing and Young Persons* (Northumbria Law Press) and co-author of *Blackstone's Guide to Landlord and Tenant Covenants: Understanding the New Law and Conveyancing in Practice* (Northumbria Law Press).

THE LAW REPORTS AND ABBREVIATIONS REFERRED TO IN PART A

Part A

RECENT CASES

---

1 *ADVERSE POSSESSION*

1.1 Ofulue v Bossert

[2008] EWCA Civ 7; The Times, 11 February 2008

The facts:

In 1976, the appellants became the registered owners of a property.
Soon afterwards they went to live in Nigeria. In 1981, a former
tenant let the respondent and her father into the property. The
property was in a state of disrepair and, in June 1981, a closing order
was made. The father looked after the property, carried out repairs
and paid the rates, but did not pay any rent. In 1983, the appellants
became aware that the respondent and her father occupied the
property, but it was not until 1987 that they began proceedings
for possession. The father counterclaimed, arguing that he had
undertaken extensive work on the property having been offered a 14-
year lease in return for completion of the work. In 1991 and 1992,
the father made, without prejudice, offers to purchase the freehold
of the property, but these were rejected. In 1996, the father died
and the appellants failed to pursue their action for possession, which
was automatically stayed in 2000 under the Civil Procedure Rules.
In August 2000, they served a notice to quit on the respondent and
applied unsuccessfully to lift the stay on their possession proceedings.
In 2001, the appellants returned to the UK and asked that the
respondent vacate the property. She refused and they issued a further
notice to quit, followed by proceedings seeking possession of the
property. In her defence, the respondent contended that ownership
of the property had been passed to her by way of adverse possession.
The county court held that the respondent had acquired the property
by adverse possession, which meant that the appellants' title had
been extinguished. The appellants appealed.

1

The decision:

The appeal was dismissed. It was necessary to show only that the person who claimed to have acquired the property by adverse possession was in possession without the consent of the paper owner and intended to possess. A person who wrongly believed that he was a tenant could occupy property in such a way that he had possession, just as much as a squatter. He did not have to show that he had an intention to exclude the paper owner. The service of the defence and counterclaim did not prevent the running of time in the respondent's favour for the purposes of the 1980 Act. There was no reason in principle why a statement in the pleading could not constitute an acknowledgement. Starting proceedings stopped time running for the purpose of those proceedings.

Comment:

This is an interesting case as the Court of Appeal considered the role of the English courts when applying the decision of the European Court of Human Rights in *Pye v United Kingdom* [2007] ECHR 44302/02. It demonstrates how facts that are unusual or different from those in *Pye* will need to be exceptional to justify a departure from the Grand Chamber decision. There is likely to be little scope for arguing that *Pye* should not be applied to adverse possession cases heard by the English Courts.

2   *BOUNDARIES*

2.1 Haycocks v Neville

[2007] EWCA Civ 78; [2007] 12 EG 156

The facts:

This case involved the determination of the boundary between the parties' properties. The court had rejected both parties' experts' methods of determining the boundary and had reached its decision by reference to a plan prepared by the developers, a subsequent plan that was prepared at the request of the parties' predecessor in title to settle the boundary, and the actual location of a driveway

2

and trees he/she later. The appellants appealed on the basis that the judge had wrongly rejected their expert's recommended methodology and wrongly used a method of her own which depended both on the position of the driveway built after the preparation of the developers' plan, and on the plan prepared by the predecessor in title.

The decision:

The appeal was dismissed. The case was not one in which the judge had rejected the expert evidence of both parties and substituted her own expertise. Instead the judge had concluded that the experts had proceeded from the wrong starting point. She had been entitled to reject the sole use of the developers' plan, if she gave sufficient reasons for doing so, and if such a decision flowed from the evidence before her. Where a conveyance was unclear or ambiguous with respect to the land covered by it, the court could have reference to subsequent conduct, such as, in the instant case, the predecessor in title's conduct in locating the driveway and border trees. The plan prepared by the predecessor in title could also be considered.

Comment:

Had the respondent agreed with its predecessor in title that the plan the predecessor in title had prepared properly represented the boundary, that would have resolved the litigation.

3   BREAK CLAUSES

3.1   KPMG v Network Rail Infrastructure Ltd

[2007] EWCA Civ 363; [2007] L & TR 32

The facts:

A rent review clause gave the tenant three possible opportunities to end the lease following a rent review. The lease generally followed the form of a draft that was attached to an agreement for a lease, except that some words had been omitted from a parenthesis in the clause as executed compared with the earlier version. The earlier version provided a further limitation on the tenant's right to determine; not only must there have been a rent review, but it must have resulted in an increase in the rent. The tenant claimed that the clause as drafted, without the relevant words relating to the increased rent condition, gave it two 'free-standing' opportunities to break the lease, in addition to the three opportunities dependent on a rent review. The judge upheld the landlord's application for rectification of the lease, based on mutual mistake, so as to supply the missing words. The tenant appealed.

The decision:

The appeal was dismissed. The tenant's solicitor had spotted the change and advised it of its effect, as he believed it to be. The evidence showed that the tenant accepted its solicitor's view of the change and was content for the transaction to proceed on that basis. The court dismissed the landlord's claim for rectification as there had been neither a unilateral nor mutual mistake.

Comment:

This case illustrates that where a solicitor notices or suspects that a provision in a document does not reflect the other party's objectives, he should advise his client of the consequences of not drawing the mistake to the other side's attention and seek clear instructions from his client as to how to deal with the mistake.

4   BUSINESS TENANCIES

4.1 Ultimate Leisure Ltd v Tindle

[2007] EWCA Civ 1241; [2008] 1 P + CR DG11

The facts:

The appellant owned the freehold of premises which were let on a 99-year lease to its wholly owned subsidiary. Under an option agreement, the respondents were given an option to purchase the freehold and to grant a new lease. The respondents exercised the option within the option period, but the appellant argued that it was not obliged to complete the sale. A clause in the agreement required that, immediately prior to completion, the subsidiary would surrender its lease to the appellant. The appellant argued that this was an agreement to surrender and it was void for non-compliance with section 38(1) of the Landlord and Tenant Act 1954. The appellant therefore claimed that the agreement for sale arising out of the option agreement was also void. The judge held that the clause was void and that the clause, which provided that the seller would sell the property free from encumbrances, was not conditional upon any other condition. The appellant appealed.

The decision:

The appeal was dismissed. The appellant was contractually bound to sell the property free from the lease and to deliver a deed of surrender to the respondents on completion. The 1954 Act only rendered void the agreement to surrender, and not the sale contract itself. If the appellant was unable to provide the deed of surrender, it was prima facie in breach of its obligation under the contract of sale arising under the option.

Comment:

Whilst there is nothing new in this decision, it does serve as a useful reminder of the importance of serving a landlord's warning notice on the tenant before entering into an agreement to surrender a 1954 Act protected tenancy. A buyer should require evidence that this procedure has been followed prior to exchange.

4.2 Picture Warehouse Ltd v Cornhill Investments Ltd

[2008] EWHC 45 (QB); [2008] 12 EG 98

The facts:

The appellant occupied business premises under a 25-year lease from January 1980. The respondent purchased the headlease in 1997. Much of the building was used as a multi-storey car park. In 1999, negotiations took place for a new lease under which the appellant would vacate its space on the second floor and move to the ground floor. The appellant also agreed to give up two of its three parking spaces on the first floor, and to use two designated spaces on land at the front of the building. The respondent agreed to carry out the necessary building work and, in consequence, the rent was reduced by £500. There was then a dispute with the council about parking at the front of the building and the appellant sought an assurance that parking would be available. By a letter dated 20 October 2000, the respondent told the appellant that parking there would be allowed for a maximum of 30 minutes, a restriction that had to be adhered to in order to avoid further conflict. The move took place but the preparation of the new lease went into abeyance. A new lease was finally entered into in 2003, but it made no reference to the allocated parking spaces in front of the building. In 2005, problems arose when the appellant's parking area was occupied by other tenants. The appellant applied for a new business tenancy under Part II of the Landlord and Tenant Act 1954 on the same terms as the previous lease. The county court found that the appellant had obtained two advantages following the move: a reduction in rent and greater visibility for its business. The judge concluded that the 2003 lease had been drafted in the way it had because the respondent did not want a formal grant, which the appellant had accepted. It would be a wrong exercise of the court's wide discretion under the 1954 Act to insert the right requested by the appellant when it had been provided with a bare licence only, which it could determine at any time. The appellant appealed, contending, *inter alia*, that a term relating to parking should be included in the new lease by virtue of section 32(3) of the 1954 Act, which provided that rights enjoyed by a tenant in connection with its holding should be included in a tenancy granted under section 29.

The decision:

The appeal was dismissed. The judge was right to hold that the 2003 lease had correctly made no provision for outside parking and that the right to outside parking, whatever it was, was to be found in the terms of the letter of 20 October 2000. The transaction had to be considered as a whole; what was granted was a licence or permission, supported by consideration, for customers or deliverymen to park for up to 30 minutes. The problem under section 32(3) was that the 2003 lease did not include any rights as to external parking. From the plain wording of the statute, it was clear that the appellant's rights were outside the lease and so outside section 32(3). There was no reason to strain the wording of the section to give it a wider meaning, particularly given the court's wider discretion under section 35 to determine the terms of a tenancy in default of agreement between the landlord and the tenant. The object of Part II of the 1954 Act was to give security of tenure to business tenants by, *inter alia*, conferring power on the court to order a new tenancy of the property comprised in the holding. No matter how widely section 35 is expressed, it could not be construed as enabling the court to enlarge the holding. In the present case, it would be permissible to include a provision in the lease conferring on the tenant a right no greater than that given by the letter of 20 October 2000. The appellant had failed to establish any case for having a term in the lease giving it an irrevocable right to park two cars outside the building.

Comment:

This case reinforces the precarious nature of side letters. A tenant cannot use a lease renewal under the 1954 Act to change informal rights into full easements.

4.3 Lay v Drexler

[2007] EWCA Civ 464; [2007] 31 EG 82

The facts:

The respondent tenant held a five-year lease of business premises. Before it expired the respondent indicated that he was considering renewing the lease. When the lease had expired, the appellant landlord served a section 25 notice and indicated that, if there was no response from the respondent, he would issue proceedings for renewal. There was no response and so the appellant issued proceedings under section 24 of the 1954 Act. The respondent filed an acknowledgement of service, not opposing the renewal, but opposing its terms. The proceedings continued for almost another year. The amount of interim rent if the respondent vacated was agreed. Before trial the respondent gave notice to the court that it no longer wanted a new lease, and the proceedings were dismissed under section 29(5) of the Act. The appellant appealed against a decision to make no order for costs after the dismissal.

The decision:

The appeal was allowed. The judge had been wrong to conclude that the case amounted to a compromise and, in particular, a compromise of the respondent's claim for a new lease. The only matter that had been compromised was the interim rent. Before the judge, the main issue, namely the terms of any new lease, had already been dismissed pursuant to section 29(5). The scheme of the provisions introduced by the Regulatory Reform (Business Tenancies) (England and Wales) Order 2003 was that, by entering an acknowledgement of service not opposing the grant of a new tenancy, the respondent was effectively launching proceedings for the grant of a new tenancy on more favourable terms than those put forward by the appellant. Those proceedings were then terminated as a result of the respondent's change of mind.

Comment:

This is a fair decision in the light of the respondent's continued delay. The Court of Appeal's view in this case was that, essentially, the tenant had effectively discontinued a claim he had brought, when he had acknowledged service and indicated that he wanted the new lease to be on different terms. This interpretation fits with the policy behind the changes to the 1954 Act, and conveyancers must now be aware that acknowledging service might, in these circumstances, be treated as equivalent to commencing proceedings.

5 CONTRACTS

5.1 Chinnock v Hocaoglu

[2007] EWHC 2933 (Ch)

The facts:

The defendant had agreed to sell the claimant the freehold of three flats. The contract between the parties provided that the claimant was responsible for the defendant's legal costs. The claimant failed to complete on the contractual completion date and the defendant served a notice to complete. The claimant then tendered the completion monies on the last day for completion under the notice, but did not pay the defendant's legal costs. The claimant sought the rectification and specific performance of the contract.

The decision:

The claimant had not tendered the correct amount and therefore the defendant was not obliged to complete. As the deadline for completion had passed without the claimant re-tendering the right amount, the defendant was entitled to rescind the contract and forfeit the deposit.

Comment:

This case illustrates that, where a notice to complete has been served and time is of the essence for completion, there can be serious consequences for the buyer.

5.2 Business Environment Bow Lane Ltd v Deanwater Estates Ltd

[2007] EWCA Civ 622; [2007] 30 EG 90

The facts:

The respondent tenant had entered into negotiations with the appellant landlord's predecessor for the grant of a new lease of business premises. The respondent subsequently terminated the lease and thereafter the appellant acquired a long lease of the property. The appellant issued proceedings for breach of the repairing covenants in the new lease. The judge found that the respondent had relied on assurances by the appellant's predecessor that it would not serve a schedule of dilapidations in consideration for the surrender of the old lease, and that the appellant was therefore precluded from enforcing the repairing covenants by a collateral contract arising from communications between the parties leading up to the execution of the new lease. It was common ground that all the correspondence between the parties was subject to contract.

The decision:

The respondent had no defence to the claim based on collateral contract. If the promise said to be binding as a collateral contract was, in truth, one of the terms for the sale or other disposition of land, it would be unenforceable unless it was contained in the written contract provided by section 2 of the Law of Property (Miscellaneous Provisions) Act 1989. Such a promise might be binding on successors in title of both parties, without the need for notice or registration as a land charge or in the Land Registry. However, the court did not think that the correspondence showed, objectively, that the parties did intend to make any contract other than that arising from the grant of the new lease.

Comment:

This case demonstrates the court's unwillingness to divert from a strict interpretation of section 2 when deciding whether a collateral contract exists. It also highlights the importance of ensuring that a contract accurately and clearly reflects the heads of terms and any other matters that are agreed before contract.

5.3 Eyestorm Ltd v Hoptonacre Homes Ltd

[2007] EWCA Civ 1366; [2007] PLSCS 269

The facts:

The parties had agreed that the appellant would lease 14 residential flats in a new development from the respondent. The appellant failed to complete on the contractual completion date. The parties then agreed to extend the completion date and the respondent also agreed to cease marketing the flats. The appellant then failed to complete on the revised date for completion, and the respondent served a notice to complete which was not complied with. The respondent therefore rescinded the contract and forfeited the deposit. The appellant argued that the respondent was in breach of contract as it had continued to market the flats and so the notice to complete was invalid as the respondent was not 'ready, able and willing' to complete. The appellant appealed against the rejection of its claim for damages for breach of contract and for the return of its deposit.

The decision:

The appeal was dismissed. The agreement to extend the completion date and for the respondent to stop the marketing of the flats did not create a binding contract as it did not comply with section 2 of the Law of Property (Miscellaneous Provisions) Act 1989.

Comment:

The appellant had suggested that the respondent was estopped from denying that it was bound by the agreement. The court doubted whether anything other than a proprietary estoppel would be sufficient to avoid the consequences of failing to comply with section 2. This decision makes it clear that the safest course of action is to assume that any variation to a contract that falls within section 2 must itself comply with section 2.

5.4 RHJ Ltd v FT Patten (Holdings) Ltd

[2007] EWHC 1655 (Ch); [2007] 4 All ER 744

The facts:

The property in this case was an office block situated between two parallel streets with a short frontage to another adjoining street. There was a car park on the corner of one parallel street, with a building and its car park on the other side. The local authority had owned the property, the car parks and the building, and had granted a lease of the property to a company. A clause in the lease of the property excluded any implied grant of easement and reserved the right to build on adjoining land, but no express right to light was granted. Until the local authority transferred the property to the claimant, and the other parcels of land to the defendants, the property had enjoyed 20 years' light between the date of its construction and the date when a light obstruction notice was registered. The issue was whether the right to light was enjoyed by some consent or agreement so that right to light could not be deemed absolute and indefeasible under section 3 of the Prescription Act 1832.

The decision:

Case law did not provide any statement to the effect that an agreement or consent for the purpose of section 3 had to expressly refer to light. The reservation was intended to allow the local authority to build on the adjoining land, and was not restricted to the rights existing at the date of the grant of the lease. The test applied was whether the clause made it clear that the claimant's enjoyment of light was not 'absolute and indefeasible'. The local authority had reserved a 'full and free' right to build on the adjoining land, as it 'may think fit'. As a right to build that could be thwarted by a right to light would not be 'full and free', the claimant's enjoyment of light was not 'absolute and indefeasible'.

Comment:

This case highlights how important it is to draft a reservation of a right to build in a way that prevents the tenant acquiring a right to light by prescription. The court has provided useful guidance on what wording may constitute an agreement under section 3 so as to prevent the acquisition of an easement by prescription.

5.5 Aribisala v St James Homes (Grosvenor Dock) Ltd

[2007] EWHC 1694 (Ch); [2007] 37 EG 234

The facts:

The parties had entered into a contract for the sale and purchase of a leasehold property. The contract incorporated the Standard Conditions of Sale (4th edition), however, condition 7.5.2 was amended to provide that section 49(2) of the Law of Property Act

1925 did not apply. The buyer did not complete on the contractual completion date and the seller served a notice to complete, which the buyer also did not comply with. The seller rescinded the contract and forfeited the deposit. The buyer issued proceedings for repayment of the deposit under section 49(2) and the seller sought summary dismissal of this claim on the ground that the contract excluded section 49(2).

The decision:

The application for summary dismissal was refused. Section 49(2) conferred a jurisdiction on the court, exercisable at its discretion, to order the repayment of any deposit paid by a buyer. It did not confer a right on either party to the contract. A contractual provision which purported to exclude section 49(2) purported to oust the court's jurisdiction, and was therefore void and of no effect on the ground of public policy. Section 49(2) did not purport to confer any benefit on the buyer, but a jurisdiction on the court that could be exercised in favour of the buyer. It was not open to the buyer to waive this jurisdiction.

Comment:

This is a helpful decision confirming that section 49(2) cannot be excluded in a contract. This is a point of significant importance in relation to contracts for the sale of land, so it is surprising that there has been no authority on this issue in over 80 years.

5.6 Ross River Ltd v Cambridge City Football Club Ltd

[2007] EWHC 2115 (Ch); [2007] 41 EG 201 (CS)

The facts:

The defendant, which was a football club, had become insolvent. The value of its assets still exceeded its liabilities, however, because of the potential of its ground for development. The defendant's Chief Executive represented it in negotiations for the sale of the ground to the claimant. The defendant then sold the freehold in the ground for £1.3 million plus a share in the anticipated overage attributable to the obtaining of residential planning permission. At the same time, the claimant granted the defendant a contracted-out lease of the ground. Subsequently, the defendant sold its share in the overage to the claimant in order to alleviate its cashflow problems. During negotiations leading to that sale, the defendant's surveyor had sought information from the claimant's Project Manager in order to evaluate the claimant's offer for the defendant's share in the overage. During these negotiations, the Project Manager had arranged a payment of £10,000 to the defendant's Chief Executive who told only one of the other three directors of the club about the payment. The defendant registered a unilateral notice against the claimant's title to the ground, and so the claimant brought proceedings to have the unilateral notice removed.

The decision:

The defendant was entitled to rescind the overage agreement as the claimant's Project Manager had made fraudulent misrepresentations of fact when he responded to the request from the defendant's surveyor for information to allow him to advise the defendant on the sale of its share in the overage, and the payment of £10,000 to the Chief Executive undermined his undivided loyalty as the defendant's chief negotiator. The defendant was entitled to a new lease of the ground in place of the lease that had been surrendered under the overage agreement. However, the defendant was entitled to rescind the sale agreement as it had been negotiated as an arms' length commercial deal, and it would be unjust to require the claimant to transfer the ground back to the defendant.

Comment:

This case is a useful summary of the things that can go wrong when the interests of parties who were originally working together on a project diverge, and illustrates how conveyancers must remain alert to the possibility of conflicts of interest arising as a transaction progresses.

5.7 Midill (97PL) Ltd v Park Lane Estates Ltd and Another

[2008] EWHC 18 (Ch); [2008] 03 EG 178 (CS)

The facts:

The claimant agreed in writing to purchase all the shares in the first defendant company from the second defendant for £4 million. The first defendant's only asset was a commercial property on Park Lane, London W1. The claimant paid a deposit of £400,000 on signing the agreement, followed by a further £800,000. The balance was payable on completion. The Standard Conditions of Sale (4th Edition) applied, subject to clause 5.9 of the agreement. Clause 5.9 provided that the claimant would not be obliged to complete on the completion date if the second defendant failed to comply with the other provisions of clause 5 regarding the provision of documentation and other matters, including the resignations of the directors and secretary of the first defendant and the appointment of replacements nominated by the claimant. The claimant was unable to complete on the contractual completion date or within the time specified in a notice to complete served by the second defendant. The second defendant accordingly purported to rescind the agreement, and sold the property to another purchaser for the higher price of £4.3 million. The claimant brought proceedings in which it disputed the second defendant's right to rescind. It contended that the notice to complete had been invalid since, at the time of giving that notice, the second defendant had not been ready, willing and able to complete because it could not provide all the documentation required by clause 5. It claimed the return of the sums paid to the second defendant, together with interest, as well as damages for breach of contract in the sum of £300,000, which represented the difference between the contractual price and the figure at which the second defendant had sold to the other purchaser. The defendant repaid the £800,000 but disputed its liability for the other sums and submitted that it had been ready, willing and able to complete in circumstances where it was able to effect the necessary administrative arrangements for completion within a reasonable time.

The decision:

The claim was dismissed. The question of whether a party was ready, willing and able to complete was one of fact and it would not necessarily be useful to compare the court's approach on the facts of past cases, given the shifts in conveyancing practices over time and the changes in technology. The burden of proof lay on the party seeking to establish that the other was not ready, willing and able to complete. The second defendant had been ready, willing and able to complete on the day it served the notice to complete, in the light of its evidence that the claimant's nominated directors had been appointed and the stock transfer form and share certificates had been signed and ready to hand over; all other formalities could have been dealt with on or before that day. The claimant had not discharged the burden of proving otherwise with regard to that date or the date upon which the notice to complete expired. Accordingly, the claimant was not entitled to the relief sought with regard to its damages claim, or in respect of the £800,000 payment. With regard to the £400,000 deposit, although section 49(2) of the Law of Property Act 1925 potentially applied, so that the court had a discretion to order its repayment, there was no justification for doing so where the deposit had been set at the conventional 10%, where there had been a failure to complete and where the parties were sophisticated professionals. A failure to complete was a classic circumstance in which a deposit was liable to be forfeited, and it should not be recovered in the absence of special reasons. The court would not ordinarily order repayment, even if the seller had made a profit on a subsequent sale. There was nothing to justify a departure from the normal approach.

Comment:

This decision is an illustration of the distinction between being ready to complete immediately and being ready to complete subject to minor administrative matters, and recognises that the efforts made by one party to prepare for completion, often depend on the indications from the other party as to whether they will be ready to complete on the contractual completion date. The prudent approach is always to work towards completion as if it will occur on the completion date, regardless of the other party's behaviour.

5.8 The Prudential Assurance Co Ltd v Ayres and Another

[2008] EWCA Civ 52; [2008] PLSCS 32

The facts:

The appellant was the tenant of office premises and the respondents were the original undertenants. In 2001, the appellant agreed to the assignment of the underlease to a firm of US attorneys who covenanted with the claimant to pay the rents 'in the manner and at the respective times appointed for payment thereof and [to] perform and observe all the covenants on the part of the lessee and the covenants and provisions contained in the underlease'. The respondents guaranteed that, should the assignees default in payment of the rents due before any lawful assignment of the underlease, they would pay the rent notwithstanding any time or indulgence granted by the appellant to the assignees, or any neglect or forebearance on the part of the appellant or any variation in the terms of the underlease. In June 2001, the appellant and the assignees entered into a supplemental deed, which provided (by clause 2.1) that the liability of the tenant under the lease and under any authorised guarantee agreement should be limited to the assignees, including but not limited to all its assets, income and accounts. Any recovery by the landlord against the tenant or any previous tenant for such default was limited to the assets of the assignees and was not to extend to the personal assets of any individual partners, other than their capital and current accounts. The landlord would not require any tenant to loan, or contribute, personal money or property to discharge any obligation to the landlord. The assignees subsequently became bankrupt leaving approximately £1.5 million in unpaid obligations under the underlease. The appellant sought to recover from the respondents in their capacity as the assignees' guarantors. The judge held that the respondents were entitled to take advantage of the limited recovery provisions, even though they were not party to the supplemental deed. Since clause 2.1 was a term that purported to confer a benefit on previous tenants within section 1(1)(b) of the Contracts (Rights of Third Parties) Act 1999, the respondents were entitled to enforce its provisions against the landlord in their own right.

17

The decision:

The appeal was allowed. Properly construed, the supplemental deed did not purport to confer any benefit on the respondents, but limited their rights against the individual partners of the assignees. As such, it provided no defence to the appellant's claim and no question arose as to the operation of the 1999 Act. Given the background to the supplemental deed, it was difficult to accept that the parties had intended to limit the scope of the respondents' liability to the appellant, or the appellant's right to enforce that liability in the ordinary way. If that had been their intention, they would have made the respondents a party to the supplemental deed and would have included a provision that clearly limited the scope of their liability to the appellant. Although the drafting of the supplemental deed had gone awry, there were no sufficiently strong objections that outweighed the conclusion that the parties to the deed had intended to assimilate the position of the respondents to that of the appellant in relation to claims against the partnership. It was impossible to accept that the parties had intended to alter the nature of the relationship between the appellant and the respondents that had been established under the licence in any significant way.

Comment:

Cases on the 1999 Act have been rare. This decision does not necessarily mean that any claim to rights by virtue of section 1(1)(b) of the 1999 Act will fail. It suggests that, for a claim to be successful, there may have to be very clear drafting.

5.9 Yewbelle Ltd v London Green Developments Ltd

[2007] EWCA Civ 475; [2007] 23 EG 164 (CS)

The facts:

The contract provided for the appellant to sell a property to the respondent whereupon the respondent would develop it and then lease back parts of it to the appellant. The respondent was not bound to complete until the appellant had obtained planning permission by entering into a section 106 agreement with the

18

local authority. Difficulties arose regarding the terms under which a library to be built on the site would be transferred to the local authority, and it emerged that part of the site that the local authority was assumed to own was actually owned by a third party. Under the contract, the appellant was required to use 'all reasonable endeavours' to obtain the section 106 agreement. A year after the contract was agreed, no section 106 agreement had been put in place and the appellant told the respondent that it considered that the agreement should therefore be discharged. The appellant then sought a declaration that the contract had come to an end, arguing that there was an implied term that the contract came to an end automatically in the circumstances. The appellant now appealed against the decision, ordering specific performance in favour of the respondent.

The decision:

The appeal was allowed. The High Court had used the correct legal test in judging whether the appellant had used all reasonable endeavours, and was right to imply the term that it did. On the facts, the appellant had not used all reasonable endeavours to deal with the library amendment. The issue of the library amendment was, however, irrelevant in light of the third party land problem. A section 106 agreement, which excluded the third party land, would not have been substantial in the form agreed by the contract. The appellant was not obliged to spend significant funds on buying the third party land to comply with its obligations under the contract, and so it was difficult to see what else the appellant could have done. The appellant had given the respondent the opportunity to waive satisfaction of the condition and the appellant was entitled to treat the contract as being discharged because of the third party land problem.

Comment:

It is surprising that neither party was aware of the fact that part of the development land was owned by an independent third party. This case illustrates the importance of carrying out a full investigation to ensure that there are no defects in the title that would adversely affect the buyer's interests or prevent development.

6 CO-OWNERSHIP

6.1 Stack v Dowden

[2007] UKHL 17; [2007] 2 AC 432

The facts:

The parties had bought a house in their joint names which they lived in together with their four children. They had been co-habiting for 18 years when they bought the house. The transfer to them did not contain a declaration of trust, but did contain a declaration that the survivor could give a good receipt for capital money arising from a disposition of the property. The purchase had been funded by the sale of their previous property, which had been in the respondent's sole name, plus savings in the respondent's (her) name, and a mortgage held in both names. The appellant paid the interest on the mortgage and the premiums for the endowment policy. They both paid off the capital, with the respondent contributing a greater proportion. Nearly all aspects of their respective finances had been kept separate. Nine years after buying the house, their relationship broke down and they agreed a Court Order that excluded the appellant from the house and required the respondent to pay for the cost of his alternative accommodation. The appellant then obtained a declaration that the house was held upon trust by the parties as tenants in common in equal shares. He also obtained an Order for the sale of the house. The respondent appealed. The Court of Appeal ordered that the net proceeds be divided 65% to her and 35% to the appellant, on the basis that the declaration as to the receipt for capital money in the transfer document could not be taken as an express declaration of trust, nor could it infer an intention that the beneficial ownership be equal, because there was no evidence that either of them had understood the declaration to carry such significance. The appellant appealed against this Order. The main issue before the House of Lords was whether a transfer into joint names established a *prima facie* case of joint, and equal, beneficial interests.

The decision:

The appeal was dismissed. The starting point where there was joint legal ownership was joint beneficial ownership. The onus was upon the person seeking to show that the parties intended their beneficial interests to be different from their legal interests and in what way. Context was everything, and each case would turn on its own facts. Many more factors than just financial contributions could be relevant to their intention, and the court gave a non-exhaustive list. A case in which the joint legal owners were to be taken to have intended that their beneficial interests should be different from their legal interests would be very unusual. Accordingly, it was for the respondent to show that the common intention when they bought the house was that they should hold the house otherwise than as joint beneficial tenants, and there were, on the evidence, many factors for her to rely on. The fact that the parties had lived together for such a long time and had children together, yet had kept their affairs rigidly separate, was strongly indicative that they did not intend their shares, even in the property that was put into their joint names, to be equal, and she had made good her case for a higher share.

Comment:

This is an important case, not only as it considers what happens to the family home where unmarried couples live together and then subsequently split up, but also because of the implications for co-owners who buy together but have no relationship with one another. When buying a property together, the parties should consider how they intend the property to be divided should they fall out, and this should be properly documented.

7   DEFECTIVE PREMISES

7.1 Alker v Collingwood Housing Association

[2007] EWCA Civ 343; [2007] 1 WLR 2230

The facts:

The respondent had pushed the front door of the property which had been let to her and, in doing so, had put her left arm through the ribbed glass panel of the door, sustaining serious injuries. The glass panel was made not of safety glass but of ordinary annealed glass. Before the accident, the glass was neither broken nor in disrepair. However, the use of ordinary annealed glass in doors presents a safety hazard, a matter which has been understood since at least 1963. The tenancy agreement provided that the appellant 'must keep your home in good condition'. The issue was whether the state of the glass panel constituted a 'relevant defect' within the meaning of section 4 of the Defective Premises Act 1972. The appellant appealed against a decision that it had acted in breach of section 4.

The decision:

The appeal was allowed. Neither a duty to maintain nor a duty to repair could possibly be said to encompass or include a duty to make safe. A duty to keep 'in good condition' could not encompass a duty to put in safe condition. A house might present many hazards, but it could not be said that the 1972 Act required a landlord, on proof only of the conditions for the application of section 4, to make safe any such dangerous feature.

Comment:

This is a welcome decision for landlords. If the court had decided that section 4 extended to an implied warranty that the property was reasonably safe, this would have resulted in a major liability for landlords.

8   EASEMENTS

8.1   Megaro v Di Popolo Hotels Ltd

[2007] EWCA Civ 309; [2007] 2 P & CR 28

The facts:

The parties owned adjoining properties that had formerly been in common ownership. Under the terms of the transfer to the respondent, it had the right, in the case of emergency, to cross the appellant's roof and to use his external staircase to exit to ground level, provided that the roof and external staircase still existed. The appellant's right to change the route of the emergency exit from time to time was also reserved in the transfer. The appellant subsequently obtained planning permission to change the use of his property and proposed plans for redevelopment. He then removed both the roof and the external staircase. It was held that it would be a nonsense if the right granted to the respondent could simply be terminated by the appellant's decision to remove the roof or staircase. The judge declared that the respondent's right was extant and he ordered that the appellant must provide an alternative means of escape. The appellant appealed and the issue was whether the judge had erred in his interpretation of the agreement.

The decision:

The appeal was allowed. The judge had erred as the terms of the arrangement were plain. The right was granted only so long as the roof and the staircase existed; when those features ceased to exist, the right came to an end. In addition, when the judge described it as a nonsense that the right could be extinguished on a whim, he seemed to have overlooked the fact that there was no evidence to show that the removal of the roof or the staircase would render the respondent's property unusable.

Comment:

This decision emphasises the need, at the drafting stage, to look ahead and identify circumstances where a dispute may arise, especially where a provision is likely to create an obvious disadvantage for one of the parties.

8.2 Adealon International Corp Proprietary Ltd v Merton London Borough Council

[2007] EWCA Civ 362; [2007] 1 WLR 1898

The facts:

The appellant owned a strip of land (the red land) that was bounded by a road to the south. The respondent owned the land adjacent to that plot (the green land), which was bounded

23

by a road to the north. The red land had no direct access to the northern road and access to the southern road could not be obtained without planning permission. Both plots of land had been owned by a company, the shares of which had been acquired by another company, of which the appellant's director was the beneficial owner. The original company transferred the green land to the respondent's predecessor in title, which was a company in which the appellant's director also had a beneficial interest. The respondent's predecessor in title then sold the green land to the respondent. The original company then transferred the red land and assigned all causes of action pertaining to the land to the appellant. The appellant claimed that, on the severance of the two plots, it became entitled, by operation of law, to an easement of necessity over the green land to give it access to the northern road. The judge dismissed the claim and the appellant appealed.

The decision:

The appeal was dismissed. The principle of an easement of necessity was one of implication from the circumstances of a grant of land and not a free-standing rule of public policy. The classic case of an easement of necessity was where land owned by one party was entirely surrounded by that of another. Where there was a realistic possibility of alternative access over the land of third parties, the case for an easement of necessity was less clear. The presumption was that any rights that the grantor required over the land transferred would have been expressly reserved in the grant and the burden lay on the grantor to establish an exception. This case concerned implied reservation, not implied grant. The appellant's director had not been concerned about the need to reserve a specific right of access to the north, rather his concern appeared to have been to control the possibility of future access to the south on the prospect of future planning permission. That was far from creating the basis for an implied right and there was nothing to overcome the ordinary presumption that, had he required an easement to the north, he would have made a specific reservation in the grant.

Comment:

Whilst this case was decided on its facts and does not introduce any new principles of law, it provides a useful summary of the law on easements of necessity. In particular, it highlights the heavier burden of proof required to imply the reservation of an easement.

8.3 Wall v Collins

[2007] EWCA Civ 444; [2007] Ch 390

The facts:

The appellant owned the freehold of a house and the respondents owned an adjoining property. The appellant also owned a leasehold interest in a plot of land to the rear of the house on which he had built a garage. The original leasehold of both the house and the respondent's property had been granted for a term of 999 years in 1910. The appellant bought the house in 1999 and the freehold interest was transferred to him, however, the leasehold interest was not separately registered and the reference to the 1910 lease in the charges register was removed. The appellant claimed a right of way over a passageway running between the house and the respondent's property, on the basis that it had been granted by way of an assignment made in 1911. It was held that the right of way granted by the 1911 assignment could only attach to the leasehold interest in the house, which was what was being assigned, and that if a leasehold estate was merged with a freehold estate, any easements or covenants attached to the leasehold interest were extinguished. The judge further found that the leasehold interest in the house had ceased to exist by way of a merger and that, in any event, the leasehold interest was surrendered by operation of law in 1999 when the appellant bought the freehold. The appellant appealed.

The decision:

The appeal was allowed. The judge's reasoning was that the right of way was attached to the 1910 lease and that therefore, when the lease was extinguished by merger, the right was lost. That was the wrong approach. An easement had to be appurtenant to a dominant tenement but, for the time being, not necessarily to any particular interest. All that mattered was that the grantee had an interest at least co-extensive with the period of the easement. Thus the merger of the lease into a larger interest in the dominant tenement was not in itself fatal to the continued existence of the easement for the period for which it was granted. The dominant tenement remained unchanged and there was no legal impediment to the continued enjoyment of the easement by the occupier for the time being of that tenement. The merger of the lease in 1999 did not destroy the easement, at least to the extent of the 1911 grant, and the 999-year right was amply sufficient for the appellant to benefit from the right of way. As to whether an equivalent right of way passed with the conveyance of the freehold of the house, section 62 of the Law of Property Act 1925 supported the argument that the appellant's right of way was not limited by the extent of his former leasehold interest. In the absence of any indication of contrary intention, the right of way, which was capable of being the subject of an easement, should in principle be treated as having passed with the freehold. The disappearance by merger of the lease of the house in 1999 did not affect the continuation of the right for the benefit of the freehold. Even where the original dominant tenement was extended, the enjoyment of the easement could continue for the benefit of the enlarged property if the additional use was merely ancillary. There was no reason for holding that the use of the garage on the plot of land was anything other than ancillary to the ordinary residential use of the house and the right of way could therefore be used to benefit the use of the garage. The appropriate declaration was that the appellant, as owner of the house and of the plot of land, enjoyed a right of way over the passageway to the extent that it was reasonably required for the convenient enjoyment of the house.

Comment:

Careful consideration is now required as a result of this decision when leasehold easements are granted. Whilst the easement may be granted for a term equivalent to the term of the lease, the easement is not 'attached to the lease' but attaches to the dominant tenement. On merger, the easement may continue to exist and continue to be enjoyed by the freeholder, either for the term for which the easement was originally granted, or permanently if section 62 applies. Following this decision, the Land Registry published an Addendum to Practice Guide 26: Leases-determination, which advises that the information about easements being determined on merger is not correct.

8.4 Risegold Ltd v Escala Ltd

[2008] EWHC 21 (Ch); [2008] PLSCS 13

The facts:

The claimant and the defendant owned adjacent industrial units, to the rear of which was a yard that lay within the defendant's ownership. The claimant's land had the benefit of an easement, which had been granted by a 1993 conveyance by the parties' mutual predecessor in title, to enter upon 'such part of the yard ...as is necessary for the purpose of carrying out maintenance, repair, rebuilding or renewal to the Property'. That right was subject to 'the minimum disturbance and inconvenience being caused to the owners and occupiers of the Adjoining Property'. The claimant had planning permission to demolish the existing single-storey building on its land and to construct a five or six-storey block containing commercial units and flats. The works would necessitate entry into the yard, the temporary erection thereon of fencing and scaffolding, and the overhead intrusion of the arm of a tower crane to be erected on the claimant's land. The defendant objected to the proposals and disputed whether the intrusions into the yard were within the terms of the right granted by the 1993 conveyance. The claimant applied for a declaration that it was entitled to enter upon the yard for the purpose of its proposed works.

The decision:

The claim was dismissed. Although the claimant was entitled to build on the site whatever was permitted by the planning permission, its entitlement to enter the yard did not depend upon what was required for that purpose, but upon the construction of the express grant in the 1993 conveyance. The terms of the grant indicated that it was intended to be construed strictly and to derogate to the minimum possible extent from the servient owner's enjoyment of its land. The right did not extend to redevelopment by the construction of something different. The term 'rebuild' did not necessarily require the new building to be identical to the old in every respect. However, implicit in that term was that there should be a substantial replacement of the exiting property, and that the points of similarity should be sufficient to make the new building recognisable as being broadly equivalent to what had been there before the works had been carried out. Whether a proposed development fell within the scope of the right was a question of fact. In the instant case, the claimant's proposed development was neither a rebuilding nor a renewal of the property and, accordingly, the claimant did not have the rights over the yard that it sought in respect of those works.

Comment:

This case does not lay down anything new but it is an interesting example of the approach a court is likely to take when construing the scope of an easement and emphasises the reliance a court is likely to place on the circumstances and likely intention of the parties at the date of grant when establishing the purpose of an easement.

8.5 Moncrieff v Jamieson

[2007] UKHL 42; [2007] 1 WLR 2620

The facts:

The respondents owned a property which adjoined the third appellant's land and was situated a short distance from a property owned by the first and second appellants. The respondents' land had no direct access to a public road and they relied on a right of way over the third appellant's land, which was set out in a 1973 transfer by which the then owner of both properties had disposed of the respondents' land. It was agreed that the right included both pedestrian and vehicular traffic and the ancillary right to stop vehicles on the servient tenement for turning purposes, the loading and unloading of goods and the picking up and setting down of passengers. The respondents claimed that the right of way also included a right to park vehicles on the servient tenement. It was not physically possible to bring vehicles onto the respondents' property because it was located between the foot of an escarpment and the foreshore and was accessible only by boat or on foot by way of a gate and steps. The Scottish courts held that the right of way did include an ancillary right to park on the servient tenement. On appeal to the House of Lords, the issues were a) whether a right to park was ever capable of existing ancillary to a servitude of vehicular access and b) if so, whether such a right existed in the particular circumstances of the case.

The decision:

The appeal was dismissed. There was no fundamental objection in principle to the right that the respondents sought to establish. The essence of a servitude was that it existed for the reasonable and comfortable enjoyment of the dominant tenement. Practical considerations might indicate that it should carry with it other rights that, although they would not qualify as servitudes on their own, were necessary if the dominant owners were to make reasonable and comfortable use of their property. The right to turn, load and unload vehicles fell within that principle. Although the express grant in the 1973 transfer fell to be construed in the circumstances existing in 1973, it was not necessary to show that all the rights claimed for the comfortable use and enjoyment of the servitude had actually been in use at that date. In this case, it was not possible to park a vehicle on the dominant tenement. If there were no right to park on the servient tenement, ancillary to the right of way, the owners of the dominant tenement would be required to deposit any goods or passengers, leave the servient tenement in order to park elsewhere, and walk back from their parking place to their property and back again when they next wanted to use their vehicle. That would entail a walk of 150 yards, in all weathers and at any time of the day, involving a steep descent or climb in exposed countryside. Therefore, a right to park on the servient land was reasonably necessary to the comfortable enjoyment of the expressly granted vehicular right of way and was included within the rights ancillary to the express grant. Parking pursuant to that right should primarily be on the area of the third appellant's land that the parties had already agreed would be suitable for the purpose; that did not necessarily bar the third appellant from parking there from time to time, nor did it bar the respondents, if there were no space in the agreed area, from parking elsewhere on the servient land in the vicinity of the gate leading to their property. That would not place an unacceptable burden upon the servient tenement, nor would it deprive its owners of any reasonable use of the land in question. It was unlikely that a large number of vehicles would be parked, given that the right was in favour only of the owners of the dominant tenement and their guests and visitors, and did not extend beyond what was reasonable for the purposes of their ownership of the dominant tenement.

Comment:

In this case, the House of Lords has provided helpful guidance on rights to park which have long been without a clear legal status. The decision establishes that a right to park can be an easement and also suggests that this is equally true of exclusive car-parking spaces.

9   GUARANTEES

9.1   Prudential Assurance Co Ltd v PRG Powerhouse Ltd

[2007] EWHC 1002 (Ch); [2007] 19 EG 164 (CS)

The facts:

Powerhouse was an electrical retailer which, with financial support from its parent company, had acquired a number of high street stores and superstores. The landlord had taken parent company guarantees or indemnities. Powerhouse had got into financial difficulties and wished to close a number of stores and to enter into a company voluntary arrangement. The company voluntary arrangement contained provisions designed to release all those creditors' claims against Powerhouse relating to the closed premises and to release the parent company's guarantees in respect of the closed premises. At a creditors' meeting, attended by all the creditors including those whose rights and obligations were not affected by the company voluntary arrangement, the company voluntary arrangement was approved by the requisite statutory majority. The landlord challenged the company voluntary arrangement on the ground that it was unfairly prejudicial under section 6 of the Insolvency Act 1986, and sought declarations that it was invalid or ineffective in so far as it purported to affect the landlord's rights.

The decision:

The terms of the company voluntary arrangement, which provided that a payment from the fund to any scheme fund creditor would immediately and automatically release all liability of the parent company under the guarantees, were not effective. Powerhouse had the benefit of, and could enforce, the rights and obligations conferred by the company voluntary arrangement. There was nothing in the 1986 Act that made a company voluntary arrangement binding and enforceable as between the parent company and the landlord. However, a company voluntary arrangement is binding between the company and its creditors. This meant that, in this case, Powerhouse could enforce an obligation on the landlord not to claim against the parent company under the terms of the guarantees.

Comment:

The decision that a company voluntary arrangement that removes the landlords' rights under such guarantees is unfairly prejudicial is a welcome relief to landlords.

10   HIGHWAYS

10.1 R (on the application of Godmanchester Town Council) v Secretary of State for the Environment, Food and Rural Affairs

[2007] UKHL 28; [2007] 3 WLR 85

The facts:

The appellants claimed that land owned by the respondent had achieved the status of a public path by 20 years of public use. The issue was whether the landowners had shown 'sufficient evidence' that they had no intention during the relevant 20-year period to dedicate the land as a public path. The issues for determination were whether the 'intention' in section 31(1) of the Highways Act 1980 had to be communicated contemporaneously to members of the public using the way or whether an intention held by the landowner but not revealed to anybody could constitute 'sufficient evidence', and whether the phrase 'during that period' in the proviso to section 31(1) meant 'during the whole of that period' or 'at some point during that period'.

The decision:

The appeal was allowed. On the true construction of section 31(1), 'intention' meant what the relevant audience, namely the users of the way, would reasonably have understood the landowner's intention to be. This was an objective test: the reasonable user would have to understand that the landowner was intending to disabuse him of the notion that the land was a public highway. The phrase 'during that period ' in the proviso to section 31(1) meant 'at some point during that period'. The intention not to dedicate did not have to be continuously demonstrated for the whole 20-year period.

Comment:

This is not a welcome decision for landowners as it establishes that it is necessary to have communicated a lack of intention to dedicate to users of the right of way to be able to defeat a dedication claim. As a result, landowners will have to be more pro-active in communicating the lack of intention to dedicate to the users of the right of way.

11 LAND REGISTRATION

11.1 Anderson Antiques (UK) Ltd v Anderson Wharf (Hull) Ltd

[2007] EWHC 2086 (Ch); [2007] PLSCS 203

The facts:

The claimant was the registered proprietor of a site with potential for development. The second defendant was the sole shareholder and director of the first defendant, which was a single purpose vehicle with nominal assets that had been formed to acquire and develop the site. The claimant's sole director visited the second defendant's home and the first defendant alleged that an oral agreement had been reached at that meeting, under which the first defendant would purchase the site from the claimant for £2 million. The first defendant argued that it had subsequently relied upon that agreement to its detriment, which was sufficient to give rise to a proprietary estoppel or constructive trust in its favour. Whilst the claimant accepted that a meeting had taken place, it denied that any agreement had been reached and stated that the only reference to the site was an assertion that the first defendant could match an offer that was rumoured to have been made for the site. Following the meeting, the claimant started an informal tendering process to sell the site. The defendants challenged the accuracy of the particulars of sale but made no reference to a purported oral agreement, accepting that they had no legal interest in the site. When their two bids for the site were both rejected, the defendants lodged notices against the titles registered in respect of the site, on the grounds that they had an equitable interest as a result of the alleged oral agreement for its sale and that they had incurred expense to their detriment in reliance upon that agreement. The claimant brought proceedings for a declaration that the defendants had no interest in the site, the cancellation of the notices, and the damages under section 77 of the Land Registration Act 2002. The claimant applied for summary judgment of its claim.

The decision:

The application was granted. The claimant was entitled to a summary judgment of its claim for a declaration that the first defendant had no interest in the site and to an Order leading to the cancellation of the notices. The defendants had failed to demonstrate the existence of any agreement for the sale of the site to them, the detrimental reliance upon which made it unconscionable for the claimant to resile from the agreement. Accordingly, the court had no basis upon which to exercise its broad equitable power to give effect to any promise by the claimant that the first defendant would have an interest in the property. Although it was not appropriate at this stage for the court to give judgment for damages to be assessed when it had yet to be proven that any loss had been suffered, it was appropriate to make a declaration that the notices in question had been applied for without reasonable cause, contrary to the statutory duty in section 77 of the 2002 Act. The person owing the primary duty under section 77 was the first defendant, being the party that had exercised the right to apply for the entry of a notice. The question was whether the second defendant was also liable for damages. The relevant test was whether his activities would constitute procurement even if he had not been a director or shareholder of the company. The first defendant was nothing more than a special purpose vehicle (SPV) with no relevant personnel other than the second defendant, who had acted on its behalf in all matters relating to the registration of the notices. Accordingly, the second defendant's actions disclosed a clear case of procurement of the commission of the tort of the application for a notice without reasonable cause by the first defendant, sufficient to make him personally liable in damages under section 77(2).

Comment:

This decision is a useful reminder of the basic position that individuals who are in control of companies have to take personal responsibility for their actions on appropriate occasions.

12 LEASEHOLD COVENANTS

12.1 Glen International Ltd v Triplerose Ltd

[2007] EWCA Civ 388; [2007] L & TR 28

The facts:

Believing that the appellant had not given an address for service pursuant to section 48 of the Landlord and Tenant Act 1987, the respondent had served a notice under section 42 of the Leasehold Reform, Housing and Urban Development Act 1993 on the appellant at the address contained in its rent demands. No counter-notice was given, so the court had made an order granting a new lease to the respondent. Over the course of the two years prior to the service of the notice, the respondent's solicitors had been in correspondence with the appellant's agents about dilapidations and insurance matters. In the course of that correspondence, the respondent's solicitors had asked the agents to confirm which address was to be used for 'all future correspondence'. The agents had replied referring to a 'correspondence address' and saying 'please write to us at ...', followed by an address different from the one that the appellant had supplied for the purposes of the payment of rent. The issue was whether the respondent should have served the notice at that address or whether its service at the address contained in the rent demands amounted to proper service within the meaning of section 99 of the 1993 Act. The appellant appealed.

The decision:

The appeal was dismissed. The agents' letter did not constitute a notice for the purposes of section 48 of the 1987 Act, and the relevant address for the purposes of section 99 of the 1993 Act was the address which the respondent had in fact used for service. The terms of the agents' letter could not reasonably have been regarded by its recipient as conveying the message that all future documentation relating to the lease, of whatever nature, should be sent to the address it contained.

Comment:

This case is a useful reminder of the steps that a tenant should go through to ascertain the correct address for service of the section 42 notice.

12.2 Ravengate Estates Ltd v Horizon Housing Group Ltd

[2007] EWCA Civ 1368; [2008] 1 EG 135 (CS)

The facts:

The appellant owned a building, part of which comprised six flats that were let to the respondent housing association on a six-year lease. The demised property was described in the lease as 'the rear section of the ground floor, the rear section of the first floor and the whole of the second and third floors'. Floor plans were attached showing the areas demised; the plans for the second and third floors showed a line running around the entire outline of the building. After the expiry of the respondent's lease, the appellant obtained vacant possession of the six flats. It received planning permission to redevelop the flats and the associated airspace by building up from the flat roof of the second floor to the level of the third-floor roof and on the area of the second and third-floor balconies, to produce a total of 14 flats. In proceedings against the respondent for dilapidations, the appellant sought to recover the cost of the remedial works. The respondent contended that the cost of the works would exceed the amount by which the value of the reversion had been reduced by the disrepair, and that the damages should be capped at the latter amount, pursuant to section 18(1) of the Landlord and Tenant Act 1927. It contended that any potential purchaser would wish to develop the property in accordance with the planning permission that the appellant had obtained, and would therefore require no reduction in price in respect of the majority of the disrepair. The appellant submitted that section 18(1) was concerned only with the value of the reversion to the demised premises, and that notional development of the airspace could not be taken into account since the airspace fell outside the respondent's demise. The judge found that the airspace was excluded from the demise but that it was appropriate to have regard to the prospects of developing it in order to assess the diminution in value of the reversion. He found that anyone purchasing the premises would do so with a view to redevelopment. Accordingly, he applied the cap and awarded damages of £61,349, which was less than half the sum claimed by the appellant. On appeal, the issues were whether the airspace was included in the demise and the effect of the potential development on the damages to be awarded.

The decision:

The appeal was dismissed. On the correct construction of the lease, the relevant airspace was expressly included in the demise. Just as the plans did not operate only at floor level but were intended to denote the volume occupied by the flat, they also included the volume occupied by the balconies and the airspace from the second-floor roof up to the third-floor roof level. Had the parties intended to exclude it, the line on the plans could have been drawn so as to make that clear. The inevitable inference from the plans was that the entire volume of the building, bounded by the horizontal plane of the uppermost part of it, was intended to be included within the demise. The judge had correctly found that any purchaser of the premises would purchase with a view to redevelopment. Such a purchaser would not require or expect a reduction in respect of a large part of the repairs. It followed that the diminution in the value of the reversion brought about by the disrepair was less than the cost of repairs and was the appropriate measure of damages. The judge had properly assessed that value by reference to items of repair that a developer purchaser would have to carry out itself.

Comment:

This case is a warning to landlords who might intend to use payment of a dilapidations claim to pay for redevelopment of the property.

12.3 Jackson v J H Watson Property Investment Ltd

[2008] EWHC 14 (Ch); [2008] 02 EG 147 (CS)

The facts:

The claimant was the tenant of a basement flat under a 125-year lease that the defendant's predecessor had granted in September 1996. The defendant company became the assignee of the reversion in 1997. Under clause 3(b) of the lease, the claimant covenanted to pay 8.333% of the cost of fulfilling the landlord's obligations under the fifth schedule and its reasonable administrative costs in complying with those obligations. Under paragraph 2 of Schedule 5 of the lease, the lessor covenanted, *inter alia*, 'at all times during the term well and substantially to repair … and maintain … the exterior of the estate … and the entrance ways paths and staircases, main walls, party walls, roof foundations and all structural parts thereof … with all necessary reparations and amendments whatsoever'. Between 1997 and 2002, water had entered into the flat as a result of a defect in the concrete light wells adjoining the flat. The light wells were not within the claimant's demise but came under the defendant's control. The claimant carried out works to the flat at a cost of £5,547.13 and suffered inconvenience and/or a diminution in the value of the flat, which he assessed at £3,900. He sought to recover those sums from the defendant. The claimant did not suggest that the repairing covenant had been breached *per se*, but argued that its wording went beyond a mere covenant to repair. Further, he contended that there was a continuing nuisance on the part of the defendant, which was liable for failing to take reasonable steps to abate it. The defendant accepted that the defect giving rise to the ingress of water might amount to a nuisance, but denied that it did so in this case. It argued that, since the defect in the concrete had been present prior to the grant of the lease, the principle of caveat lessee applied so that the original landlord would not have been liable to the claimant. In those circumstances, no liability for a continuing nuisance could have been created on the assignment to the defendant in 1997.

The decision:

The claim was dismissed. In the absence of an effective covenant to repair in the lease, the claimant could not rely upon the law of nuisance to impose an obligation to rectify faulty construction work by the defendant's predecessor in title. Since, on the evidence, the premises demised were at all times in the same physical condition for present purposes as they were when constructed, no want of repair had been proved for which the defendant could be liable under the repairing covenant. On the proper construction of the covenant, it was not possible to hold that the wording went beyond a mere covenant to repair. The principle of caveat lessee applied to a nuisance involving interference with the physical enjoyment of land and damage resulting from defective premises. In the absence of statutory intervention, parties were free to let and to take a lease of poorly constructed premises and allocate the rectification costs as they saw fit. The principle applied whether the complaint related to the state and condition of the demised premises or of other parts of the building in which the demised premises were located.

Comment:

This case illustrates that tenants of new commercial buildings should obtain the benefit of collateral warranties from the construction and design team to ensure that they are not left without a remedy in this situation.

12.4 Princes House Ltd v Distinctive Clubs Ltd

[2007] EWCA Civ 374; [2007] L & TR 34

The facts:

Under a 1998 lease of basement premises, service charges were payable by the respondent to the appellant for specified services, including the repair and maintenance of the roof of part of the building known as the BAFTA block. The respondent's liability was capped for the first five years of the lease. The appellants were to use all reasonable endeavours to provide the services, so far as was consistent with good estate management. By clause 5.5.2, the landlord was not liable to the tenant for any failure to provide the specified services 'unless and until the Tenant has notified the Landlord of such failure and the Landlord has failed within a reasonable time to remedy the same'. In 2002, the appellants informed the tenants that they intended to replace the roof of the BAFTA block in summer 2003, however, the works were then delayed until the following summer. The appellants then claimed £425,000 from the respondent in service charge arrears, plus interest. The respondent counterclaimed for breach of the appellants' repairing covenant, contending that the works should have taken place before the end of 2003, thereby enabling it to benefit from the service charge cap. The court awarded £201,000 on the appellants' claim but awarded a greater sum on the respondent's counterclaim. The judge found that the works could, with reasonable endeavours, have been completed by the end of 2003, and that the appellants were unable to rely upon the notice requirement in clause 5.5.2 in all the circumstances. On appeal, the appellants further contended that any award of damages should have been confined to the cost of patch repairs until 2004.

The decision:

The appeal was dismissed. The appellants' obligation to repair the roof existed independently of any notice given under clause 5.5.2 because it was created by other provisions in the lease. The breach of covenant occurred when the appellants failed to provide the specified services. The purpose of clause 5.5.2 was to protect the appellants by providing that liability would not arise until it was notified by the respondent and a reasonable time had passed. Since that provision was to protect one party, that party could waive it unilaterally. By informing the respondent that they intended to repair the roof in the summer of 2003, the appellants had made it clear that they were not relying upon the requirement for notice. Furthermore, what constituted a reasonable time was not linked to the giving of notice but depended upon all the circumstances, including the fact that the appellants knew of the need for repair without having been notified. The judge had been entitled to find that, had the appellants used all reasonable endeavours, they could have completed the roof works by the end of 2003 in circumstances that met the reasonable requirements of the tenant immediately below. It was not appropriate to restrict damages to the cost of patch repairs until 2004. Patch repairs were reasonable while the appellants were working up a scheme for replacement, but were no longer sufficient once the appellants had been advised that replacement was required and had devised a scheme.

Comment:

The tenant successfully argued that the landlord had delayed the repairs and therefore denied it the benefit of a service charge cap. However, where a prospective tenant wishes to exclude its liability to contribute towards particular costs, consideration should be given to negotiating a limit on service charge costs relating to that specific item of expenditure rather than a cap that applies during a specified period.

12.5 Carmel Southend Ltd v Strachan & Henshaw Ltd

[2007] EWHC 1289 (TCC); [2007] 35 EG 136

The facts:

The defendant had taken a lease of industrial premises for a term of 15 years in which it covenanted to keep the premises, and to yield them up, in good and substantial repair. It was agreed that, when the lease expired, the roof was in disrepair. In 2005, the claimant landlord arranged for the roof to be 'overcladded'. The defendant argued that patch repairs represented a cheaper repair option which had been reasonably and sensibly possible and that the patch repairs should therefore form the basis of the calculation of damages. The claimant argued that patch repairs would not have been an appropriate method of repair and/or would have been futile and impracticable.

The decision:

The claim was allowed. However, patch repairs, which were very common in the industry, were the appropriate repair works, given the particular disrepair to the roof and the terms of the covenants. Such a conclusion was supported by the vast majority of the oral expert evidence heard at trial. The overcladding of the roof had been the result of the claimant's decision, who had had the position of the incoming tenant firmly in mind, without any advice to the effect that the cost of such work would be recoverable from the defendant. Damages would be assessed accordingly.

Comment:

Whilst the landlord was successful in his claim, he only obtained damages on the basis of patch repairs.

12.6 Lyndendown Ltd v Vitamol Ltd

[2007] EWCA Civ 826; [2007] 47 EG 170

The facts:

The appellant was the landlord and the respondent was the tenant under a headlease of two industrial units for a term expiring in January 2002. In late 1999, the appellant granted a licence to the respondent to sublet. The subtenant covenanted with the appellant to observe, and perform, all the covenants contained in the headlease. The respondent's parent company had previously given an undertaking to the subtenant, in a letter, that the subtenant's repairing obligations would be limited to making the property wind and watertight, and that any greater obligation contained in the sublease or the licence to sublet would be performed at the parent company's expense. Following the expiry of the headlease, the subtenant remained in possession under the terms of the sublease pursuant to Part II of the Landlord and Tenant Act 1954. The appellant brought a dilapidations claim against the respondent. The respondent denied any liability for damages on the ground that there had been no diminution in the value of the reversion within section 18 of the Landlord and Tenant Act 1927. It was accepted that, unless the letter sent by the parent company altered the position, any damage to the reversion was nil or nominal since, at the date upon which the headlease expired, the subtenant was in occupation under a sublease, to which Part II of the 1954 Act applied, containing the same or similar repairing covenants, which the appellant could enforce directly by virtue of section 65(2) of the 1954 Act. The appellant maintained that the letter adversely affected its interest and it relied on an admission of the respondent's expert that, had he been advising the appellant at the time of the licence, he would have advised it to take a guarantee from the parent company. Determining a preliminary issue, the county court held that the existence of the letter did not affect the value of the reversion and that the appellant was not entitled to substantial damages. The appellant appealed.

The decision:

The appeal was dismissed. The county court had been entitled to accept the evidence of the respondent's expert and to conclude that the letter had not adversely affected the value of the reversion. The arrangement between the parent company and the subtenant, as set out in the letter, could have no effect upon the subtenant's obligations to repair under the sublease. Although there was a degree of uncertainty in the letter, and a potential for a falling out between the parent company and the subtenant, that was not a significant risk and would not worry a potential purchaser. The court had been entitled to infer that the advice that the respondent's expert would have given would have been aimed at taking commercial advantage, at a time when the subtenant was not yet bound by the sublease, of the parent company's willingness to indemnify the subtenant. The position had been quite different by 2001 and 2002.

Comment:

This case illustrates that when granting a licence to assign or sublet, a landlord should ask to see any side letters so that it can identify whether there can be any current or eventual prejudice to the landlord.

13 LEASEHOLD ENFRANCHISEMENT

13.1 Kensington Heights Commercial Co Ltd v Campden Hill Developments Ltd

[2007] EWCA Civ 245; [2007] Ch 318

The facts:

The appellant appealed against an Order that it transfer, to the respondents, the term granted by a lease of a property pursuant to Part 1 of the Landlord and Tenant Act 1987, and the respondents cross-appealed against an Order that the transfer was subject to a sub-underlease. The appellant had held the property, which it had developed into flats and houses, under a 1973 lease from Thames Water. The respondents were qualifying tenants within the meaning of the 1987 Act and so if the appellant wished to dispose of its interest, the respondents had to be offered first refusal. In 2000, the freehold reversion was transferred by Thames Water to another company, which agreed with the appellant that it would accept a surrender of the 1973 lease and grant it a new lease. No offer notices under the 1987 Act were served. In 2004, the appellant granted a 10-year lease of part of the roof of the property to Vodafone, to allow Vodafone to erect telecommunications apparatus on the property. The respondents served notice requiring the property to be transferred to them free from the sub-underlease to Vodafone. The judge found that the 2000 agreement was a relevant disposal, that the appellant had been in breach of its obligations under Part I of the Act, and ordered that the 2000 lease should be transferred to the respondents, subject to the sub-underlease to Vodafone.

The decision:

The appeal was allowed and the cross-appeal dismissed. The 2000 agreement, which contained the agreement to surrender, was the relevant disposal. An offer notice should have been, but had not been, served on the respondents. The appellant was the head lessee before the transaction and remained the head lessee after the transaction. On this basis, the commercial effect of the 2000 agreement was not a disposal of the appellant's interest.

Comment:

This case illustrates the complexity of the 1987 Act. Although the court acknowledged that the landlord had failed to serve notice in breach of the 1987 Act, the tenants were left without a remedy. It is vital that the correct notices are served to protect the tenants' interests.

13.2 Renshaw v Magnet Properties South East LLP

[2008] 4 EG 170

The facts:

The claimants were the tenants of a house containing four flats. In September 2006, as qualifying tenants, they served notice on the defendant's predecessor in title, the then registered owner, of their claim to exercise the right to acquire the freehold of the house under section 13 of the Leasehold Reform, Housing and Urban Development Act 1993. The notice specified 26 November 2006 as the last date upon which a counter-notice under section 21 of the 1993 Act could be served. On 8 November 2006, the defendant completed the purchase of the reversion from its predecessor, although it did not register that acquisition until 12 January 2007. Meanwhile, on 20 November 2006, the defendant served a counter-notice under the Act, although its predecessor remained the registered owner. The claimants' initial notice sought acquisition at a price of £27,799 plus £1, whereas the counter-notice suggested that the appropriate price was £120,000. The claimants issued an application under section 25(1) of the 1993 Act, for the court to determine the terms upon which they were to acquire the freehold of the property in the absence of a valid counter-notice. The defendant applied for the claim to be struck out and/or summary judgment since the claim was misconceived in law. The claimants argued that the only person on whom notices were to be served, and who could serve notices under the 1993 Act, was the registered proprietor, and that position was not affected in the present case by section 19 of the Act. Section 19 addressed the possibility of one or more disposals of the reversion during the tenant's initial notice period.

The decision:

The application was dismissed. The basic principle underlying the law of land registration, which applied equally in the present case, was that a purchaser, even with actual notice of an encumbrance that needed to be registered, took free of that encumbrance unless it was registered. A tenant had to know on whom he was to serve notice, and who was serving notices on him. In principle, the reversioner for the purposes of both receiving and giving notices had to be the registered proprietor. By section 19(3) of the 1993 Act, at the date of the disposal on 12 January 2007, the defendant, having acquired the reversion and legally perfected its title, took over everything that had been done up to that date by its predecessor. The legal status of what had or had not been done enured to the benefit or disadvantage of the new owner. It was not sensible to hold that the defendant could do something prior to 12 January 2007 that it had no legal right or power to do and have it validated retrospectively. The position had to be clear as at the date upon which the notice was served. Once that position was clear and regularised, a purchaser merely acquired a clear and regularised position from its vendor, which was the way in which section 19 operated.

Comment:

This decision illustrates how it is crucial that time-critical notices are served by or on the right person.

13.3 Earl Cadogan v Sportelli

[2007] EWCA Civ 1042; [2007] 44 EG 180 (CS)

The facts:

This case involved a number of appeals about the price payable to the landlords in respect of several leasehold enfranchisement claims by tenants of properties in central London. Three of the appeals were collective enfranchisement claims under the Leasehold Reform, Housing and Urban Development Act 1993; one was a lease extension claim under the 1993 Act; and the other involved the enfranchisement of a single house, under section 9(1A) of the Leasehold Reform Act 1967. The issues to be decided were, first, the deferment rate to be applied when valuing the freehold interest with vacant possession and, secondly, whether an addition should be made to the price to reflect hope value, that is, the value arising from the option that a freeholder would have had, in the real market, to sell the freehold or a leasehold extension to the tenant in the future. The Lands Tribunal applied a general deferment rate of 4.75% for houses and 5% for flats, setting a new guideline and departing from the standard rate of 6% that had been applied in previous cases involving properties within the prime central London area. It also decided that, on the correct construction of the 1993 Act, hope value was to be excluded from the collective enfranchisement and lease extension cases, although it could be included in respect of the single house enfranchisement under section 9(1A) of the 1967 Act. The landlords appealed on the hope value point in respect of the 1993 Act cases.

The decision:

The appeals were dismissed. Hope value was not a permissible element in the valuations under Schedules 6 or 13 to the 1993 Act for lease extensions or collective enfranchisement respectively. It represented no more than the anticipation of future marriage value. The scheme of the 1993 Act differed from its predecessors in making detailed provision for the definition and allocation of marriage value, as a separate element of the price payable to the landlord. The statute acknowledged the special value that the lessee was likely to receive by the enlargement of its interest, whether by coalescence with, or control of, the freehold, or by adding a 90-year extension onto the lease. It recognised that, in the real world, the respective shares of that special value would be a matter for negotiation between landlord and tenant. The purpose of the statute was to reduce uncertainty by separately identifying that special value and fixing the landlord's share at 50%, or excluding that element altogether for leases with 80 years left to run.

There was no scope for the separate inclusion of hope value. The appellants' narrow interpretation, upon which the exclusion of the tenant's overbid was directed only at the present, led to absurdity. In excluding tenants' bids from consideration in the valuation process, the statute referred to the acquisition of any interest from the landlord either now or in the future. It was not disputed that the assumed market was different from the real market. Once that was accepted, the degree of difference, and its relevance to the valuation, was a matter of judgment for the Lands Tribunal. Its approach was not irrational, and was in line with that of the majority of the experts who had given evidence. Moreover, it had been appropriate for the Lands Tribunal to lay down guidelines as to the deferment rate to be applied in future cases. An important part of the Lands Tribunal's role was to promote consistent practice in land valuation matters. In future cases involving property outside the prime central London area, the deferment rate adopted by the Lands Tribunal would be the starting point, although evidence might be called to show that a different rate should be applied.

Comment:

The Court of Appeal's decision is of great interest, as deferment rates have a direct impact on the price payable by tenants when enfranchising or extending their leases. Unfortunately, whilst the court went some way towards clarifying why market evidence is not an appropriate guideline for setting deferment rates, it did not comment on what forms of evidence may be more relevant to areas outside central London. It agreed that there is now a need for Parliament to legislate on the issue of deferment rates so as to give greater certainty to the market.

14   MORTGAGES

14.1 Scottish and Newcastle plc v Lancashire Mortgage Corporation Ltd

[2007] EWCA Civ 684; [2007] All ER (D) 68 (Jul)

The facts:

The appellant brewery had a charge over club premises. The owner of the club sought to re-finance his indebtedness to the brewery by remortgaging the club and his house. The respondent was prepared to make a loan on the security of a first legal charge on both the house and the club, and it advanced £30,000 of which £20,000 was paid to the appellant. Both the appellant and the respondent took legal charges over the house and the appellant's charge was registered first. The owner then fell into arrears with the loan repayment, both the club and the house were sold and the proceeds were insufficient to meet both lenders' claims in full. The appellant asserted priority for its charge over the house as it was registered first. The respondent argued that its charge ranked in priority. The judge held that the appellant was estopped from denying the respondent's priority.

The decision:

The judge had been entitled to make the findings of fact on which the respondent's case of proprietary estoppel was based. Prior to the granting of the legal charges, the owner's solicitor had direct contact with the appellant's recoveries manager. As a result, the appellant understood that its charges would rank second and, in that knowledge, the appellant acquiesced in and benefited from the respondent's loan to the owner. The post-completion documents were also consistent with the appellant knowing that its charges ranked second. It was a case of passive acquiescence rather than positive representation, encouragement or promise.

Comment:

The dispute in this case could have been avoided if the parties had entered into a deed regulating the priority between their legal charges. This case also demonstrates how important it is to check the register once an application to register a transaction has been completed by the Land Registry, so that any errors can be identified and the Land Registry can be asked to correct them.

15 OPTIONS

15.1 Rennie v Westbury Homes (Holdings) Ltd

[2007] EWCA Civ 1401; [2007] 2 EGLR 95

The facts:

On 17 September 1992, the claimant and his wife entered into an agreement with the defendant, a developer, whereby, in return for £50,000, they granted it an option to purchase 21.53 acres of agricultural land that had development potential for 50% of its market value. The option was exercisable during a period of ten years from the date of the agreement, which additionally provided that: 'At any time during the last year of the Option Period ... the intending Purchaser may by notice in writing ... require such period to be extended by 5 years and upon service of such notice and payment to the intending Vendor of the additional sum of ... £20,000 this Agreement shall be construed as if the Option Period was 15 years'. The claimant's wife died in 1998 and her interest in the land passed to the claimant. On 12 September 2002, the defendant's solicitors wrote to the claimant's solicitor stating that they would shortly be placed in funds for the extension of the option for a further five years, and requesting bank account details in order to arrange payment. The claimant did not reply, but, on 17 September 2002, £20,000 was transferred to the client account of the claimant's solicitor, which acknowledged receipt of the payment. The claimant sought a declaration that the option agreement had determined because notice and payment to extend it had not been given in time. It was by then agreed that the original option period had ended on 16 September 2002.

The decision:

The claim was dismissed. The option agreement set out what the notice had to convey to the recipient, without prescribing the inclusion of any particular form of words or any particular details. A reasonable recipient of the letter of 12 September 2002, with knowledge of the terms of the option agreement, would have understood that the defendant required the option period to be extended by five years. The defendant's subjective intentions were irrelevant and, accordingly, it made no difference that the defendant might have intended the letter to be merely preparatory to a later notice. A document that was not intended by its sender to be a valid notice could nevertheless operate as one. The letter therefore constituted a valid notice to extend the option period. There was no express requirement to pay the sum of £20,000 before the expiry of the ten-year period, and no such requirement could be included by necessary implication. The making of the payment was merely a further obligation that had to be performed before the option agreement could be construed as though the option period were 15 years instead of 10. The appropriate implication was that such payment would be made within a reasonable time. Such a term provided the claimant with sufficient certainty. Payment the day after the expiry of the original option period was reasonable.

Comment:

This decision emphasises the need to take care when drafting an option agreement and, in particular, in respect of what will constitute a valid notice, whether for the purposes of exercising a right to extend, or a right to exercise the option.

15.2 Ahmed v Wingrove

[2007] EWHC 1777 (Ch); [2007] 31 EG 81 (CS)

The facts:

The claimants granted the defendant an option to purchase land to the rear of their house. The option land consisted of an access strip and an irregular plot. The claimants would retain a 25-foot wide strip along the rear boundary of their property. The claimants fenced the option land to separate it from the rest of their property. The defendant later purported to exercise the option. In subsequent proceedings, the judge rejected the claimants' argument that the option was unenforceable, or that it ought to be rectified in terms that rendered the defendant's attempt to exercise it ineffective. The judge made an Order for specific performance, as requested by the defendant, in terms that 'Upon the Defendant paying to the Claimants on 20th October ... the sum of £100,000 ... the Claimants shall ... execute a proper transfer of the Property to the Defendant'. The parties' solicitors then corresponded about completion. Issues were raised concerning the defendant's wish to inspect the land prior to completion to ensure that the fence correctly reflected the boundaries, and concerning a claim by the claimants to be entitled to an implied right of way for the benefit of their retained land. The completion date specified in the Court Order, 20 October 2006, passed without the sale taking place. Five days later, the claimants' solicitor wrote to the defendant, expressing the view that time was of the essence of the Order, that they had been ready and willing to complete on that date, and that the defendant's failure to do so amounted to a repudiatory breach of contract that entitled the claimants to rescind the option agreement. The claimants then applied to the court for an Order that the contract was discharged owing to the defendant's failure to complete. At the hearing, the claimants finally abandoned their claim to an implied right of way.

The decision:

The application was dismissed. As a matter of contract, time was not of the essence on 20 October 2006 and failure to complete by that date was not a repudiatory breach of contract. That failure did not give rise to any contractual right on the part of the vendor to treat the contract as at an end. The Court Order was not in the form of an 'unless' order and there was no suggestion in it that the defendant was to lose the contract altogether just because he

was a few days late in completing. The defendant had been unable
to complete since the completion date because the claimants had
purported to terminate the contract only five days after that date
and had thereafter refused to consider completion. The court
should consider whether it was appropriate to allow the defendant
further time to complete the contract, in the same manner as it
would with any other application for an extension of time, having
regard to the justice of the case and the overriding objective. In the
instant case, it was appropriate to extend the time for completion.
In the face of the claimants' claim to a right of way, which was
unwarranted and totally spurious, it had not been unreasonable
for the defendant to seek to get to the bottom of that issue before
completion. His request for access to check the position of the
fences was likewise reasonable. An order would be made setting a
new timetable for completion. A declaration would also be made
that there was no right of way over the property to be transferred in
favour of the claimants' retained land.

Comment:

In this case, the claimants failed in their final bid to avoid an option
agreement granting a developer the right to buy land to the rear of
their house for £100,000.

15.3 Coles v Samuel Smith Old Brewery (Tadcaster) (an unlimited company)

[2007] EWCA Civ 1461; [2007] PLSCS 247

The facts:

The appellants were the trustees of a working men's club and
held a tenancy of the club premises and a long-standing option
to purchase the freehold from the first respondent landlord. The
option had not been registered under either the Land Charges Act
1972 or the Land Charges Act 1925. In 2002, the appellants sought
to exercise the option. The first respondent did not wish to sell to
them and, instead, sold the property to the second respondent, its

wholly owned subsidiary, for £7,996, on the basis that the option would be void against a purchaser of the legal estate for money or money's worth. The appellants brought proceedings against the respondents, seeking specific performance of the contract for sale that had been created by the exercise of the option. Refusing that relief, the judge held that the sale to the second respondent was not a sham, notwithstanding that the purchase price was below the value of the property and that the sale had taken place for the sole purpose of avoiding the obligations under the option. The judge accepted the respondents' arguments that the specific performance could not be ordered against either the first respondent, which no longer owned the property, or the second respondent, against which the option was not binding. He instead awarded damages for breach of contract.

The decision:

The appeal was allowed. The judge had correctly refused to order specific performance against the second respondent. The transaction with the second respondent had been a genuine sale to a genuine company, albeit at a low price, and could not be regarded as a sham. However, specific performance could have been ordered against the first respondent. It would have been possible to order the first respondent to procure a transfer by the second respondent to the appellants; the first respondent could, if necessary, have changed the directors of the second respondent to overcome any objection from their side.

Comment:

Although the appellants were able to enforce their option, this case illustrates how important it is to register an option immediately after exchange. There might be considerable time between exchange of the option agreement and completion of the sale and this case illustrates the problems that can arise.

16 PLANNING

16.1 M & M (Land) Ltd v Secretary of State for Communities and Local Government

[2007] EWHC 489 (Admin); [2007] 2 P & CR 18

The facts:

The applicant had purchased a site in respect of which a certificate of lawful existing use as a 'scrap yard' had previously been granted by the waste planning authority. The applicant unsuccessfully applied for planning permission to redevelop the site as a scrap yard. The planning inspector determined that the main issue before him was whether the use of the site for the buying and selling of scrap metal and salvage had been abandoned or not. After hearing evidence, the planning inspector decided that the site had been used on a 'low-key ' basis as a scrap yard, but that that use had been abandoned approximately ten years earlier following a fire on the site. The planning inspector concluded that, given that use of the site as a scrap yard had been abandoned, the proposed redevelopment of the site as a scrap yard was contrary to planning policy and should be refused. The applicant applied to quash the decision on the basis that it was not possible in law, pursuant to section 191 of the Town and Country Planning Act 1990, to abandon the use of land that had received a certificate of lawful existing use.

The decision:

The application was refused. Section 191 merely declared that at a particular point in time a use referred to by the certificate was lawful. It could not be said that a use dignified with a certificate of lawful existing use was in a stronger position than a use conferred by a grant of planning permission and, accordingly, such a use could, like a use conferred by a grant of planning permission, be abandoned.

Comment:

This decision confirms that, even where land benefits from a certificate of lawful use, it is not sufficient, when the use is challenged, to produce the certificate as conclusive proof that the use is authorised. Thus, where a seller provides a buyer with a certificate of lawful use, enquiries should be raised concerning the actual use of the property in question.

17   PROFESSIONAL NEGLIGENCE

17.1 Earl of Malmesbury v Strutt and Parker (a partnership)

[2007] EWHC 999 (QB); [2007] 21 EG 130 (CS)

The facts:

The claimants brought an action for negligence against the defendant which had negotiated four leases of the claimants' land for airport car parking. The claimants alleged that a surveyor employed by the defendant had been negligent and in breach of his duty to exercise skill and care in relation to three of those leases for the years 2000, 2002, and 2003. The leases were due to run until August 2026, and the evidence was that earnings from the car parks for the years 2005 and 2006 would be £845,000 and £1.804 million respectively. It was alleged that the surveyor should have negotiated the leases with rents that reflected the earnings of the car park, and provided for the claimants to receive 80% of those earnings. The claimants' solicitor was also joined into the case on the basis that if the surveyor was in breach of his duty, the solicitor must also have failed in his duty. The claimants sought to recover the difference between the rents that they would receive under the leases as negotiated and the rents that they would have received had the surveyor performed his duty. The defendants argued that the correct approach was to value the reversions that the claimants had and those that they might have had if the surveyor had performed his duty. The questions for the court were, *inter alia*:

i)   whether the defendants were in breach of duty; and if so

ii) whether the claimants had lost a significant chance of obtaining a rent with a turnover element;

iii) the value of that chance; and

iv) the date from which damages should be assessed.

The decision:

Judgment was given for the claimants. On the evidence, the surveyor had failed in his duty to the claimants in negotiating the 2002 and 2003 leases, but not in respect of the 2000 lease. No contributory negligence arose on the part of the claimants. The solicitor was not in breach of his duty to the claimants and the claims against him failed. The claimants were entitled to damages on the basis of what the surveyor was most likely to have obtained in negotiations had he done no more or less than was required to fulfil his duty. Considering the relative strengths and weaknesses of the negotiating positions of the parties, the claimants had lost the chance of a turnover rent as a result of the breach of duty. Where property was acquired as a result of negligent advice, whether the advice came from a surveyor, solicitor or other professional, the usual measure of loss was the difference in value between the purchase price paid and the value as properly described at the date of purchase. The grant or acquisition of a lease was of an interest in land and, where the complaint was of negligent advice to a tenant as to rent, the court was bound to hold that damages were to be assessed on the basis of the values at the transaction date, unless particular circumstances made that inappropriate in that such an approach would not accurately reflect the overriding compensatory rule. There were no special circumstances to show that a valuation basis should not be applied. There was no justification for assessing the value at dates later than the transaction dates. Nothing had happened that required the taking of a later date to satisfy the overriding rule that the measure of damages should put the injured party in the same position as it would have been in had it not sustained the wrong.

Comment:

The court said that the surveyor was retained to give commercial advice and the solicitor was retained to give legal advice. It fell within the surveyor's expertise, and not the solicitor's expertise, to know that a turnover rent was appropriate. This will be a welcome relief for conveyancers.

17.2 Funnell v Adams & Remer (a partnership)

[2007] EWHC 2166 (QB); (2007) 104(40) LSG 27

The facts:

The claimants had instructed the defendants, a solicitors' partnership, to negotiate a 25-year lease of business premises. The initial rent charged was reduced as the claimants were required to remove a large amount of waste over the first five years. There was also an informal agreement that there would be a six-month rent holiday as, under clause 4.31 of the lease, the claimants had to complete certain works. The lease was subject to five annual rent reviews when the rent was to be set in accordance with open market rental values, disregarding the effect of any improvement carried out otherwise than in fulfilment of an obligation to the landlord. During negotiations, the claimants indicated that they wished to perform further works. In accordance with the landlord's wishes, the works were referred to under clause 4.31 as 'new works' and were added to the list of works under that clause. The defendants did not advise the claimants that this amendment imposed an obligation on them to perform the works and that, therefore, any improvement in the land resulting from those works would fall to be reflected in the rent review. This later came to light when the claimants instructed another company in relation to subletting part of the premises to alleviate their financial difficulties. The claimants then decided to extricate themselves from the lease by assigning it. They moved out of the premises one year before the first review date and had to abandon the works. It was accepted that the rent would have been approximately £24,000 per annum at the date of the first review but there was disagreement as to whether, had the new works not been carried out, it would have been £18,000 or £12,600. The claimants submitted that an increase to £12,600 would have been borne by the business.

The decision:

The claim was allowed. The mere act of extricating oneself by taking reasonable steps from a predicament did not break the chain of causation. Accordingly, if the consequences of flowing from that course of action were reasonably foreseeable, they were, in principle, recoverable. However, that could not undermine the primary principle that there had to be a causal link between the loss suffered and the fault giving rise to the claim. Any other conclusion would place the claimants in a better position than they would have been in had the negligence not occurred, because they would be compensated for a loss that they would still have suffered even if the defendants had not been negligent. On the evidence, there was a causal link between the defendants' negligence and the losses suffered by the claimants in abandoning the lease and moving to smaller premises. It was plain that the cause of the decision to assign the lease and abandon that size of premises with that level of security had been triggered by the news concerning the rent review clause and the unexpected high rent that would be payable from the time of the first five-year rent review resulting from the defendants' negligence.

Comment:

This decision illustrates that when conveyancers give advice to a client on the negotiation of a document or specific wording within a document, they need to consider whether the document gives effect to the commercial bargain that their client thinks that it has struck.

18 RENT REVIEW

18.1 Scottish & Newcastle plc v Raguz (No. 3)

[2007] EWCA Civ 150; [2007] 2 All ER 871

The facts:

The appellant appealed against a decision that the respondent was entitled to an indemnity in respect of sums which it had paid to the reversioner under two underleases. The respondent was the original tenant of two underleases of hotel premises and had assigned both leases to the appellant, which had in turn assigned the leases. The premises were in fact occupied by a later assignee that had gone into administrative receivership. There had been two rent reviews and, as the occupier could not pay, the reversioner demanded the rent from the respondent, which paid it. The reversioner required that the rent be paid as a condition of agreeing to the assignment of the leases to a purchaser of the business as a going concern. At first instance, the judge held that, although the reversioner had not served the notices under section 17(2) of the Landlord and Tenant (Covenants) Act 1995 which were necessary to preserve the respondent's liability in respect of large parts of the money claimed, the respondent, having paid the arrears so that the assignment could proceed, was entitled to be indemnified for them by the appellant.

The decision:

The appeal was dismissed. If a landlord wished to preserve the possibility of claiming against an original tenant when the rent was subject to review, he had to serve section 17(2) notices within six months after each rent day in turn, specifying that the sum intended to be recovered was then nil, but that this was subject to paragraph 4 of the notice and the possibility of the rent being determined to be a greater sum.

Comment:

As a result of this decision, if a rent review has not been determined by the relevant rent review date, a landlord should, as a precautionary measure, serve a section 17 notice on any former tenants (and any guarantors of those tenants) who remain liable for the payment of fixed charges. This notice should be served within six months of each rent payment date until the rent review has been determined. A further notice should be served once the final amount has been determined, unless the current tenant has actually paid any shortfall that was due following the rent review being finalised. This is an unwelcome additional property management task on landlords. It should be noted that leave to appeal to the House of Lords was granted on 12 July 2007.

18.2 Coors Holdings Ltd v Dow Properties Ltd

[2007] EWCA Civ 255; [2007] 2 P & CR 22

The facts:

The appellant's predecessor had entered into an agreement with the respondent that a lease would be granted once the respondent had constructed a public house. The building was completed and the lease was granted. The rent review clause in the lease provided that there would be a rent review every ten years that would bring the rental value of 'the site comprised in the demised premises' in line with an open market valuation. A declaration was sought as to whether that clause required the open market rental value to be determined by reference to land and building or land alone. It was held that the phrase 'the site comprised in' meant that, for rent review purposes, only the part of the demised premises that consisted of the site excluding the building should be valued to determine the open market rental value. The judge accordingly made a declaration that in establishing the rental value of the demised premises, the valuation should be carried out under the assumption that the building did not exist. The appellant appealed.

The decision:

In construing a rent review clause, the correct starting point was the terms of the lease and the assumption that one would normally expect the rent on review to be for the whole premises. There had to be a very clear indication of a contrary intention in the lease for it to be otherwise. In this case, on the proper construction of the lease, the phrase 'the site comprised in' could only be referring to the land without the building.

Comment:

This decision highlights the need for clear drafting to give effect to the intention of the parties. If the building was intended to be excluded from the valuation, then an express term to this effect in the lease would have made this clear.

18.3 Level Properties Ltd v Balls Brothers Ltd

[2007] EWHC 744 (Ch); [2008] 1 P & CR 1

The facts:

The rent review clause in the defendant's lease provided that, on review, the rent was the higher of the passing rent and the open market yearly rent. The review was referred to an independent expert for determination. Clause 3.13 of the lease stated that the claimant's written licence to assign the whole of the demised premises should not be unreasonably withheld, subject to its entitlement to require a surety in certain circumstances. The court was required to determine the interpretation of certain provisions within the lease. On an application for a licence to assign, could the claimant have insisted on the provision of a surety on assignment even if it was unreasonable to do so? On the true construction of the lease should the open market yearly rent be determined either on the basis of a single letting, or if it produced a higher figure, on the basis of two lettings, one of the ground floor and one of the basement, the open market yearly rent being the aggregate of the rents payable under those two lettings? Were the parties bound by the expert's determination?

The decision:

Clause 3.13 set out the agreement of the parties as to what alienations were not absolutely prohibited and could be made with consent and, accordingly, restrict the circumstances in which a tenant could properly apply for consent to an assignment. It did not set out a condition which the claimant could impose for the giving of consent to an assignment, nor did it set out a circumstance in which a refusal of consent was deemed to be reasonable. Therefore, the claimant could insist on a surety. The correct interpretation of the clause that defined the open yearly market rate was that it was to be determined on the basis of two lettings, one for the ground floor and one for the basement if it produced a higher figure. Finally, the parties were not bound by the expert's determination as the lease did not confer upon him the sole and exclusive power to interpret the lease.

Comment:

The preliminary issues are an interesting reminder of how a court will construe rent review provisions and the fact that, in the absence of ambiguity, or a lack of clarity, the rent review provisions will be interpreted on the basis of the words used in the context of the lease as a whole. The decision also revisited the role of an independent expert appointed to determine the new rent at rent review.

19 RESIDENTIAL TENANCIES

19.1 Andrews v Cunningham

[2007] EWCA Civ 762; [2008] L & TR 1

The facts:

The appellant was the tenant of the ground floor flat in a property divided into flats. The owner of the property had occupied the basement flat. The tenancy had been given orally and the owner had given the appellant a rent book which had the words 'Assured Tenancy' on the cover. Some three and a half years after the owner's death the executors of his estate, the respondents, had served the appellant with a notice under section 21 of the Housing Act 1988 purporting to end his tenancy. The appellant claimed that his tenancy was a non-shorthold assured tenancy and that accordingly the notice was of no effect. The district judge decided that the owner had intended that the appellant was to have security of tenure on a long-term basis and that the rent book was a notice to that effect. On appeal, the judge determined that the appellant was an assured shorthold tenant.

The decision:

The appeal was dismissed. The words 'assured tenancy' on the cover of the rent book were not a statement 'that the assured tenancy to which it relates is not to be an assured shorthold tenancy' because an assured shorthold tenancy was itself a type of assured tenancy.

Comment:

This case highlights the requirement of serving the correct statutory notice, without which there may be uncertainty and arguments over what was intended.

20 RESTRICTIVE COVENANTS

20.1 Re Vince's Application

(2007) 151 SJLB 1264

The facts:

This was an application under section 84(1)(aa) and (c) of the Law of Property Act 1925 for the modification of restrictive covenants affecting a large house and its grounds. The covenants, which benefited two adjoining properties, prevented the applicants from using their property for any purpose other than as a single private dwellinghouse in the occupation of one family, from doing anything that could be a nuisance to the owners of the adjoining properties, or from obstructing or interfering with the access and user of light and air to and for the adjoining properties. The applicants had obtained planning permission to convert their house into five dwellings, including two-storey and first-floor extensions, with off-street parking for ten cars. The owner of one adjoining property objected. The applicants required a modification of the covenants solely to allow the development for which they had permission so that the adjoining owner would be protected from any future redevelopment proposals.

The decision:

The application was refused. The proposed development would reduce the value of the adjoining house by £5,000 to £10,000, which was not a significant impact. There would be no loss of view from inside the adjoining house and the loss of the view from its garden that would result from the proposed development was not material. The development would increase the residential floor space of the applicants' house by at least a third and there would be five dwellings instead of one. It was highly likely that the vehicular movements and activity generated by five households, in two three-bedroom houses and three two-bedroom houses, would exceed that of a single household. Although vehicles travelling to and from the applicants' property would not normally pass the front of the adjoining house, it was likely that there would be an increase in total vehicular movements but the placement of windows in the applicants' proposals meant that the privacy of the adjoining owner would be maintained as far as possible. Whilst the amount of sunlight and diffuse light available to some of the rooms in the adjoining house would be reduced, the affected rooms would be the utility room, cloakroom, half-landing, bathroom and attic and therefore their use was essentially transitory. There was nothing in the restrictive covenants that justified giving special weight to the issue of noise and disturbance caused by the building works, which would be short-term, and therefore was not an issue to be considered under section 84(1)(aa), which was concerned with the long-term user of land. The proposed development, despite their best efforts to minimise its impact by considerate design, would lead to increased occupancy, activity and vehicular movement and to some loss of light to the adjoining house, which would have a significant combined effect. The maintenance of peace and quiet and the access of light, both of which had remained largely unchanged since the covenants were imposed, were practical benefits that were of substantial value or advantage to the adjoining owner. The applicants had failed to satisfy the requirements of section 84(1)(aa) and also section 84(1)(c).

Comment:

This case is a useful example of the weight that the Lands Tribunal will give to the various arguments put forward by a party seeking to oppose the discharge or modification of a restrictive covenant. The Lands Tribunal was not really swayed by arguments relating to the value of the land, nor by the aspect and view enjoyed by the property. Instead, it gave greater emphasis on the adverse impact of a reduction of light to the property and the increased activity and resulting noise that would be generated if the covenant was modified to allow development.

20.2 Lawntown Ltd v Camenzuli

[2007] EWCA Civ 949; [2008] 1 EG 136

The facts:

The respondent, a developer, had obtained planning permission to convert a house into two flats. The house was one of a pair of semi-detached houses on an estate of similar houses built as family houses. The house was subject to restrictive covenants that prevented the conversion into flats. The benefit of the covenants extended to all the properties on the estate. The respondent applied to the county court under section 610 of the Housing Act 1985 to vary the covenants. The appellants, who lived next door, opposed the application. The judge held that the court should normally proceed on the assumption that the planning permission had been properly granted and should not have regard to matters that had already been considered by the planning authority. The judge considered the loss of the benefit of the covenant, the setting of a precedent and negative effect on property values, and conducted a balancing exercise in which the crucial factor was the urgent demand for more housing in London. None of these matters had been taken into account by the planning authority. He therefore allowed the application.

The decision:

The appeal was dismissed. The court's discretion under section 610 was broad but not unfettered. The statute did not create a presumption in favour of a variation of the restrictive covenant or any duty to vary. Instead, the court was to carry out a balancing exercise, taking into account all relevant factors and giving such weight to them as it judged appropriate. The court was to have regard to the interests that were protected by the restrictive covenant and the extent to which those would be harmed by the proposed variation, as well as to the interests of the person seeking the variation and the advantages that would accrue from it. The latter factor could engage matters of public as well as private interest, particularly where policy considerations favoured the more intensive use of existing dwellinghouses. The court had to make its own assessment of the relevant factors. It should not leave matters out of account merely because they had already been considered by the local planning authority when granting planning permission. The judge had erred in confining his attention to those matters that had not been taken into account in the planning process. Determining the question afresh, the matters raised by the appellants as objections were outweighed by the factors in favour of variation, including the existence of an urgent demand for more housing in London. To take account of such matters did not involve straying into the impermissible area of planning judgment. The development plan reflected a matter of wider public interest in that respect, and it was appropriate for the court to have regard to the public benefit of meeting the need for additional homes through the conversion of existing houses into flats. Such an approach was in line with the underlying policy of section 610.

Comment:

Whilst an application to the Lands Tribunal under section 84 of the Law of Property Act 1925 is a well-known procedure for modifying a restrictive covenant, the provisions of section 610 of the Housing Act 1985 are relatively unknown and are rarely used. This case illustrates that section 610 can be a useful tool for potential developers to circumvent a requirement only to use a property as a single private dwellinghouse.

20.3 Dobbin v Redpath

[2007] EWCA Civ 570; [2007] 4 All ER 465

The facts:

The appellant appealed against a decision of the Lands Tribunal refusing his application to modify a restrictive covenant affecting his land so as to permit the erection of a detached bungalow and garage. The restrictions had been imposed by a conveyance and the land formed part of a building scheme. The appellant obtained planning permission to build on the land but the respondent, who owned the adjoining property, objected. The Lands Tribunal held that the appellant had not satisfied section 84 of the Law of Property Act 1925, that the proposed construction would have an adverse effect on the surrounding area, and that the existence of a building scheme increased the presumption that the restrictive covenant would be maintained.

The decision:

The appeal was dismissed. All the Tribunal did was to apply the relevant guidance for these type of cases and to take a different approach in its consideration of the test under section 84 where a building scheme was in existence. It was true that to speak of an 'increased presumption' where a building scheme existed was misleading and it was preferable that the Tribunal instead considered the weight to be attached to objections in light of the existence of a building scheme. However, the Tribunal found the existence of the scheme to be highly relevant and there were no grounds for interfering with its decision.

Comment:

This case provides a useful summary of the approach taken by the Lands Tribunal when considering an application to modify a restriction imposed by a building scheme. The scenario in this case is not unusual, and the decision shows that the existence of a planning permission for a proposed development does not mean that the neighbours will not enforce the benefit of a restriction under the building scheme.

21 SERVICE CHARGE

21.1 Brown's Operating System Services Ltd v Southwark Roman Catholic Diocesan Corporation

[2007] EWCA Civ 164; [2008] 1 P & CR 7

The facts:

The appellant appealed against a decision upholding the claim of the respondent for unpaid service charges. The respondent's policy in relation to the service charge was to build up a surplus to cover future expenditure by retaining the excess of the service charges paid by tenants over the amount actually spent. When the surplus reached a substantial sum, the appellant felt that it should be entitled to a service charge 'holiday'. When the respondent refused this, the appellant gave six months' notice to quit and refused to pay the last two quarters' service charge on the basis that the surplus held by the landlord more than covered those two quarters. The respondent sued and it was held that the surplus was for the benefit of the building and that the appellant had not been entitled to refuse to pay it.

The decision:

The appeal was allowed. The lease did allow the respondent to include in the total service cost a sum as reasonable provision for expenditure likely to be incurred. However, it did not provide for the creation of a reserve fund. The money held by the respondent was either held in reserve under the lease, or was the excess of the appellant's payments on account over actual expenditure, which the respondent was entitled to retain only on account of future service rent payable. The money was to be used to meet any authorised expenditure in each succeeding year and only when that money was exhausted could a further demand for more be made. It was to be inferred that any money unspent at the end of the lease belonged to the tenants.

Comment:

This case does not establish a point of law, rather it concerns the wording of a particular lease and highlights the need for clear drafting that sets out the purpose, application and fate of excess service charge monies paid by a tenant.

Part B

RECENT LEGISLATION

| 1 | AGRICULTURAL LAND |

1.1 The Agricultural Holdings (Units of Production) (Wales) Order 2007

SI 2007/2398 (W 199)

Commencement date: 7 September 2007

This Order prescribes units of production for the assessment of the productive capacity of agricultural land situated in Wales and sets out the amount which is to be regarded as the net annual income from each such unit for the year 12 September 2006 to 11 September 2007 inclusive.

This Order revokes the Agricultural Holdings (Units of Production) (Wales) Order 2006.

An assessment of the productive capacity of agricultural land is required in determining whether or not the land in question is a 'commercial unit of agricultural land' for the purposes of the succession provisions in the Agricultural Holdings Act 1986.

A 'commercial unit of agricultural land' is land which, when farmed under competent management, is capable of producing a net annual income which is not less than the aggregate of the average annual earnings of two full-time male agricultural workers aged 20 years or over (paragraph 3 of Schedule 6 to the 1986 Act).

Article 2 of this Order provides that in determining this annual income figure, whenever a particular farming use mentioned in column 1 of the Schedule is relevant to the assessment of the productive capacity of the land in question, the units of production and the net annual income specified in columns 2 and 3 respectively will form the basis of that assessment.

The net annual income figures in column 3 of the Schedule prescribe the net annual income from one unit of production. In some cases the net annual income is derived from a unit which will be on the land for the full 12-month period. In other cases the net annual income is derived from a unit which will be on the land for only part of the year, and there may be more than one production cycle in the 12-month period. The assessment of the productive capacity of the land will take account of the total production in the course of a year.

This Order includes net annual income figures for land which was in 2005 an eligible hectare for the purposes of Council Regulation (EC) No. 1782/2003 (O.J. No. L270, 21.10.2003, p.1), which establishes the Single Payment Scheme. There are separate figures in the Schedule for severely disadvantaged land, disadvantaged land and other land. There are also separate figures for land which was set aside from production in 2005.

2 COMMONHOLD

2.1 The Commonhold and Leasehold Reform Act 2002 (Commencement No. 6) (England) Order 2007
SI 2007/1256

This Order brings into force, on 1 October 2007, section 153 of the Commonhold and Leasehold Reform Act 2002 in relation to England. Section 153 inserts section 21B into the Landlord and Tenant Act 1985, which requires that a demand for service charges must be accompanied by a summary of the rights and obligations of the tenant.

2.2 The Commonhold and Leasehold Reform Act 2002 (Commencement No. 4) (Wales) Order 2007
SI 2007/3161 (W 272)

This Order brought into force on 30 November 2007, section 153 of the Commonhold and Leasehold Reform Act 2002 in relation to Wales. Section 153 of the Act inserts section 21B into the Landlord and Tenant Act 1985, which requires that a demand for service charges must be accompanied by a summary of the rights and obligations of the tenant.

3   COMMONS REGISTRATION

3.1   The Commons Act 2006 (Commencement No. 2, Transitional Provisions and Savings) (England) Order 2007

SI 2007/456

The principal purpose of this Order was to bring section 15 of the Commons Act 2006, which makes new provision about the registration of land as a town or village green, into force in relation to England on 6 April 2007.

It also brought into force in relation to England:

a) on 20 February 2007, section 52 (partially) and paragraphs 4 and 6(a) of Schedule 5; and

b) on 6 April 2007, sections 4, 5 and 24, and Schedule 6 (partially).

The Order also contains transitional and saving provisions to:

a) require that a green registered under section 15 is, until section 1 of the 2006 Act is brought into force in relation to the relevant area, entered in the registers maintained under the Commons Registration Act 1965;

b) ensure that the existing provisions for registration of new greens and common land under section 13(b) of the 1965 Act remain effective in certain cases (such as on an exchange of land consequential on a compulsory purchase order);

c) preserve any application to register a green made under the 1965 Act before 6 April 2007, so that such applications must be determined under that Act.

3.2   The Commons (Registration of Town or Village Greens) (Interim Arrangements) (England) Regulations 2007

SI 2007/457

Commencement date: 6 April 2007

Until sections 1–3 of the Commons Act 2006 come into force, section 15 of the Commons Act 2006 provides a revised basis for seeking registration of land as a town or village green. These Regulations enable registration authorities to register land, which meets the criteria for registration set out in section 15(1) or 15(8) of the 2006 Act, in the register of town or village greens maintained pursuant to the Commons Registration Act 1965.

These Regulations:

a) specify the procedure for applying to register land as a town or village green (Regulation 3);

b) specify the procedure for dealing with applications for registration (Regulations 4–7); and

c) specify the manner of registration of land as a town or village green following the granting of an application (Regulation 8).

These Regulations replace the relevant provisions in the Commons Registration (New Land) Regulations 1969 (SI 1969/1843) for the registration of new town or village greens under the Commons Registration Act 1965. However, the 1969 Regulations remain in force to enable the registration of new greens and new common land for the purposes specified in the savings contained in Article 4(3) of the Commons Act 2006 (Commencement No. 2, Transitional Provisions and Savings) (England) Order 2007 (SI 2007/456).

3.3 The Commons Registration (Objections and Maps) (Amendment) (England) Regulations 2007

SI 2007/540

Commencement date: 6 April 2007

These Regulations amend the Commons Registration (Objections and Maps) Regulations 1968 so as to enable the registration of certain land or rights, whose provisional registration in the register of common land or town or village greens could not otherwise become final in consequence of a court order, either to be made final or be removed from the register.

3.4 The Commons (Severance of Rights) (Wales) Order 2007

SI 2007/583 (W 55)

Commencement date: 1 March 2007

Section 9 of the Commons Act 2006, which is deemed, by section 9(7) of that Act to have come into force on 28 June 2005, prevents, subject to exceptions, the severance of a right of common from the land to which it is attached. This Order permits the temporary severance of a right of common to graze animals from the land to which the right is attached by enabling the leasing or licensing of the right to a third party for no more than three years or by a lease or licence of the land without the right.

This Order came into force on 1 March 2007, but has effect as from 28 June 2005 so that any lease or licence of a right of common to graze animals granted after that date for a period of three years or less is not void for those purposes by virtue of section 9(3) of the Act.

3.5 The Commons Registration (General) (Amendment) (England) (Revocation) Regulations 2007

SI 2007/1553

Commencement date: 31 May 2007

These Regulations revoke the Commons Registration (General) (Amendment) (England) Regulations 2007. The latter Regulations would have revoked on 1 June 2007, in relation to England, provisions of the Commons Registration (General) Regulations 1966 relating to official searches of the commons registers and certificates of search.

3.6 The Works on Common Land, etc. (Procedure) (England) Regulations 2007

SI 2007/2588

Commencement date: 1 October 2007

These Regulations, which apply in relation to England only, prescribe the procedure for applications to the Secretary of State under section 38 of the Commons Act 2006 for consent to carry out restricted works on common land, and certain related types of applications.

They enable the Secretary of State to appoint a person to exercise his functions in relation to such applications (Regulation 3).

They include provisions about:

a) making and publicising applications (Regulations 5, 7–8, 18, 21(1) and 23(1));

b) making representations in relation to applications (Regulation 9); and

c) the management and determination of applications, including provision for holding site inspections, hearings or inquiries in appropriate cases (Regulations 6, 10–17 and 19).

3.7   The Deregistration and Exchange of Common Land and Greens (Procedure) (England) Regulations 2007

SI 2007/2589

Commencement date: 1 October 2007

These Regulations, which apply in relation to England only, prescribe the procedure for applications to the Secretary of State under section 16 of the Commons Act 2006 for the deregistration, or the deregistration and exchange, of areas of registered common land.

They enable the Secretary of State to appoint a person to exercise his functions in relation to such applications (Regulation 3).

They include provisions about:

a) making and publicising applications (Regulations 5(1)–(2) and 7-8);

b) making representations in relation to applications (Regulation 9);

c) the management and determination of applications, including provision for holding site inspections, hearings or inquiries in appropriate cases (Regulations 6 and 10–18); and

d) the fee payable by applicants (Regulation 5(3)).

3.8 The Commons Act 2006 (Commencement No. 3, Transitional Provisions and Savings) (England) Order 2007

SI 2007/2584

This Order brings the following provisions of the Commons Act 2006 into force on 1 October 2007 in relation to England:

a) sections 16 and 17, which make provision about the deregistration and exchange of land registered as common land or as a town or village green;

b) sections 38 to 43, and section 44 and Schedule 4 (insofar as they are not already in force), which make provision about works on common land; and

c) section 48, and section 53 and Schedule 6 (both partially), which contain repeals.

3.9 The Commons (Deregistration and Exchange Orders) (Interim Arrangements) (England) Regulations 2007

SI 2007/2585

Commencement date: 1 October 2007

Sections 16 and 17 of the Commons Act 2006 make provision for applications to deregister land which is registered as common land or as a town or village green, and to register other land in replacement. Such applications are, in England, to be determined by the Secretary of State or a person appointed by him. Where he grants an application, section 17(1) and (2) of the 2006 Act requires him to make an order directing the commons registration authority to amend its register of common land or town or village greens accordingly. Part 1 of the 2006 Act has not yet been fully brought into force. Until sections 1 to 3 are brought into force, an order under section 17 is to be treated as an order directing the registration authority to amend the registers which it maintains pursuant to the Commons Registration Act 1965 by virtue of transitional provisions contained in the Commons Act 2006 (Commencement No. 3, Transitional Provisions and Savings) (England) Order 2007.

These Regulations specify the manner in which a registration authority must amend the registers which it maintains pursuant to the 1965 Act, when it receives an order under section 17.

3.10 The Works on Common Land (Exemptions) (England) Order 2007

SI 2007/2587

Commencement date: 1 October 2007

This Order, which applies in relation to England only, prescribes exemptions to the prohibition in section 38(1) of the Commons Act 2006 on the carrying out, without the consent of the Secretary of State, of any restricted works on land to which that section applies.

Exemptions are prescribed (Article 2 and Schedule 1) which, subject to certain conditions, allow specified persons to erect temporary fencing for the purposes of:

a) restricting the movement of animals which are grazing on the land;

b) allowing recovery of vegetation; and

c) nature conservation.

An exemption is also prescribed for the installation, in certain circumstances, of permanent regularly spaced obstacles (such as bollards or stones) to prevent or restrict vehicular access to common land.

Where works are carried out pursuant to an exemption contained in this Order, there are requirements for a notice to be displayed at the site of the works and for notification to be given to the Secretary of State (Article 4 and Schedule 2).

The exemptions only apply in relation to registered common land (Article 2), and not in relation to other classes of land to which section 38 applies. Nothing in this Order authorises any person to carry out works which are prohibited by any other enactment or rule of law, nor exempts any person from complying with any other requirement to obtain consent or permission which may exist independently from section 38.

3.11 The Commons Registration (General) (Amendment) (Wales) Regulations 2007

SI 2007/2597 (W 220)

Commencement date: 1 October 2007

These Regulations revoke, on 1 October 2007, the provisions in the Commons Registration (General) Regulations 1966 (SI 1966/1471) relating to official searches of the commons registers and certificates of search insofar as those provisions apply in relation to Wales and make a related amendment to those Regulations.

A search of the commons registers will instead be possible through the new question which has been added to Part II of the revised Supplementary Enquiries of Local Authority Form, CON29O.

Regulation 35 (supply of certain forms) of the 1966 Regulations is also revoked in view of the discontinuance of the arrangements for the Office of Public Sector Information (formerly HM Stationery Office) to supply the forms specified in that Regulation.

4 COMPULSORY PURCHASE

4.1 The Home Loss Payments (Prescribed Amounts) (England) Regulations 2007

SI 2007/1750

Commencement date: 1 September 2007

These Regulations increase the amount of home loss payments payable under section 30 of the Land Compensation Act 1973. A person is entitled to a home loss payment when he is displaced from a dwelling by compulsory purchase or in the other circumstances specified in section 29 of the Act.

Section 30(1) of the Act provides that in cases where a person occupying a dwelling on the date of displacement has an owner's interest, the amount of home loss payment is calculated as a percentage of the market value of the interest, subject to a maximum and minimum amount. Section 30(2) specifies the amount of the home loss payment in any other case.

Regulation 2(2)(a) of these Regulations increases the maximum amount payable under section 30(1) from £40,000 to £44,000 and Regulation 2(2)(b) increases the minimum amount from £4,000 to £4,400. Regulation 2(3) increases the home loss payment under section 30(2) from £4,000 to £4,400.

These increases have been calculated by reference to the Department for Communities and Local Government's house price index, which varies in line with changes to house prices.

The revised amounts apply where the displacement occurs on or after 1 September 2007.

Regulation 3 revokes, with savings, the Home Loss Payments (Prescribed Amounts) (England) Regulations 2006.

4.2 The Home Loss Payments (Prescribed Amounts) (Wales) Regulations 2007

SI 2007/2372 (W195)

Commencement date: 1 September 2007

These Regulations, which apply to Wales, increase the maximum and minimum amounts of home loss payments payable under the Land Compensation Act 1973 to those with an owner's interest in a dwelling. They also increase the amount of home loss payment payable in any other case.

A person who is displaced from a dwelling by compulsory purchase or in other circumstances specified in section 29 of the Act is entitled to a home loss payment. The present basis for assessing the amount of home loss payment was established by amendments to the Act in the Planning and Compensation Act 1991.

Section 30(1) of the Act provides that in cases where a person occupying a dwelling on the date of displacement has an owner's interest, the amount of home loss payment is calculated as a percentage of the market value of that interest, subject to a

80

maximum and minimum amount. Section 30(2) prescribes the amount of the home loss payment in any other case.

Regulation 2(a) of these Regulations increases the maximum amount payable under section 30(1) from £40,000 to £44,000 and Regulation 2(b) increases the minimum amount from £4,000 to £4,400. Regulation 2(c) increases the home loss payment payable, under section 30(2), in any other case from £4,000 to £4,400.

Only the maximum and minimum amounts of home loss payments are changed and there is no change to the percentage payable of the market value of the displaced person's interest in the dwelling.

The revised amounts apply where the displacement occurs on or after 1 September 2007.

These Regulations provide that the Home Loss Payments (Prescribed Amounts) (Wales) Regulations 2006 will continue to have effect in relation to a displacement occurring before the date on which these Regulations come into force but are otherwise revoked.

5 COUNTRYSIDE AND RIGHTS OF WAY

5.1 The Countryside and Rights of Way Act 2000 (Commencement No. 12) Order 2007

SI 2007/1493 (C 61)

This Order brings into force on 21 May 2007, in relation to England, section 57 of, and Schedule 6 to, the Countryside and Rights of Way Act 2000 to the extent that those provisions insert the following provisions into the Highways Act 1980:

a) section 119D, which provides for the diversion of certain highways for the protection of the special features of sites of special scientific interest; and

b) section 119E, which makes provisions supplementary to section 119D.

This Order also brings into force the consequential amendments in Schedule 6 to the Act relating to the above sections.

5.2 The Rights of Way (Hearings and Inquiries Procedure) (England) Rules 2007

SI 2007/2008

Commencement date: 1 October 2007

These Rules set out the procedures for hearings and inquiries afforded or caused to be held by the Secretary of State in connection with the confirmation, or modification and confirmation, of certain disputed orders made by certain local authorities, relating to the creation of footpaths, bridleways and restricted byways, the modification of the definitive map and statement (relating to certain public rights of way), and the stopping up, diversion or extinguishment of footpaths, bridleways and restricted byways.

Rule 4 relates to the initial stages of a hearing or inquiry and provides for notification in relation to the hearing or inquiry to be given by the Secretary of State to the authority which made the order, to any applicant for the order, to every person who has made (and not withdrawn) representations or objections to the order and to certain other persons required to be notified in consequence of the 1980 Act, the 1981 Act or the 1990 Act.

Part 3 of these Rules (rules 5 to 14) sets out the procedure for hearings afforded by the Secretary of State and includes provision for submission of statements of case for the hearing (rule 6), appearances at the hearing (rule 8) and site inspections and adjourning the hearing to the land (rule 10).

Part 4 of these Rules (rules 15 to 26) sets out the procedure for inquiries caused to be held by the Secretary of State and includes provision for pre-inquiry meetings (rule 15), submission of statements of case for the inquiry (rule 17), appearances at the inquiry (rule 19), proofs of evidence (rule 20) and site inspections and adjourning the inquiry to the land (rule 22).

Part 5 of these Rules (rule 27) sets out the procedures for hearings and inquiries resulting from a proposal by the Secretary of State to modify a rights of way order.

Part 6 of these Rules (rules 28 to 32) relates to general matters and includes provision for allowing further time for taking steps under the Rules (rule 28), inspection and copying of documents (rule 29) and the use of electronic communications (rule 31).

Rule 32 (transitional provision) provides that these Rules do not apply to any hearing or inquiry held in relation to an order submitted to the Secretary of State for confirmation before the coming into force of these Rules.

5.3 The Countryside and Rights of Way Act 2000 (Commencement No. 14) Order 2007

SI 2007/2595 (C 99)

This Order brings into force on 1 October 2007, in relation to England, the remainder of section 69 of the Countryside and Rights of Way Act 2000.

Section 69(1) inserts subsections (2A) and (2B) in section 147 of the Highways Act 1980. Section 147(2A) requires a competent authority exercising their powers under section 147(2) (in considering whether to authorise the erection of stiles, gates or other works) to have regard to the needs of persons with mobility problems. Section 147(2B) permits the Secretary of State to issue guidance to competent authorities as to matters to be taken into account by competent authorities when exercising their powers under section 147(2) and requires those authorities to have regard to any such guidance.

Section 69(3) inserts a new section 147ZA into the 1980 Act which enables competent authorities to enter into agreements with owners, lessees or occupiers of land for the replacement or improvement of stiles, gates or other structures so as to result in a structure that is safer or more convenient for use by persons with mobility problems.

6   ENERGY PERFORMANCE CERTIFICATES

6.1   The Energy Performance of Buildings (Certificates and Inspections) (England and Wales) Regulations 2007
SI 2007/991

Commencement date: various

These Regulations implement in England and Wales Articles 7 (energy performance certificates), 9 (air-conditioning system inspections) and 10 (energy assessors) of the Energy Performance of Buildings Directive, OJ No L 1, 4.1.2004 which lays down requirements for the production of energy performance certificates when buildings are constructed, sold or rented out, display of certificates in large public buildings, and regular inspections of air-conditioning systems.

Part 2 of these Regulations implements Articles 7(1) and (2) of the Directive and requires the production of energy performance certificates when buildings are constructed, sold or rented out. In particular:

- Sellers and prospective landlords are required to make available energy performance certificates to prospective buyers and tenants at the earliest opportunity (Regulation 5).

- Where the Housing Act 2004 imposes a duty on sellers or their agents to have a home information pack, sellers and their agents must ensure that energy performance information is included in any written particulars of the dwelling for sale (Regulation 6).

Regulation 8 and Schedule 2 amend the Building Regulations 2000 and the Building (Approved Inspectors etc) Regulations 2000. In addition to various consequential amendments, Regulation 17E is inserted into the Building Regulations 2000. It requires energy performance certificates to be produced when buildings are constructed. Paragraph 1(5) of Schedule 2 revokes Regulation 16 of those Regulations. Paragraph 2(2) of Schedule 2 substitutes

Regulation 12 of the Building (Approved Inspectors etc) Regulations 2000. The Regulations that are revoked and substituted (which each required an energy rating for new dwellings) are superseded by the requirement to produce an energy performance certificate. Regulation 9 requires certificates for those buildings to which the Building Regulations 2000 do not apply.

Schedule 2 also amends Regulation 17A of the Building Regulations 2000, which implemented Article 3 of the Directive. The amendment requires the Secretary of State to approve a methodology of calculation of the energy performance of buildings and ways in which the energy performance of a building shall be expressed.

Energy performance certificates must be accompanied by recommendations for the improvement of the energy performance of the building (Regulation 10).

Regulation 11 sets out the minimum requirements for energy performance certificates. In particular, certificates must be no more than ten years old, except in circumstances where the Housing Act 2004 requires a home information pack, in which case a certificate is only valid if it is less than three months old at the first point of marketing, as that term is defined in the Home Information Pack Regulations 2007.

Regulation 14 imposes restrictions on the circumstances in which certificates and recommendations may be disclosed, and creates an offence for unlawful disclosure.

Part 3 implements Article 7(3) of the Directive. In particular, occupiers of large buildings occupied by public authorities and by institutions providing public services to a large number of persons, must display a display energy certificate and obtain an advisory report containing recommendations for the improvement of the energy performance of the building (Regulation 16).

Part 4 implements Article 9 of the Directive. In particular, the person who has control of the operation of an air-conditioning system with an 'effective rated output' (defined in Regulation 20(3)) of at least 12 kW must ensure the system is inspected at regular intervals not exceeding five years (Regulation 21).

Part 5 implements Article 10 of the Directive. Energy assessors who produce certificates or inspect air-conditioning systems must be members of an accreditation scheme approved by the Secretary of State (Regulation 25).

Part 6 requires certain documents produced by energy assessors to be entered onto a register maintained by the Secretary of State. Regulations 34 to 37 set out who may access the register.

Part 7 deals with enforcement and makes provision for enforcement by way of civil penalties. Regulation 38 imposes a duty on local weights and measures authorities to enforce the duties relating to certificates and air-conditioning inspections. Regulation 40 empowers enforcement authorities to issue penalty charge notices for any breach.

Regulation 49 makes provision to bind the Crown. Regulation 50 imposes a general duty to co-operate with and allow reasonable access to any person who is under a duty relating to certificates or inspections.

6.2 The Energy Performance of Buildings (Certificates and Inspections) (England and Wales) (Amendment) Regulations 2007

SI 2007/1669

Commencement date: 2 July 2007

These Regulations amend the Energy Performance of Buildings (Certificates and Inspections) (England and Wales) Regulations 2007 in relation to various requirements related to energy performance certificates and recommendation reports. The principal Regulations implement Articles 7 (energy performance certificates), 9 (air-conditioning system inspections) and 10 (energy assessors) of Directive 2002/91/EC of the European Parliament and of the Council of 16 December 2002 on the Energy Performance of Buildings (OJ No. L 1 4.1.2003 p.65).

Regulation 3(4)(a) extends from 3 months to 12 months the validity of an energy performance certificate where the property is first marketed in circumstances where the Housing Act 2004 requires a home information pack.

Paragraphs (2), (3), (4)(b) and (c), (5) and (6)(a) and (c) of Regulation 3 make changes by way of minor correction or clarification or consequential amendment.

Paragraph 3(6)(b) postpones from 1 October 2007 to 1 January 2008 the coming into force of the provisions listed in paragraphs 8 and 9 of Schedule 1 to the principal Regulations. Paragraphs 8 and 9 replace the energy rating requirements of the Building Regulations 2000 (SI 2000/2531) with requirements for energy assessment and energy performance certificates, in order to implement requirements of Directive 2002/91/EC in respect of newly constructed dwellings.

Regulation 4(1) provides that in circumstances where, but for the temporary exception in Regulation 34 of the Home Information Pack (No. 2) Regulations 2007, both a duty under section 155(1) or 159(2) of the Housing Act 2004 would apply to any person, and a duty under the principal Regulations to make available a valid energy performance certificate to any prospective buyer or tenant would apply to the relevant person, the relevant person shall, before entering into a contract to sell or rent out a building, ensure that a valid energy performance certificate is given free of charge to the prospective buyer or tenant. The Regulation 34 exception disapplies the requirement to have a home information pack where an energy performance certificate cannot be obtained by the responsible person despite all reasonable efforts before a property is placed on the market or thereafter.

Paragraphs (2) and (3) of Regulation 4 ensure that the interpretation, enforcement and all other ancillary provisions in the principal Regulations relating to an energy performance certificate shall have effect in relation to a certificate provided under the duty imposed by Regulation 4(1).

7   ESTATE AGENTS

7.1   Consumers, Estate Agents and Redress Act 2007

The Consumers, Estate Agents and Redress Act 2007 received Royal Assent on 19 July 2007.

The Act's main provisions are as follows:

- To create a new statutory National Consumer Council to replace the existing National Consumer Council (a company limited by guarantee), the Gas and Electricity Consumers Council ('energywatch') and the Consumer Council for Postal Services ('Postwatch'). The Act also contains a power to dissolve the Consumer Council for Water and transfer its functions to the new body established by the Act.

- To enable the Secretary of State to require service providers in the electricity and gas (in Great Britain), postal services (in the United Kingdom) and water (in England and Wales) sectors to belong to redress schemes to ensure resolution of complaints in those sectors and to award compensation where warranted. The energy and postal services regulators (the Gas and Electricity Markets Authority and the Postal Services Commission respectively) are given a duty to prescribe complaint handling standards which will be binding on regulated providers in Great Britain (and the United Kingdom in relation to postal services).

- To enable the Secretary of State to require estate agents to join an ombudsman scheme and strengthen the Regulation of estate agents through measures such as: requiring estate agents to keep records, allowing trading standards officers to inspect those records, expanding the circumstances in which the Office of Fair Trading can take regulatory action against estate agents.

- To enable the Secretary of State to make Regulations giving individuals similar rights to cancel contracts for goods or services made during a solicited sales visit to their home or workplace as they have in relation to an unsolicited visit.

8 HOME INFORMATION PACKS

8.1 The Home Information Pack (Redress Scheme) (No. 2) Order 2007

SI 2007/1946

Commencement date: 1 August 2007

This Order requires estate agents in England and Wales to be members of an approved redress scheme for the purpose of dealing with complaints related to Home Information Packs. Before such an Order can be made the Secretary of State must have approved one or more redress schemes pursuant to section 173 of the Housing Act 2004. Details of every approved scheme are available on the Department for Business, Enterprise and Regulatory Reform website.

The requirement to belong to an approved redress scheme applies:

a) in respect of those properties for which a Home Information Pack is required under Part 5 of the Housing Act 2004, as that Part is brought into force from time to time in respect of different types of property – from 1 August 2008, this will be in respect of residential properties with four or more bedrooms; and

b) only to persons who engage in estate agency work as defined in section 1 of the Estate Agents Act 1979.

8.2 The Home Information Pack (No. 2) Regulations 2007

SI 2007/1667

Commencement date: 2 July 2007

These Regulations prescribe the documents to be included in home information packs and the circumstances in which they are included (Parts 1 to 5 of the Regulations). They provide for exceptions and enforcement (Parts 6 and 7) and make further provision in relation to home condition reports (Parts 8 and 9). The duties to have a home information pack which complies with these Regulations are found in sections 155 to 159 of the Housing Act 2004. The Regulations apply in England and Wales.

The Regulations make a distinction between 'required' documents which must be included in home information packs and 'authorised' documents which may be included. A pack must not include any documents not required or authorised (Regulation 4) and advertising information must not be included (Regulation 12). Part 2 of the Regulations makes provision about the source and clarity of documents included in the original home information pack and in copies of the pack.

Regulations 8, 9 and 10 are the Regulations that set out which documents are required and authorised to be included in packs. The required documents specified in Regulation 8 include an index, information about the energy efficiency of the property, a sale statement, title information, additional information for commonhold and leasehold properties and property searches. Schedules 1 to 10 to the Regulations make further provision about these documents, and in some cases prescribe minimum terms necessary for documents to comply with the Regulations. Not all documents are required in every case, and Regulation 8 describes this further.

Regulation 9 describes the information authorised to be included in a home information pack. This information may be included in a separate document or within a required document. Authorised information includes a home condition report, translations, Braille versions, summaries or explanations of pack documents, additional title information, additional information relating to commonhold and leasehold properties and additional information about physical condition. It includes further property searches. Searches relating to other premises may be included. Schedule 10 to the Regulations specifies a number of other types of relevant information which may be included. Regulation 10 deals with the required information for new properties where the legal commonhold or leasehold interest being sold has not yet been registered or created.

Part 4 of the Regulations deals with the assembly of home information packs. Regulation 13 prescribes the required order of documents included in a pack and Regulation 15 prescribes the age of certain documents at the 'first point of marketing' (defined in Regulation 3). Under Regulations 14, 16 and 17, some required documents must be included before the 'first point of marketing' and others should be included within 28 days of that point. In the circumstances specified in Regulations 16 and 17 a home information pack temporarily need not include a particular document, so long as reasonable efforts are being made to obtain it. Regulations 18 and 19 make provision for requests for and delivery of documents in relation to the obtaining of documents under Part 4. Regulation 20 makes provision for the event that a document is completely unobtainable.

Part 5 of the Regulations deals with the accuracy of home information packs. Regulations 21 to 23 deal with the circumstances in which the pack or pack documents must or may be updated. The effect of Regulation 24 is that a responsible person must provide a seller with a copy of any pack documents requested by him for the purposes of checking their accuracy.

Part 6 of the Regulations makes exceptions from the home information pack duties. These exceptions relate to seasonal accommodation, sales mixed with sales of non-residential premises, dwellinghouses used for both residential and non-residential purposes, portfolios of residential properties, unsafe properties and properties to be demolished. The exception under Regulation 33 ensures that, where a person makes public that a property is on the market before the date the home information pack duties are brought into force, a person does not become a responsible person for the purposes of the home information pack duties if it was put on the market before then, so long as marketing was sustained to a reasonable extent before the date. The exception under Regulation 34 applies temporarily with the effect that the home information pack duties do not apply until all the required documents have been commissioned before the property is put on the market, and the responsible person has at least obtained energy information about the property.

Part 7 of the Regulations specifies that the level of penalty charge for penalty charge notices which may be given by enforcement authorities is £200 (for a breach of a home information pack duty). Regulation 36 specifies that penalty charge notices do not apply where the content of a pack document fails to comply with these Regulations, but a responsible person believes on reasonable grounds that it does.

The Regulations require that home condition reports (which may be included in home information packs under Regulation 9(a)) must be made by members of certification schemes (home inspectors) approved by the Secretary of State under Part 8. Before approving a scheme, the Secretary of State must be satisfied that it contains appropriate provision for the matters described in Regulation 3.

Part 9 of the Regulations makes provision for the keeping of a register of home condition reports and the circumstances in which information may be disclosed from that register. Under section 165(7) of the Housing Act 2004, a disclosure from a register which is not in accordance with Regulations is a criminal offence.

8.3 The Home Information Pack (Amendment) Regulations 2007
SI 2007/3301

Commencement date: 14 December 2007

These Regulations amend the Home Information Pack (No. 2) Regulations 2007. Under sections 155 to 159 of the Housing Act 2004, a home information pack must comply with the Regulations.

Regulation 2 adds a new Regulation 10A to the Regulations, the effect of which is to treat required leasehold documents, other than the lease, as authorised documents for a temporary period until 1 June 2008. The amendments in paragraph (2) are consequential upon that amendment.

The amendment in Regulation 3(1) extends the period described in Regulation 34 of the Regulations (first day marketing during a temporary period), until 1 June 2008. The amendment in paragraph (2) consequentially amends the date when Regulation 16 of the

Regulations applies (energy information unobtainable before or at the first point of marketing).

Regulation 4 amends the Regulations to take account of the transfer of functions from the National Assembly for Wales to Welsh Ministers, effected by the Government of Wales Act 2006.

9   HOUSING

9.1   Approval of Code of Practice (Private Retirement Housing) (Wales) Order 2007

SI 2007/578 (W 50)

Commencement date: 2 March 2007

By this Order the National Assembly for Wales approves, subject to the exception mentioned below, a code of practice relating to the management of private retirement housing by landlords and others who discharge the management function. The approved code is *The Code of Practice for Private Retirement Housing (Wales)* (ISBN 0-9526691-3-7) and is published by Chain and Pyle, Unit 3, King James Court, King James Street, London SE1 0DH. Appendices 4 to 6 of the Code have not been approved as they are not relevant for the purposes of section 87 of the 1993 Act.

Approval for *The Association of Retirement Housing Managers' Code of Practice for the Management of Leasehold Sheltered Housing* (ISBN 0-9526691-0-2) is withdrawn, as are modifications to *The Association of Retirement Housing Managers' Code of Practice for the Management of Leasehold Sheltered Housing* (ISBN 0-9526691-1-0).

Section 87(7) of the Leasehold Reform, Housing and Urban Development Act 1993 provides that failure to comply with any provision of an approved code of practice does not of itself render any person liable to any proceedings, but in any proceedings the code of practice is admissible as evidence and any provision which appears to be relevant to any question arising in the proceedings will be taken into account.

The approval and withdrawal provided for in this Order apply to the management of private retirement housing in Wales and are subject to the transitional provision in Article 4. The Code that was approved in 1995 and modified in 1998 continues to have effect for the purpose of proceedings relating to acts or omissions that are alleged to have occurred before this Order comes into force.

9.2 The Housing (Right to Buy) (Prescribed Forms) (Amendment) (England) Regulations 2007

SI 2007/784

Commencement date: 3 April 2007

Regulation 2 of these Regulations substitutes the form of notice to be used by a tenant claiming to exercise the right to buy his or her dwellinghouse in accordance with section 122 of the Housing Act 1985. The Regulations apply in relation to houses and flats in England only.

The new form RTB1 is set out in the Schedule to these Regulations and replaces the form set out in Schedule 1 to the Housing (Right to Buy) (Prescribed Forms) Regulations 1986. By virtue of Regulation 2 of the 1986 Regulations, a form substantially to the same effect as that set out in the Schedule to these Regulations may be used.

References to civil partners have been included in the new form to reflect the coming into force of the Civil Partnership Act 2004.

Other minor drafting changes have been made to the form, including changes to the list of public sector landlords.

10 INCOME TAX

10.1 The Energy-Saving Items Regulations 2007

SI 2007/831

Commencement date: 6 April 2007

Section 312 of the Income Tax (Trading and Other Income) Act 2005 provides that the Treasury may make Regulations to specify other descriptions of energy-saving items in respect of which expenditure may be deducted by residential landlords when calculating the profits of their property business. Section 314 further provides that the Treasury may make Regulations providing for the apportionment and restriction of the amount of such a deduction. These Regulations exercise the powers contained in those sections.

Regulation 1 deals with citation, commencement and interpretation.

Regulation 2 specifies that hot water system insulation, draught proofing, solid wall insulation and floor insulation are to be classed as items of an energy-saving nature.

Regulation 3 restricts the maximum amount of expenditure for which a deduction is allowed to £1,500 per property (dwellinghouse) per tax year.

Regulation 4 provides for a just and reasonable apportionment of the allowable deduction where two or more people each own or have interests in the property in question. This Regulation also deals with contributions to expenditure, and provides an appeal mechanism in cases where there is a dispute.

Regulation 5 revokes previous Regulations that have dealt with the treatment of items of an energy-saving nature.

11   LAND REGISTRATION

11.1   The Land Registration (Proper Office) Order 2007

SI 2007/3517

Commencement date: 1 April 2008

This Order, which comes into force on 1 April 2008, designates particular offices of the land registry as the proper office for the receipt of specified descriptions of application under the Land Registration Act 2002. It replaces the Land Registration (Proper Office) Order 2003 and the Land Registration (Proper Office) (Amendment) Order 2005.

As a consequence of this Order, on and after 1 April 2008, the Land Registry's Durham (Boldon), Harrow and York Offices will cease to be proper offices and there will be one Durham proper office, administered initially from the Southfield House and Boldon House buildings. The following table shows the effect of the changes:

Administrative area	Former proper office	New proper office
Brent	Harrow	Swansea
Camden	Harrow	Croydon
City of Westminster	Harrow	Croydon
East Riding of Yorkshire	York	Kingston upon Hull
Harrow	Harrow	Swansea
Islington	Harrow	Stevenage
North Yorkshire	York	Durham
City and County of the City of London	Harrow	Stevenage
The Inner Temple and the Middle Temple	Harrow	Stevenage
York	York	Durham
Those administrative areas previously dealt with by the Durham (Boldon) or Durham (Southfield) proper offices	Durham (Boldon) or Durham (Southfield)	Durham

12 LANDLORD AND TENANT

12.1 The Service Charges (Summary of Rights and Obligations, and Transitional Provision) (England) Regulations 2007

SI 2007/1257

Commencement date: 1 October 2007

These Regulations prescribe the content of the summary of tenants' rights and obligations relating to service charges, which must accompany any demand for such charges made by a landlord, under section 21B of the Landlord and Tenant Act 1985. The

96

Regulations also make provision for minor matters in respect of the form of the summary.

Regulation 4 provides transitional provisions relating to demands for service charges sent to tenants prior to 1 October 2007.

12.2 The Administration Charges (Summary of Rights and Obligations) (England) Regulations 2007

SI 2007/1258

Commencement date: 1 October 2007

These Regulations prescribe the content of the summary of tenant's rights and obligations relating to administration charges, which must accompany any demand for such charges made by a landlord. The Regulations also make provision for minor matters in respect of the form of the summary.

12.3 The Licensing and Management of Houses in Multiple Occupation (Additional Provisions) (England) Regulations 2007

SI 2007/1903

Commencement date: 1 October 2007

Regulations 3 to 11 of these Regulations apply to houses in multiple occupation in England that are converted blocks of flats to which section 257 of the Housing Act 2004 applies. These are buildings that have been converted into and consist of self-contained flats where the building work undertaken in connection with the conversion did not comply with the appropriate building standards and still does not comply with them, and less than two-thirds of the self-contained flats are owner-occupied.

The Regulations impose duties on a person managing such section 257 HMOs in respect of:

a) providing information to occupiers (Regulation 4);

b) taking safety measures, including fire safety measures (Regulation 5);

c) maintaining the water supply and drainage (Regulation 6);

d) supplying and maintaining gas and electricity, including having it regularly inspected (Regulation 7);

e) maintaining common parts (defined in Regulation 7(6)), fixtures, fittings and appliances (Regulation 8);

f) maintaining living accommodation (Regulation 9); and

g) providing waste disposal facilities (Regulation 10).

The manager's duties do not extend to the parts of the HMO over which the manager cannot reasonably be expected to exercise control (Regulation 3).

Regulation 11 imposes duties on occupiers of an HMO for the purpose of ensuring that the person managing it can effectively carry out the duties imposed on him.

By section 234(3) of the Act, a person who fails to comply with Regulations 3 to 11 of these Regulations commits an offence punishable on summary conviction with a fine not exceeding level 5 on the standard scale.

Regulation 12 amends the Licensing and Management of Houses in Multiple Occupation and Other Houses (Miscellaneous Provisions) (England) Regulations 2006 (SI 2006/373), so that, with some exceptions, those Regulations now apply to all HMOs to which Part 2 of the Act applies, including section 257 HMOs. Some additional provisions are relevant only to section 257 HMOs. Regulation 12 also amends those Regulations in respect of the standards relating to washing and bathing facilities that are prescribed for deciding the suitability of a house for multiple occupation by a particular maximum number of households or persons. It also makes a minor amendment to the information that needs to be provided concerning fire safety at the HMO or house in an application for a licence.

12.4 The Houses in Multiple Occupation (Certain Converted Blocks of Flats) (Modifications to the Housing Act 2004 and Transitional Provisions for section 257 HMOs) (England) Regulations 2007

SI 2007/1904

Commencement date: 1 October 2007

These Regulations modify Part 2 (licensing of houses in multiple occupation) and Part 4 (additional control provisions in relation to residential accommodation) of the Housing Act 2004 and section 263 of the Act in its operation for the purposes of those Parts, in relation to a house in multiple occupation to which section 257 of the Act applies.

Section 257 of the Act applies to a building or a part of a building which has been converted into, and consists of, self-contained flats if the building work undertaken in connection with the conversion did not comply with appropriate building standards and still does not comply with them, and less than two-thirds of the self-contained flats are owner-occupied. A flat is owner-occupied if it is occupied by a person who has a lease granted for a term of more than 21 years or by a person who has the freehold estate in the converted block of flats, or by a member of the household of a person within either of those two descriptions.

The Regulations modify, for the purposes of Part 2 of the Act, in respect of a section 257 HMO:

a) the definition of 'person having control' (Regulations 3 and 9);

b) the matters about which a local housing authority must satisfy itself when deciding whether or not to grant a licence (Regulations 4 and 5);

c) the licence conditions (Regulations 6 and 11);

d) the person in respect of whom a rent repayment order may be made (Regulation 7); and

e) the circumstances when a notice under section 21 of the Housing Act 1988 may be served (Regulation 8).

These Regulations also modify section 139 of the Act in respect of the service of overcrowding notices in respect of section 257 HMOs (Regulation 11).

The Regulations also make transitional provisions in respect of section 257 HMOs which were previously registered in a registration scheme under Part 11 of the Housing Act 1985 (Regulation 13). Part 11 of the Act was repealed by the Housing Act 2004 (Commencement No. 5 and Transitional Provisions and Savings) (England) Order 2006 (SI 2006/1060) on 6 April 2006 in respect of all HMOs other than section 257 HMOs. That Order provided that the repeal of Part 11 of the Housing Act 1985 would take effect in respect of a building or a part of a building which is both a section 257 HMO and a house in multiple occupation for the purpose of Part 11 of the Housing Act 1985 on the date on which Regulations made under section 61(5) come into force.

Nothing in these Regulations affects a local authority's licensing functions under Part 2 of the Act in relation to a flat that is situated within a section 257 HMO.

12.5 The Administration Charges (Summary of Rights and Obligations) (Wales) Regulations 2007

SI 2007/3162 (W 273)

Commencement date: 30 November 2007

These Regulations prescribe the content of the summary of tenants' rights and obligations relating to administration charges which must accompany any demand for such charges made by a landlord. The Regulations also make provision for minor matters in respect of the form of the summary.

12.6 The Service Charges (Summary of Rights and Obligations, and Transitional Provisions) (Wales) Regulations 2007

SI 2007/3160 (W 271)

Commencement date: 30 November 2007

These Regulations prescribe the content of the summary of tenants' rights and obligations relating to service charges, which must accompany any demand for such charges made by a landlord, under section 21B of the Landlord and Tenant Act 1985. The Regulations also make provision for minor matters in respect of the form of the summary. Regulation 4 provides transitional provisions relating to demands for service charges sent to tenants prior to 30 November 2007.

13 LEGAL SERVICES

13.1 Legal Services Act 2007

The Legal Services Act received Royal Assent on 30 October 2007 and will establish a new framework for the Regulation of legal services in England and Wales.

The Act makes provision for:

- A new regulatory framework replacing the existing framework, comprising a number of oversight regulators with overlapping responsibilities.

- The establishment of the Legal Services Board. This will be a single oversight body, independent both from Government and from the 'front-line' approved regulators such as the Law Society and Bar Council.

- The establishment of an independent Office for Legal Complaints. This will be a body with statutory power to establish a scheme for handling complaints about services provided by persons subject to oversight Regulation by the Legal Services Board, and to award redress in appropriate circumstances.

- Alternative Business Structures to enable lawyers and non-lawyers to work together to deliver legal and other services. New business structures are expected to give legal providers greater flexibility to respond to market demands within the UK and overseas. Licences will be conferred by licensing authorities, with various safeguards in place.

The Act is in 9 Parts as follows:

Part 1: The Regulatory Objectives – this sets out the eight regulatory objectives, which guide the Legal Services Board, the approved regulators, and the Office for Legal Complaints in exercising their functions.

Part 2: The Legal Services Board – this sets out the structure and functions of the Legal Services Board, including its duty to act compatibly with the regulatory objectives, to assist in the maintenance and development of standards in regulation, education and training and to establish a Consumer Panel. It also sets out the requirements for both appointment to, and membership of, the Board and the powers that the Lord Chancellor has in relation to these processes.

Part 3: Reserved Legal Activities – this lists and defines the reserved legal activities. It explains who is entitled to carry out these activities, and the penalties for those who carry out, or pretend to be entitled to carry out, these activities where they are not entitled. It provides for transitional arrangements for those currently allowed to carry on reserved legal activities. It also explains the process for altering the scope of the reserved legal activities. Approved regulators are the bodies that authorise and regulate persons to carry on reserved legal activities. This Part of the Act explains what an approved regulator is, lists those bodies designated by the Act as approved regulators, and explains how other bodies can become an approved regulator in the future.

Part 4: Regulation of Approved Regulators – this prescribes the general duties of approved regulators and the powers that the Legal Services Board has to ensure that these are being properly carried out. It details how the Legal Services Board can intervene when there is a problem, the procedures that it must follow, and the persons that it must consult. The Legal Services Board's powers include target-setting, censure, financial penalties, direct intervention in the approved regulator's Regulation of its members and, ultimately, the power to recommend to the Lord Chancellor that an order be made cancelling the approved regulator's designation.

Part 5: Alternative Business Structures – this makes provision for the licensing of new business structures in legal services. This will allow lawyers and non-lawyers to work together to deliver legal and other services. This Part of the Act sets out the arrangements for authorisation, by the Legal Services Board, of licensing authorities and how, in the absence of an appropriate licensing authority, the Legal Services Board can license Alternative Business Structures firms directly. It makes provision for the Regulation of Alternative Business Structures.

Part 6: Legal Complaints – this establishes an independent Office for Legal Complaints, which is responsible for administering an ombudsman scheme under which all complaints will be dealt with by a Chief Ombudsman, assistant ombudsmen, and staff appointed by the Office for Legal Complaints. Part 6 removes the ability of approved regulators to provide redress to complainants and grants this power to the ombudsman scheme. The Office for Legal Complaints will draw up scheme rules setting out the detail of the ombudsman scheme. This Part makes provision for the appointment process and terms of office for members of the Office for Legal Complaints Board and the Chief Ombudsman and the assistant ombudsmen. It also makes provision for the accountability of the Office for Legal Complaints to the Legal Services Board, the framework of rules by which the Office for Legal Complaints will establish its operating procedures, and changes to the regulatory arrangements of approved regulators.

Part 7: Further Provisions Relating to the Legal Services Board and the Office for Legal Complaints – this makes provision as to the guidance that the Legal Services Board may give. It also requires the Board to make rules providing for the payment by approved regulators of a levy, to recoup the expenditure of the Legal Services Board and Office for Legal Complaints. The rules may include provision as to the rate and times at which the levy is payable, and circumstances in which the levy may be waived. This section also makes provision for the Legal Services Board to enter into voluntary arrangements with any person, for example to promote best regulatory practice.

Part 8: Miscellaneous Provisions about Lawyers – this makes provision for the following matters:

a) the requirement for alteration of the rules of the Solicitors Disciplinary Tribunal to be approved by the Legal Services Board and empowering the Legal Services Board to give a limited range of directions to the Tribunal;

b) the maintenance of the register of trademark attorneys and the register of patent attorneys;

c) the application of legal professional privilege in relation to authorised persons who are not barristers or solicitors;

d) amendment of the Immigration and Asylum Act 1999 (which regulates the provision of immigration advice services) and the Compensation Act 2006 (which makes provision in relation to claims management services), in consequence of the new regime established by the Act;

e) the making of costs orders in relation to *pro bono* legal representation; and

f) conferring competence on the Scottish Legal Complaints Commission in respect of certain reserved matters.

Part 9: General – this makes provision regarding offences committed by corporate and unincorporated bodies. It provides that certain functions conferred on the Lord Chancellor by the Act may not be transferred to another Minister by a transfer of functions order. It states how notices issued pursuant to provision made in the Act are to be given and makes provision governing the procedure for making Orders and Regulations under powers in the Act. It allows for minor and consequential amendments to be made by Order and makes provision regarding the extent, commencement and short title of the Act.

14 PLANNING

14.1 The Planning and Compulsory Purchase Act 2004 (Commencement No. 4 and Consequential, Transitional and Savings Provisions) (Wales) (Amendment No. 2) Order 2007

SI 2007/1023 (W 92)

Commencement date: 24 March 2007

This Order brings to an end the transitional arrangements made under the Planning and Compulsory Purchase Act 2004 (Commencement No. 4 and Consequential, Transitional and Savings Provisions) (Wales) Order 2005 in relation to Ceredigion County Council.

Under those arrangements, each local planning authority listed in the Schedule to the No. 4 Order is able to continue with the process leading ultimately to the adoption of its unitary development plan under the Town and Country Planning Act 1990, instead of having to start work on the preparation of a local development plan under the Planning and Compulsory Purchase Act 2004.

This Order removes the Council from the list of local planning authorities in the Schedule to the No. 4 Order and thus places the Council under a duty to prepare a local development plan for its area.

14.2 The Planning and Compulsory Purchase Act 2004 (Commencement No. 10 and Saving) Order 2007

SI 2007/1369

Article 2 of this Order brings into force on 30 June 2007, in relation to Wales, the following provisions of the Planning and Compulsory Purchase Act 2004:

a) section 42(1) and (5) to (9) (applications for planning permission and certain consents); and

b) Schedule 9, so far as it gives effect to the repeal of section 76 of the Town and Country Planning Act 1990 (duty to draw attention to certain provisions for the benefit of the disabled).

Article 3 contains a saving for the Town and Country Planning (Applications) Regulations 1988.

14.3 The Planning and Compulsory Purchase Act 2004 (Corresponding Amendments) Order 2007

SI 2007/1519

Commencement date: 24 May 2007

Section 100(5) of the Planning and Compulsory Purchase Act 2004 amends section 12 of the Acquisition of Land Act 1981. The effect of the amendment is to entitle a person who is a tenant (whatever the period of the tenancy) of land proposed for compulsory purchase by an authority other than a Minister, to receive notice of the making of a compulsory purchase order. Before that amendment, the entitlement under the 1981 Act had been restricted, so far as tenants were concerned, to those whose tenancy was for a period of more than one month.

Section 101(3) of the 2004 Act makes similar provision in relation to Schedule 1 to the 1981 Act, which applies where land is proposed to be compulsorily purchased by a Minister.

The Acts specified in the Schedule to this Order contain provisions broadly comparable to those in section 12 of, and Schedule 1 to, the 1981 Act before their amendment. The provisions of those Acts are amended by this Order, as specified in the Schedule, to reflect the amendments that have been made to section 12 of, and Schedule 1 to, the 1981 Act.

This Order extends to England and Wales only. The amendments do not affect any order of which notice was served before the coming into force of this Order.

14.4 The Planning and Compulsory Purchase Act 2004 (Commencement No. 4 and Consequential, Transitional and Savings Provisions) (Wales) (Amendment No. 4) Order 2007

SI 2007/2447 (W 203)

Commencement date: 7 September 2007

This Order brings to an end the transitional arrangements made under the Planning and Compulsory Purchase Act 2004 (Commencement No. 4 and Consequential, Transitional and Savings Provisions) (Wales) Order 2005 in relation to Carmarthenshire County Council.

Under those arrangements, each local planning authority listed in the Schedule to the No. 4 Order is able to continue with the process leading ultimately to the adoption of its unitary development plan under the Town and Country Planning Act 1990, instead of having to start work on the preparation of a local development plan under the Planning and Compulsory Purchase Act 2004.

This Order removes the Council from the list of local planning authorities in the Schedule to the No. 4 Order and thus places the Council under a duty to prepare a local development plan for its area.

14.5 Planning-gain Supplement (Preparations) Act 2007

The Planning-gain Supplement (Preparations) Act 2007 received Royal Assent on 20 March 2007 and gives power to the Commissioners for HM Revenue and Customs, the Secretary of State and the Northern Ireland Department, to incur expenditure for the purpose of, or in connection with, preparing for the imposition of a Planning-gain supplement, which is referred to in the Act as 'a tax on the increase in the value of land resulting from the grant of permission for development'. There is no specific commencement provision in the Act.

15 RATES

15.1 Rating (Empty Properties) Act 2007

The Rating (Empty Properties) Act 2007 received Royal Assent on 19 July 2007. The Act gives effect to the Government's proposals to reform relief from business rates in respect of empty property. Those proposals followed the recommendations of the Barker Review of Land-Use Planning and the Lyons Inquiry into Local Government, which were commissioned by the Chancellor of the Exchequer and the Deputy Prime Minister.

The Barker Review was asked to consider how planning policy and procedures can better deliver economic growth and prosperity alongside other sustainable development goals. The report on the outcome of the Review was published on 5 December 2006, recommending that the Government should make better use of fiscal incentives to encourage efficient use of urban land and, in particular, the reform of relief from business rates in respect of empty property.

The report of the Lyons Inquiry, published on 21 March 2007, recommended the reform and reduction of the existing reliefs from business rates in respect of empty property.

In response to the recommendations of the Barker Review and the Lyons Inquiry, the Chancellor of the Exchequer announced in his Budget report of 21 March 2007 the Government's intention to modernise the existing system of reliefs from business rates for owners of unoccupied property.

The reforms in the Act increase liability to business rates for unoccupied properties to the same basic level of liability as for occupied properties (although the Act provides for liability for unoccupied properties to be reduced by order). The reforms also provide that charities and community amateur sports clubs which own empty property will not be liable to rates for that property, as long as it appears it will next be used for charitable purposes or the purposes of the club.

The Act also makes consequential amendments to legislation. This includes inserting into the Local Government Finance Act 1988 a new section allowing the Secretary of State and the Welsh Ministers to make Regulations to prevent changes in the state of property operating as a means of avoiding unoccupied property rates.

16 STAMP DUTY

16.1 The Stamp Duty Land Tax (Zero-Carbon Homes Relief) Regulations 2007

SI 2007/3437

Commencement date: 7 December 2007

These Regulations provide relief from Stamp Duty Land Tax on the first acquisition of a dwelling which is a zero-carbon home in accordance with sections 58B and 58C of the Finance Act 2003.

Regulation 1 provides for citation, commencement and effect. The Regulations shall have effect in relation to acquisitions made on or after 1 October 2007, but before 1 October 2012. Authority for the retrospective effect is given by section 58C(7) of the Act, which provides that the relief may be granted in respect of acquisitions occurring before the date these Regulations come into force.

Regulation 2 provides for interpretation. It refers to the methodology for determining energy performance approved by the Secretary State for the Department of Communities and Local Government under Regulation 17A of the Building Regulations 2000 (SI 2000/2531 as amended by SI 2006/652 and SI 2007/991) and to any further methodology approved by the Secretary of State for the purposes of these Regulations. It also defines accredited assessors and in that context, for England and Wales, refers to the Government's *Standard Assessment Procedure for Energy Rating of Dwellings*, which is published by BRE and can be found at www.bre.co.uk/sap2005

Regulation 3 sets out the scope of the Regulations.

Regulation 4 provides for relief on a land transaction that is the first acquisition of a zero-carbon home. Where the chargeable consideration does not include rent and is no more than £500,000, the transaction is exempt from Stamp Duty Land Tax. Where the chargeable consideration includes both rent and other consideration, and the consideration other than rent is no more than £500,000, no Stamp Duty Land Tax is chargeable in respect of the consideration other than rent. Where the chargeable consideration other than rent is more than £500,000, the Stamp Duty Land Tax shall be reduced by £15,000. HM Revenue and Customs may refuse relief where they have reasonable grounds for thinking that the dwelling is not a zero-carbon home, notwithstanding that a zero-carbon home certificate has been issued in respect of that dwelling.

Regulation 5 defines zero-carbon home as a dwelling which satisfies the three aspects of energy efficiency set out in column 1 of the table. These aspects are heat loss parameter, the dwelling CO_2 emission rate and net CO_2 emissions. The evidence to be adduced to show that the dwelling is energy efficient in these areas is shown in column 2. Whether these requirements are met is to be determined by an accredited assessor using the approved methodology.

Regulation 6 provides for the issue of certificates by accredited assessors confirming where a dwelling satisfies the definition of a zero-carbon home and makes provision as to the content of those certificates. The vendor shall obtain a zero-carbon home certificate and shall pass it to the purchaser on or before the acquisition of the zero-carbon home or as soon as practicable if the acquisition predates the coming into force of these Regulations.

Regulation 7 provides that the Secretary of State may approve a methodology for the calculation of the energy performance of a dwelling for the purposes of these Regulations. Section 58C(2)(c) of the Act provides that the Regulations may provide for the approval of a scheme or process for certifying energy efficiency.

Regulation 8 provides that relief shall be claimed in a land transaction return or an amendment of such a return.

Regulation 9 provides that where the first acquisition of one or more zero-carbon homes is included in a number of linked transactions, section 55(4) of the Act shall not have effect for the purposes of these Regulations. Section 58C(4) of the Act provides that the Regulations may modify provisions of the Act about linked transactions in relation to a set of transactions of which at least one is the first acquisition of a dwelling which is a zero-carbon home.

Part C

OTHER RECENT DEVELOPMENTS

1 *AIRPORT NOISE MAPS*

On 18 December 2007, the Department for the Environment, Food and Rural Affairs published a series of noise maps showing the daytime and night-time noise levels during 2006 at 18 major airports in England and in neighbouring areas. The noise maps will be used to produce action plans to help local authorities and airport operators manage and reduce noise levels in their communities. The noise maps are available on the Defra website at www.defra.gov.uk/Environment/noise/ambient.htm#aviation

2 *AVOIDING MORTGAGE FRAUD: LAW SOCIETY NEWSLETTER FOR SOLICITORS*

On 12 December 2007, the Law Society published a newsletter entitled *Mortgage fraud – are you being targeted?*

The newsletter describes:

a) how a mortgage fraud is perpetrated;

b) how solicitors are affected by it;

c) warning signs; and

d) checks and procedures for solicitors.

It also reminds conveyancers that they should consult the Law Society's anti-money laundering practice note and the *Council of Mortgage Lenders' Handbook* for information on how to protect themselves from becoming involved in mortgage fraud.

3 LAND REGISTRY – CHANGES TO LAND REGISTER ONLINE

On 5 November 2007, the Land Registry issued a press release announcing that from midnight on 5 November 2007, documents referred to on the Register would no longer be available electronically from the Land Register Online service. Documents still on the Register are available by post or by visiting a Land Registry Office. This change does not affect business users of the Land Registry Direct service or the availability of registers and title plans from the Land Register Online.

4 CONSULTATION ON REGULATION OF ESTATE AGENTS

On 9 November 2007, the Department for Business, Enterprise and Regulatory Reform issued a consultation seeking views on implementing further regulatory changes to govern estate agents. Some of the changes were recommended by the Office of Fair Trading but were not included in the Consumers, Estate Agents and Redress Act 2007. The consultation can be found at www.berr.gov.uk/files/file42348.pdf. The consultation closed on 1 February 2008.

The consultation asks for comments on:

1. The level at which the penalty charge for failing to belong to an approved redress scheme should be set.

2. The obligation to keep certain permanent records, including additional information relating to:

   a) a client's prospective liabilities to an estate agent;

   b) the disclosure of an estate agent's personal interest in a transaction; and

   c) offers made to sellers.

3. The manner and places where the prescribed permanent records should be kept.

4. The fee that should be paid by a banned estate agent applying to have a prohibition order revoked or varied.

5. Whether sellers should be given details of all offers received from prospective buyers, which would mean that they could no longer specify that they do not want to receive details of certain kinds of offers.

6. Whether the current statutory definitions of 'sole agency', 'sole selling rights' and 'ready, willing and able purchaser' should be amended.

5 ONSHORE WIND ENERGY PLANNING CONDITIONS GUIDANCE NOTE

In October 2007, the Department for Business, Enterprise and Regulatory Reform and the Renewables Energy Board published an Onshore Wind Energy Planning Conditions Guidance Note. It is hoped that this will provide support to those involved in the planning process by providing a generic set of specimen planning conditions. The Guidance Note can be found at www.berr.gov.uk/files/file35240.pdf

6 BUILDING REGULATIONS CONSULTATION

In July 2007, the Department for Communities and Local Government published a consultation on its proposal to lengthen the time limits for prosecution of breaches of the Building Regulations. The consultation can be found at www.communities.gov.uk/planningandbuilding/publications/consultations

The consultation closed on 23 October 2007 and the DCLG have published a summary of the responses, which can be found at www.communities.gov.uk/planningandbuilding/publications/consultations. The key proposals in the consultation, to implement longer time limits for local authorities to prosecute for breach of Building Regulations, were strongly supported by the majority of the respondents.

7 COMMERCIAL PROPERTY STANDARD ENQUIRIES

A new version of STER (Solicitor's Title and Exchange Requirements) and the accompanying guidance notes has been published. Both can be found at http://property.practicallaw.com/0-103-2123. STER has been amended so that it is assumed that the contract will incorporate the Standard Commercial Property Conditions (Second Edition). There are consequential amendments to the guidance notes where these refer to particular conditions of the SCPC. The guidance notes have also been amended to refer in the note to Requirement 5 that the relevant Land Registry document is now Land Registry Practice Guide 46 (not Land Registry Leaflet 28), to remove the reference to the Land Registration Rules 1925, and to refer in the note to Requirement 6.4 to the current limit per claim on solicitors' indemnity insurance being £2 million rather than £1 million.

8 LAND REGISTRY – PROPER OFFICES

The Land Registration (Proper Office) Order 2007 was published on 13 December 2007 and comes into force on 1 April 2008. It designates the Land Registry offices that are the proper offices for the receipt of specified applications for administrative districts in England and Wales, under the Land Registration Act 2002. The 2007 Order replaces the Land Registration (Proper Office) Order 2003 and the Land Registration (Proper Office) Amendment Order 2005.

As a consequence, on and after 1 April 2008, the Land Registry's Durham (Boldon), Harrow and York Offices will cease to be proper offices and there will be one Durham proper office, administered initially from the Southfield House and Boldon House buildings.

The following table shows the effect of the changes:

Administrative area	Former proper office	New proper office
Brent	Harrow	Swansea
Camden	Harrow	Croydon
City of Westminster	Harrow	Croydon
East Riding of Yorkshire	York	Kingston upon Hull
Harrow	Harrow	Swansea
Islington	Harrow	Stevenage
North Yorkshire	York	Durham
City and County of the City of London	Harrow	Stevenage
The Inner Temple and the Middle Temple	Harrow	Stevenage
York	York	Durham
Those administrative areas previously dealt with by the Durham (Boldon) or Durham (Southfield) proper offices	Durham (Boldon) or Durham (Southfield)	Durham

9 COMPANIES ACT 2006

On 1 March 2007, the DTI published a consultation paper setting out its proposals in relation to secondary legislation to be made under the Companies Act 2006, transitional arrangements and savings for existing companies, and revised draft model articles. Comments on political donations and expenditure were due by 1 May 2007 and on all other issues by 31 May 2007. The consultation paper is available at www.berr.gov.uk/consultations/page37980.html

10 BUSINESS TENANCIES

The Department for Communities and Local Government published a consultation paper on the proposed repeal of section 57 of the Landlord and Tenant Act 1954 and the modification of section 30(1) to allow public bodies to oppose renewal of business tenancies on additional grounds. The consultation will be of interest to public bodies and also to any business occupiers whose landlords are public bodies. The consultation paper is available at www. communities.gov.uk/housing/publications/consultations. The consultation closed on 25 May 2007.

11 REGULATORS' COMPLIANCE CODE

The Legislative and Regulatory Reform (Regulatory Functions) Order 2007 was made on 18 December 2007 and came into force on 6 April 2008. The Order was made under section 24(2) of the Legislative and Regulatory Reform Act 2006 and specifies a number of regulatory functions to which sections 21 and 22 of that Act apply. In addition, those regulators whose functions are specified in the Order must have regard to the Statutory Code of Practice for Regulators when exercising any of these functions. The final version of the Code was published on 17 December 2007 by the Department for Business Enterprise and Regulatory Reform. A number of bodies connected to the property industry are affected by it.

Section 21 of the 2006 Act provides that any person exercising a regulatory function to which section 21 applies must have regard to the principles that:

a) regulatory activities should be carried out in a way which is transparent, accountable, proportionate and consistent; and

b) regulatory activities should be targeted only at cases in which action is needed.

Section 22(1) provides that a Minister of the Crown may issue, and revise, a code of practice relating to the exercise of regulatory functions. Section 22 also imposes a duty on any person exercising a regulatory function to which section 22 applies, to have regard to that code of practice when determining certain policies or principles or when exercising certain regulatory functions.

The Order specifies the regulatory functions to which the duties contained in sections 21 and 22 of the 2006 Act apply. Those functions are wide-ranging and cover the regulatory functions of a large number of bodies, including:

Charity Commission for England and Wales
Civil Aviation Authority (subject to some exceptions)
Equality and Human Rights Commission (EHRC)
Environment Agency
Financial Services Authority
Forestry Commission
Gambling Commission
Health and Safety Commission
Health and Safety Executive (subject to some exceptions)
Historic Buildings and Monuments Commission for England
     (English Heritage)
Housing Corporation
Natural England
Office of Fair Trading
Registrars of Companies for England and Wales, Northern Ireland
     and Scotland

The Order also covers regulatory functions under, or by virtue of, a variety of statutes and European Community instruments dealing with a broad range of subjects, including many that are relevant to conveyancers, such as:

Agriculture
Charities
Companies
Consumer and business protection
Environment
Estate agents
Insolvency
Licensing
Public health and safety
Road transport
Water
Wildlife

The Code can be found at www.berr.gov.uk. Its purpose is to promote efficient and effective approaches to regulatory inspection and enforcement that improve regulatory outcomes without imposing unnecessary burdens. Part 2 of the Code outlines a number of principles on which the Code is based. These principles are:

1. To allow, or even encourage, economic progress.

2. To use risk assessment to concentrate resources in areas that need them most.

3. To provide authoritative, accessible advice easily and cheaply.

4. To inspect only with a reason.

5. To require the provision of necessary information only.

6. To ensure that businesses which persistently break regulations should be identified quickly and face proportionate and meaningful sanctions.

7. To hold regulators accountable for the efficiency and effectiveness of their activities, while remaining independent.

12 TEMPORARY STOP NOTICES

The Department for Communities and Local Government issued a consultation paper on proposed amendments to the regulations on temporary stop notices. The proposed amendments would allow a local planning authority to use a temporary stop notice to prevent the occupation of residential caravans on an unauthorised development, as long as an alternative site was available. The consultation closed on 31 May 2007. The consultation paper can be found at www.communities.gov.uk/planningandbuilding/publications/consultations

13 THE CONSTRUCTION (DESIGN AND MANAGEMENT) REGULATIONS 2007

The Construction (Design and Management) Regulations 2007 came into force on 6 April 2007 and replaced the Construction (Design and Management) Regulations 1994. The 2007 regulations apply to construction projects whether commenced before or after 6 April 2007.

The Health and Safety Executive has published *The Approved Code of Practice* (ACoP) which gives practical advice for all those involved in construction work. It explains:

- The legal duties placed on clients, CDM co-ordinators, designers, principal contractors, contractors, self-employed and workers.

- The circumstances in which domestic clients do not have duties under the CDM Regulations 2007 (but explains that the regulations still apply to those doing work for them).

- The new role of CDM co-ordinator – a key project advisor for clients and responsible for co-ordinating the arrangements for health and safety during the planning phase of larger and more complex projects.

- Which construction projects need to be notified to HSE before work starts and gives information on how this should be done.

- How to assess the competence of organisations and individuals involved in construction work.

- How to improve co-operation and co-ordination between all those involved in the construction project and with the workforce.

- What essential information needs to be recorded in construction health and safety plans and files, as well as what should not be included.

Copies of the ACoP are available from HSE Books (www.hsebooks. com).

14 AMENDMENTS TO PPG 15, PLANNING AND THE HISTORIC ENVIRONMENT

The Department for Communities and Local Government has published *Circular 01/07: Revisions to Principles of Selection for Listed Buildings*. This updates and clarifies paragraphs 6.1 to 6.40 of *PPG 15: Planning and the Historic Environment*, which deals with the principles and criteria for listed buildings. The general principles have been updated to provide clarity to the listing system to ensure it is transparent and accountable. The statutory criteria and general principles set out the factors taken into account when assessing a building for listing. The Circular can be found at www.communities. gov.uk/publications/planningandbuilding/circularrevisions

15 HERITAGE PROTECTION SYSTEM

The Department for Culture, Media and Sport has published a White Paper, *Heritage Protection for the 21st Century*, which proposes measures for a unified and simpler heritage protection system with greater opportunity for public involvement. It addresses the key aims of making the system more open, transparent and accountable. The White Paper is available at www.culture.gov. uk/NR/rdonlyres/D1933A0E-14F6-4AE0-8DDF-E6745380E88B/0/ hrp_whitepaper_doc1.pdf

16 DEVELOPMENT NEAR LARGE-SCALE PETROL STORAGE DEPOTS

Before a local planning authority can consider a planning application relating to development within certain distances from a site holding certain hazardous substances, it must consult the Health and Safety Executive and take into account any advice given. Following the investigation into the fire and explosion at Buncefield in 2005, the HSE was asked to review the advice it gives to local planning authorities in relation to development near large-scale petrol storage depots. The HSE has published a consultation paper seeking views on proposed changes to when its advice is required and what advice might be given. The consultation paper can be found at http://consultations.hse.gov.uk/inovem/gf2.ti/f/4194/126533.1/PDF/-/cd211.pdf. The consultation closed on 22 May 2007.

17 CONTROL OF ADVERTISEMENTS

The Town and Country Planning (Control of Advertisements) (England) Regulations 2007 came into force on 6 April 2007 and replaced the Town and Country Planning (Control of Advertisements) Regulations 1992 in England (but not in Wales). The Regulations control the display of outdoor advertisements such as billboard hoardings.

The Regulations provide that:

a) certain categories of advertisements are excepted from control;

b) deemed consent is given for certain classes of advertisement; and

c) express consent must be obtained for any advertisement that is neither excepted from the Regulations nor covered by a deemed consent.

The changes to advertisement control made by the Regulations include the following:

- The term 'advertiser' is defined so that it is clearer which parties the local planning authority should serve discontinuance notices on.

- Where the Regulations require consideration of the effect of an advertisement on the local amenity, 'amenity' is defined to include aural amenity as well as visual amenity.

- When exercising powers under the Regulations, the local planning authority must take into account the provisions of the development plan, as far as these are material.

- An application for express consent should be made using a form published electronically by the Secretary of State.

- A local planning authority may allow applications for express consent to be made electronically.

- A local planning authority has the power to decline to determine applications for express consent for certain types of advertisement within an area of special control.

- Advertisements on a balloon are no longer excepted from advertisement control and are now a category of advertisement to which deemed consent may apply.

- Minor amendments have been made to the scope of categories of advertisements that qualify for deemed consent and some of the conditions and limitations that apply.

- A new deemed consent class has been introduced for advertisements on certain telephone kiosks.

Circular 03/07: Town and Country Planning (Control of Advertisements) (England) Regulations 2007 was published on 29 March 2007 by the Department for Communities and Local Government and can be found at www.communities.gov. uk/documents/planningandbuilding/pdf/321506. The Annex to this Circular gives a general outline of the present system of advertisement control and includes relevant advice about advertisement applications to local planning authorities, appeals to the Secretary of State, and how to deal with unauthorised advertisements.

The Regulations were amended on 20 July 2007 by the Town and Country Planning (Control of Advertisements) (England) (Amendment) Regulations 2007.

18   DEVELOPMENT OF BROWNFIELD LAND

In conjunction with the Budget 2007, HM Treasury published a consultation paper – *Tax Incentives for Development of Brownfield Land* – a consultation on a package of measures to reform land remediation relief and the exemption from landfill tax for waste from cleaning up contaminated land. The consultation paper is available at www.hm-treasury.gov.uk/budget/budget_07/ documents/bud_bud07_brownfield.cfm. The consultation closed on 14 June 2007.

19 LAND REGISTRY – CONFIDENTIAL DOCUMENTS

With effect from 19 March 2007, the Land Registry will treat communications marked 'confidential' that are received in relation to objections to registration of land as potentially disclosable. Unless it is reasonable to assume that the sender is aware of this policy, communications marked 'confidential' will be returned to the sender with an invitation to re-lodge the document on a non-confidential basis. If the correspondence is sent in response to a Land Registry notice, it will be assumed that the sender is aware of the policy, as the notice states 'note that any communications or supporting documents you supply may also be disclosed to the other parties even if marked 'confidential' or to similar effect'. In other cases, such as an unsolicited disclosure, knowledge of the policy will not necessarily be assumed. This clarification is in line with advice in *Land Registry Practice Guide 37 – Objections and Disputes* as it is important that parties are aware of the other party's arguments and evidence.

20 CML FRAUD PREVENTION POLICY OVERVIEW

On 26 February 2008, the Council of Mortgage Lenders updated its 'Fraud Prevention' policy overview. This summarises the four main types of fraud as follows:

1. Application Fraud – where an individual knowingly submits incorrect information when applying for a mortgage, for example by exaggerating income or applying for an owner-occupier mortgage for a let property.

2. Identity fraud – where someone uses another person's identity to apply for a mortgage in their name.

3. Registration fraud – where a person changes the registration of a property and takes out a mortgage against it.

4. Valuation fraud – where deliberately inaccurate valuations are submitted to lenders.

The policy is available at www.cml.org.uk/cml/policy/issues/2019

21 PPG 5: WORKS AND MAINTENANCE IN OR NEAR WATER

The Environment Agency has published guidance to help construction, demolition and maintenance companies prevent the pollution of watercourses. *PPG5: Works and Maintenance in or Near Water* is available at http://publications.environment-agency.gov.uk/pdf/PMHO1107BNKG-e-e.pdf?lang=_e

22 COMPANIES IN ADMINISTRATION AND NON-DOMESTIC RATES ON EMPTY PROPERTIES

On 26 February 2008, the Office of Public Sector Information published the Non-Domestic Rating (Unoccupied Property) (England) Regulations 2008 along with an accompanying explanatory memorandum. These Regulations include a new permanent exception which provides that companies in administration are not liable for rates in respect of empty properties they own (Regulation 4(l)). The Regulations also impose a six-month time limit on the exception from non-domestic rates for empty industrial premises (Regulation 4(b)).

23 CONSULTATION ON PART 1 OF THE COMMONS ACT 2006

Part 1 of the Commons Act 2006 provides for the registers of common land, town and village greens set up under the Commons Registration Act 1965 to be maintained, as well as containing provisions for the registration of new rights of common land and town or village greens. In July 2007, the Department for Environment, Food and Rural Affairs published a consultation paper seeking views on the timetable for implementing Part 1 and a number of other proposals relating to Part 1. The consultation closed on 28 September 2007. In January 2008, a summary of responses to the consultation was published, which indicates that Part 1 will be implemented on a pilot basis from October 2008, with national implementation likely to start in October 2010.

The consultation paper and the summary of responses are available at www.defra.gov.uk/corporate/consult/commonsact2006-registers/index.htm

24 THE CODE FOR LEASING BUSINESS PREMISES IN ENGLAND AND WALES 2007

The Code for Leasing Business Premises in England and Wales 2007 was formally launched on 28 March 2007 by Yvette Cooper, Minister of State (Housing and Planning).

The Code comprises three documents:

1. Leasing Business Premises: Landlord Code

   This sets out a series of recommendations covering the following:

   a) lease negotiations;

   b) rent deposits and guarantees;

   c) length of term, break clauses and renewal rights;

   d) rent review;

   e) assignment and subletting;

   f) service charges;

   g) repairs;

   h) alterations and changes of use;

   i) insurance; and

   j) ongoing management.

2. Leasing Business Premises: Model Heads of Terms

   This is a heads of terms checklist which all parties, their agents and solicitors can use during lease negotiations.

3. Leasing Business Premises: Occupier Guide

   This is intended to be a guide for tenants to lease negotiations, the Code and some general leasing issues.

The Code recommends that landlords should be aware of the RICS 2006 Code of Practice on Service Charges in Commercial Property and should seek to observe its guidance in drafting new leases and on renewals.

The official website of the Code is www.leasingbusinesspremises. co.uk.

25 CONSULTATION ON COLLECTION OF BUILDING CONTROL INFORMATION BY LOCAL AUTHORITIES

In March 2007, the Department for Communities and Local Government launched a consultation on the collection of building control information by local authorities. Building control can be carried out either by the local authority or by a private sector approved inspector. A local authority is only required to keep public registers containing information relating to the building control activities. They are not required to keep any information relating to their own capacity as building control bodies. The consultation proposes that local authorities should keep and maintain public registers relating to their own building control functions as well as that of approved inspectors, in order to provide consistency and a similar standard of service across local authorities. The consultation is available at www.communities.gov. uk/planningandbuilding/publications/consultations. The consultation closed on 15 June 2007.

26 AMENDED PRE-ACTION PROTOCOL FOR CONSTRUCTION AND ENGINEERING DISPUTES

A new Pre-Action Protocol for Construction and Engineering Disputes came into effect from 6 April 2007. As well as disputes under building contracts and professional appointments, the Protocol can affect, for example, a defects claim under an agreement for lease or a claim against a developer under a development agreement. A court will impose costs sanctions on a party that does not comply with the Protocol. The Protocol is available at www.justice.gov.uk/civil/procrules_fin/

27 NEW HMRC GUIDANCE ON REITS

On 26 March 2007, HM Revenue & Customs published new guidance on real estate investment trusts. This replaced the draft guidance that had been available since 29 November 2006. The new guidance includes HMRC's approach to property held by REITs through non-resident unit trusts such as Jersey Property Unit Trusts. The guidance is available at www.hmrc.gov.uk/manuals/greitmanual/index.htm

28 COMMONS REGISTRATION SEARCHES

With effect from 1 October 2007, Form CR21 is no longer used for carrying out a search of the commons registers. Instead, the commons registers may be searched by using Form CON29O – Optional Enquiries of Local Authority.

29 CONSULTATION ON PERMITTED DEVELOPMENT RIGHTS FOR MICROGENERATION EQUIPMENT

The Department for Communities and Local Government has launched a consultation on the Government's proposals for reforming certain aspects of the planning system. The Government's aim is to make it easier for householders to install energy-generating equipment, by removing the need to obtain planning permission for certain types of works. The consultation period expired on 27 June 2007. The consultation paper is available at www.communities.gov.uk/planningandbuilding/publications/consultations

30 PROPOSALS TO MODERNISE BUILDING CONTROL

On 29 March 2007, the Department for Communities and Local Government published a paper, *The Future for Building Control*, setting out its initial proposals to reform the building control system. The paper is available at www.communities.gov.uk/planningandbuilding/publications/consultations. The paper is not a formal consultation and the DCLG intends to use any responses to it to develop its proposals in more depth so that it can then publish a formal consultation.

31 WATER ACT 2003

The following provisions of the Water Act 2003 were brought into force on 1 April 2007:

- The provisions of section 62 that had not already been implemented, requiring water undertakers to prepare and maintain water resources management plans.

- Section 98, which provides for schemes for the adoption of sewers, lateral drains and sewage disposal works.

- Part of section 100, dealing with devolution in Wales.

- Provisions in section 101 dealing with certain minor consequential amendments and repeals.

32 CONSULTATION ON DRAFT RURAL DEVELOPMENT PROGRAMME FOR ENGLAND 2007–2013

On 13 April 2007, the Department for Environment, Food and Rural Affairs issued a consultation paper on a draft of the Rural Development Programme for England which will run from 2007–2013. The consultation closed on 5 July 2007. A summary of responses was published in November 2007. Both the consultation paper and the summary of responses are available at www.defra.gov.uk/corporate/consult/rural-dev2007-13/index.htm

33 SERVICE AND ADMINISTRATION CHARGE DEMANDS

From 1 October 2007, a landlord must supply long leaseholders with a summary of their rights and obligations relating to service and administration charges when sending out service and administration charge demands. A leaseholder may withhold the service or administration charge payment if a landlord fails to provide the summary with the demand.

The Commonhold and Leasehold Reform Act 2002 (Commencement No. 6) (England) Order 2007 brought section 153 of the 2002 Act into force on 1 October 2007. Section 153 inserts section 21B into the Landlord and Tenant Act 1985, which requires that a demand for service charges must be accompanied by a summary of the tenant's rights and obligations relating to service charges. Section 21B(2) of the 1985 Act provides that the Secretary of State may make regulations prescribing the form and content of such summaries of rights and obligations.

The form and content of the summary are prescribed by The Service Charges (Summary of Rights and Obligations, and Transitional Provision) (England) Regulations 2007. The Administration Charges (Summary of Rights and Obligations) (England) Regulations 2007 require landlords to use particular information for the summary of a tenant's rights and obligations relating to administration charges that must be sent when demanding payment of an administration charge.

Similar provisions came into force in Wales on 30 November 2007.

34 CONSULTATION ON DELIVERING PROPERTY SEARCHES

In May 2007, the Department for Communities and Local Government launched a consultation on draft good practice guidance for local authorities and personal searchers in the delivery of property searches to consumers. The draft guidance aims to improve access to data held by local authorities and working relationships between local authorities and personal search companies. The consultation closed on 26 June 2007 and the consultation paper is available at www.communities.gov.uk/ housing/publications/consultations

35 CHANGES TO SDLT RELIEFS FOR SURPLUS SCHOOL LAND

Certain school land transactions have been exempted from charge to SDLT by the Finance Act 2003, Section 66 (Prescribed Statutory Provisions) Order 2007 which came into force on 25 May 2007. The Order prescribes that transfers of land under certain provisions of Schedule 22 to the 1998 Act and under section 27(2)(b) of the Education and Inspections Act 2006 will be exempt from charge to SDLT if either the buyer or the seller is a public body.

36 GYPSIES AND TRAVELLERS: NEW GOOD PRACTICE GUIDANCE

The Department for Communities and Local Government (DCLG) has issued two new publications that will be of interest to local authorities, those involved with housing and anyone advising gypsies and travellers.

Local Authorities and Gypsies and Travellers: A Guide to Responsibilities and Powers explains the responsibilities and powers of local authorities in relation to Gypsies and Travellers. The Government's aim is to improve the relationships between gypsies and travellers and settled communities. The guide is available at www.communities.gov.uk/documents/housing/pdf/322684

Draft Guidance on the design of sites for Gypsies and Travellers – A Consultation Paper seeks views on good practice guidance for the design of gypsy and traveller sites. The consultation covers a number of important aspects of designing such sites including location, facilities, layout and size. The consultation closed on 22 August 2007. The consultation is available at www.communities. gov.uk/housing/publications/consultations

37 ACTING FOR THE BUYER AND THE SELLER – A CONSULTATION

On 26 April 2007, the Solicitors Regulation Authority published a consultation paper on a possible change to the rules on when a solicitor can act for both the buyer and the seller in a conveyancing transaction. The consultation paper outlined three options:

1. To keep the current rule as it is.

2. To remove the rule and rely on the general provisions on conflicts of interests.

3. To remove the rule and rely on the general provisions on conflicts of interests but with specific safeguards.

The consultation period ended on 26 July 2007. The consultation paper is available at www.sra.org.uk/securedownload/file/236

38 SMOKE-FREE PREMISES

The Health Act 2006 laid down the framework in England and Wales for a ban on smoking at work, in enclosed public places and in certain vehicles. The Health Act 2006 (Commencement No. 3) Order 2007 provided for the smoking ban to come into force in England on 1 July 2007 and it is now a criminal offence to smoke in a smoke-free place. Employers and others who manage smoke-free premises must put up no-smoking signs and prevent smoking or face criminal sanctions. The Smoke-free Premises etc. (Wales) Regulations 2007 (Wales Regulations) brought the smoking ban into force in Wales on 2 April 2007. The smoking ban came into force in Scotland on 26 March 2006 and in Northern Ireland on 30 April 2007.

The smoking ban covers the following premises:

- Premises open to the public, whether by invitation or not and whether upon payment or not. The smoking ban applies only while the premises are open to the public, unless they are also a workplace.

- Premises used as a place of work (including voluntary work) by more than one person, even if those who work there do so at different times, or only intermittently. The smoking ban applies at all times.

- Premises used as a place of work (including voluntary work) where members of the public, or a section of the public, might attend for the purpose of seeking or receiving goods or services from those working there, even if members of the public are not always present. These premises must be smoke-free at all times.

The smoking ban only affects premises to the extent that they are 'enclosed' or 'substantially enclosed' and, where premises are only partly used as a workplace, the ban only effects those parts which are used as a workplace.

Premises are enclosed where both of the following apply:

1. There is a ceiling or roof.

2. The premises are wholly enclosed either permanently or temporarily, except for doors, windows and passageways.

A 'roof' is defined as including any fixed or moveable structure or device that is capable of covering all or part of the premises as a roof, including a canvas awning.

Premises are substantially enclosed if they have a ceiling or roof and the opening(s) in the walls form less than half the area of the walls (the '50% rule'). Any other structures that 'serve as' walls forming the perimeter of the premises must be taken into account. Doors, windows or other fittings that can be opened or shut do not count as opening(s) for this purpose and they are assumed to be shut.

The following premises are exempt from the smoking ban:

- Private dwellings. This exemption includes self-contained residential accommodation for temporary or holiday use and garages, outhouses and other structures used exclusively by the occupants of a dwellinghouse. However, this exemption does not apply to any parts of the dwelling that are used:

a) in common with other premises (for example, common entrance halls, stairways or shared laundry rooms); or

b) solely as a place of work by:

  i)   more than one person who does not live there; or

  ii) a person who does not live there and someone who does; or

  iii) anyone (living there or not) who, in the course of their work, invites others in.

Personal care, domestic assistance, building maintenance, and installation, maintenance or removal of services do not count as 'work'.

- Designated smoking bedrooms in hotels, guest houses, inns, hostels or members' clubs. This exemption does not cover dormitories or rooms made available under separate arrangements for persons to share at the same time.

- Designated smoking rooms in care homes, hospices and prisons for adults.

- Performers are not subject to the smoking ban if artistic integrity makes it appropriate for them to smoke during the performance.

- Specialist tobacconist shops are not required to be smoke-free whilst being used for sampling cigars and pipe tobacco.

- Designated smoking rooms in off-shore installations.

- Designated rooms in research or testing facilities are not required to be smoke-free whilst being used for specified research or tests in connection with smoking.

- Designated smoking rooms in mental health units for the use of adult patients in residential accommodation do not have to be smoke-free until 1 July 2008.

There are a number of offences under the smoke-free legislation including smoking in a smoke-free place, a failure by anyone who controls or is concerned in the management of smoke-free premises to comply with their duty to stop anyone from smoking on the premises, and a failure by anyone who occupies or is concerned in the management of smoke-free premises with their duty to make sure that the requisite no-smoking signs are correctly displayed.

Regulation 2(1) of the Smoke-free (Signs) Regulations 2007 provides that at each entrance to smoke-free premises there must be at least one no-smoking sign displayed in a prominent position, which must comply with all of the following:

- Be at least A5 size.

- Display the no-smoking symbol (a single burning cigarette in a red circle at least 70mm in diameter with a red bar across it).

- State (so that it can be easily read by those using the entrance): 'No smoking. It is against the law to smoke in these premises'.

A no-smoking sign which displays only the no-smoking symbol may be displayed in a prominent position instead where the entrance is one of the following:

- An entrance from other smoke-free premises (e.g. a shop in an indoor arcade).

- An entrance solely for persons entering their place of work in premises which have another entrance at which a sign that complies with Regulation 2(1) is displayed.

Local authorities are responsible for enforcing the smoke-free provisions. An authorised officer who has reason to believe that a person has committed an offence of smoking in a smoke-free place or who notices a failure to display no-smoking signs may issue a penalty notice. The form of penalty notice for each offence is set out in the Smoke-free (Vehicle Operators and Penalty Notices) Regulations 2007. A person who receives a fixed penalty notice may give written notice to the local authority requesting a court hearing instead.

39 PLANNING FOR A SUSTAINABLE FUTURE: WHITE PAPER

On 21 May 2007, the Government published a White Paper, *Planning for a Sustainable Future*, setting out the Government's proposals for planning reform building on Kate Barker's recommendations for improving the speed, responsiveness and efficiency in land use planning, and taking forward Kate Barker's and Rod Eddington's proposals for reform of major infrastructure planning. The White Paper is a consultative document and comprises ten chapters and two annexes. The first chapter is an executive summary; the other chapters deal with each area of proposed reform. The first annex contains a summary of the consultation questions. The second annex is a schedule of Government responses to the Barker recommendations.

The consultation period ended on 17 August 2007. The White Paper is available at www.communities.gov.uk/publications/planningandbuilding/planningsustainablefuture

40 CHANGES TO THE POSITION OF ENTRIES IN THE REGISTER

Enhancements to the Land Registry's computer system went live on 4 June 2007. These changes affect the way that some entries are positioned in the register. Under the new system, both entries carried across and new entries will be treated in the same way. Entries will be now be placed in the next available position in the relevant part of the register. There are no priority issues with the placement of these types of entries, unless they are related to a legal charge. However, the changes implemented by the Land Registry will not affect how it deals with the registration of charges, which will continue as previously. Registered charges on the same registered estate will continue to rank as between themselves in the order shown on the register. The applications most likely to be affected by the changes are those involving entries being carried across from an existing title, or titles in the relevant part of the register, and applications to correct the register. There is no change to existing registers. Any new entries arising from an application will be placed in the next available position in the relevant register.

41 CONTROLS ON STREET LITTER

From 1 July 2007, local authorities can require occupiers of premises where food or drink are served for consumption on the premises to clear up litter that comes from their premises. Premises where food or drink are sold for consumption on either the whole or part of the premises may be subject to a Street Litter Control Notice. As a result of this change, premises such as a restaurant, café or public house where the entire eating or drinking area is inside may be subject to a Street Litter Control Notice. The previous provisions only applied to take-away outlets and restaurants, cafes or bars with tables that are outside and adjacent to the street.

A Street Litter Control Notice requires the occupier, or owner, to clear up litter where the littering is likely to cause defacement of a public space and to implement measures to ensure that the land is litter-free. Failure to comply immediately with a Street Litter Control Notice can lead to a fine or a fixed penalty notice.

42 AMENDMENTS TO THE COMMERCIAL PROPERTY STANDARD ENQUIRIES

New versions of the following documents were published in June 2007:

- CPSE.1 and GN/CPSE.1: version 2.4 has been replaced by version 2.5.

- CPSE.2 and GN/CPSE.2: version 2.1 has been replaced by version 2.2.

- RQ: version 2.3 has been replaced by version 2.4 which refers to the new versions of CPSE.1 and CPSE.2.

The changes that have been made:

a) clarify the enquiry in relation to town and village greens (CPSE.1, Enquiry 4.7);

b) refer to the Control of Asbestos Regulations 2006 (CPSE.1, Enquiry 8.3 and CPSE.2, Enquiry 10.12);

c) refer to the Construction (Design and Management) Regulations 2007 (CPSE.1, Enquiry 14.4 and 14.5);

d) refer to Tenancy Deposit Schemes (CPSE.2, Enquiry 9.1).

New versions of the following documents were published in August 2007:

• CPSE.1 and GN/CPSE.1: version 2.5 has been replaced by version 2.6.

Enquiry 21.6 (dealing with Transfers of a Going Concern) has been deleted. Enquiry 21.6 asked whether the seller intended to apply to HM Revenue & Customs for permission to retain the VAT records relating to the Property following completion of the Transaction. The enquiry is no longer appropriate because of the changes in the law relating to VAT records, which came into effect for contracts entered into on or after 1 September 2007.

43 CONSULTATION ON PROPORTIONATE DISPUTE RESOLUTION FOR HOUSING

On 29 June 2007, the Law Commission launched a consultation, *Housing: Proportionate Dispute Resolution – The Role of Tribunals*, seeking views on the role of tribunals in housing disputes. This followed from an issues paper and consultation on housing dispute resolution in 2006. The consultation examines whether there should be a specialist tribunal to adjudicate housing disputes and, if so, how such a body would work. The proposed tribunal would incorporate the Residential Property Tribunal Service tribunals and would have jurisdiction to deal with mobile home possession claims, as well as rented housing and disrepair claims. The Law Commission also proposes changes to the way appeals are handled. Consultation on this project closed on 28 September 2007. The consultation paper is available at www.lawcom.gov.uk/housing_disputes.htm

44 CONSULTATION ON PART 1 OF THE COMMONS ACT 2006

On 3 July 2007, the Department for Environment, Food and Rural Affairs launched a consultation on the implementation of Part 1 of the Commons Act 2006. Part 1 deals with the updating and maintenance of registers of common land and town or village greens by commons registration authorities. The consultation is on the proposed timetable for implementing Part 1 and on other regulations and orders that will be made in respect of Part 1. The consultation closed on 28 September 2007. A summary of responses was published in January 2008. Both the consultation paper and summary of responses are available at www.defra.gov. uk/corporate/consult/commonsact2006-registers/index.htm

45 ENCOURAGING RESPONSIBLE LETTING

The Law Commission published a consultation paper on 13 July 2007 on proposals intended to promote responsible behaviour by landlords in relation to the private residential rented sector. The proposal is that landlords would only be able to let property through an accredited scheme or if they were a member of a recognised association of private landlords or if they let through a letting agent that was a member of an accredited scheme or association. The Government would set key standards of behaviour for landlords which would initially be enforced by the accredited scheme or association but, ultimately, would be enforced by a central body. The consultation period closed on 12 October 2007. The consultation paper is available at www.lawcom.gov.uk/docs/cp181.pdf

46 CONSULTATION ON INSURANCE CONTRACT LAW

In July 2007, the Law Commission and the Scottish Law Commission published a joint consultation paper on insurance contract law, covering misrepresentation, non-disclosure and breach of warranty by the insured. This consultation paper follows a joint scoping paper published in January 2006, which explained that the law of misrepresentation, non-disclosure and breach of warranty would be considered for reform, and three subsequent Issues papers on misrepresentation and non-disclosure, warranties, and intermediaries and pre-contract information. These Issues papers were in anticipation of a single consultation on reform, planned for Summer 2007. The Commissions have decided, however, to publish two consultation papers. The second paper will be published in 2008 and will cover post-contractual good faith, insurable interest and damages for late payment of claims. The deadline for responses was 16 November 2007. The consultation paper is available at www.lawcom.gov.uk/docs/cp182_web.pdf

47 *CONSULTATION ON SHARED OWNERSHIP AND LEASEHOLD ENFRANCHISEMENT*

In July 2007, the Department for Communities and Local Government published a consultation on proposals to restrict the right of tenants under shared ownership schemes to buy additional shares in their properties, and to prevent them being able to enfranchise before they have acquired all of the additional shares under their shared ownership leases. The aim of these measures is to prevent affordable housing being sold by shared owners who have acquired the entire interest in their properties, especially in areas where the supply of affordable housing is restricted. The consultation closed on 19 October 2007. The consultation paper is available at www.communities.gov.uk/publications/housing/sharedownership

A summary of the responses received to the consultation was published on 16 January 2008 and is available at www.communities.gov.uk/publications/housing/sharedownershipenfranchise

48 HOUSING GREEN PAPER

The Department for Communities and Local Government published the following documents on 23 July 2007:

- A Housing Green Paper.

- Practice Guidance on Strategic Land Availability Assessment, which gives local authorities advice on identifying land for housing and assessing deliverability.

- An Eco-towns Prospectus, which sets out a 'vision' and specification for local authorities and developers on developing eco-towns.

- A Policy Statement confirming the Government's intention for all new homes to be zero carbon by 2016.

- A document outlining the significant and progressive changes that will need to be made to the energy efficiency requirements in the Buildings Regulations to ensure that all new homes are zero carbon by 2016.

- A consultation document on making the Code for Sustainable Homes mandatory.

- Preliminary advice on implementing Planning Performance Agreements.

- An analysis of the responses received to the consultation on the draft Planning Policy Statement on Planning and Climate Change.

- A Policy Statement on water efficiency in new buildings.

49 CONSULTATION ON THE IMPLEMENTATION OPTIONS FOR THE TRANSFER OF PRIVATE SEWERS

In July 2007, the Government issued a consultation paper looking at how the transfer of private sewers and lateral drains to the statutory water and sewerage companies could be implemented and considering different methods of transfer. The consultation period ended on 19 October 2007. The consultation paper is available at www.defra.gov.uk/corporate/consult/sewers-transfer/consultation.pdf.

The proposed methods of transfer are:

- Overnight transfer where from a set date the ownership of all private sewers and lateral drains would transfer to the statutory water and sewerage companies.

- Phased transfer where the transfer of the private sewers and lateral drains would begin on a set date but would be phased over a period of time.

- Application-based transfers where an owner of a private drain or lateral sewer would be entitled to apply for their drain or sewer to be transferred.

50 MONEY LAUNDERING REGULATIONS

On 25 July 2007, HM Treasury published The Money Laundering Regulations 2007 (Regulations), which came into force on 15 December 2007.

In summary, the Regulations:

- Extend supervision to all businesses in the regulated sector to secure greater compliance with anti-money laundering controls including, for the first time, estate agents, trust and company service providers and consumer credit businesses.

- Include strict tests to ensure money services business and firms that help set up and manage trusts and companies are not run for criminal purposes.

- Provide more detailed obligations regarding customer due diligence, such as explicit requirements for firms to monitor their business relationships on an ongoing basis and for firms to identify not just the customer but the beneficial owner of the customer.

- Require firms to vary customer due diligence and monitoring according to the risk of money laundering.

- Require extra checks on customers that pose a higher risk of money laundering, for example, foreign heads of state and non-face-to-face customers.

The Regulations also reduce regulatory burdens in low-risk areas so that firms will be able to make fewer checks in low-risk situations, and carry out fewer identity checks as they will be able to rely on checks carried out by certain other firms such as solicitors and FSA authorised financial advisers. Record-keeping requirements are also eased, enabling firms to keep only important details rather than whole documents.

51 LAW SOCIETY GUIDANCE ON REPORTING TERRORISM AND MAINTAINING CLIENT CONFIDENTIALITY

On 19 July 2007, the Law Society published a practice note explaining the nature of a solicitor's duty of confidentiality to a client and how the anti-terrorism 'failure to disclose' offence provisions in the Terrorism Act 2000 affect this duty. The practice note is available at www.lawsociety.org.uk/documents/downloads/dynamic/practicenote_terrorismact2000.pdf

52 REGISTERING CHARGES UNDER THE COMPANIES ACT 2006

From 1 October 2008, section 395 of the Companies Act 1985 will be replaced by section 860 of the Companies Act 2006. Section 395 provides that companies registered in England and Wales must register a mortgage or charge when it is created by sending Form 395 to the Registrar of Companies, together with the document creating the charge, within 21 days of creation of the charge. If the Form 395 and the document creating the charge are not delivered within the time limit, the charge is void against a liquidator or administrator and against a creditor. From 1 October 2008, Form 395 will be replaced by Form 860. The charge categories that have to be registered and the 21-day time limit for registration will not change.

On 19 July 2007, the Department for Business, Enterprise and Regulatory Reform published draft regulations setting out the information to be provided to the Registrar of Companies when registering a charge under the Companies Act 2006. It is intended that the draft regulations will come into force on 1 October 2008. The information to be provided by companies registered in England and Wales under the draft regulations is the same as that required under the 1985 Act and includes:

a) the date of the creation of the charge;

b) a description of the instrument (if any) creating or evidencing the charge;

c) the amount secured by the charge;

d) the name and address of the person entitled to the charge;

e) short particulars of the property charged.

Comments on the draft regulations were required to be made by 30 September 2007.

53 REVISED TRANSACTION FORMS

The Law Society has produced new TransAction forms for use from 1 August 2007. The forms have been extended and adapted to comply with the Home Information Pack Regulations. The forms may be used to prepare a HIP, but can also be used in the conveyancing process where a HIP is not required.

The new TransAction forms consist of the following:

TA1 Home Information Pack Index
TA2 Sale Statement
TA3 Required leasehold information
TA4 Required commonhold information
TA5 Proof of requests for missing documents and information
TA6 Property information form
TA7 Leasehold information form
TA8 New home information form
TA9 Commonhold information form
TA10 Fittings and contents form
TA11 Additional property information

TA12 Buyer information
TA13 Completion information and requisitions on title
TA14 Leasehold information request
TA15 Commonhold information request

Forms TA6, TA7, TA9, TA10, TA13 are adapted and updated versions of the current TransAction forms. The other forms are new HIP documents, or forms authorised for inclusion in a HIP.

The forms are available from Shaw & Sons Limited.

54 WATER EFFICIENCY IN NEW BUILDINGS: A JOINT DEFRA AND COMMUNITIES AND LOCAL GOVERNMENT POLICY STATEMENT

On 23 July 2007, the Department for Communities and Local Government, and the Department for Environment, Food and Rural Affairs, published a joint policy statement outlining how they propose to set minimum standards for water efficiency in new buildings. This followed a joint consultation document published in 2006. In 2008 the two departments are proposing to do the following:

- For new homes – amend the Building Regulations to set a minimum whole building performance standard. The standard is to be set at 125 litres per day.

- For non-domestic buildings – amend the Water Supply (Water Fittings) Regulations 1999 to set new performance standards for key fittings that can be installed in buildings (such as taps and toilets).

55 NEW FORMS OF ENQUIRIES OF LOCAL AUTHORITIES

On 1 August 2007, two new forms of enquiries of local authorities came into force and replaced the 2002 editions:

1. Form CON29R – Enquiries of Local Authority (2007). This replaces CON29 – Part I Standard Enquiries of Local Authority (2002 edition). It contains a set of standard questions that should be raised in every case. Replies to these enquiries are needed for the purposes of compiling a Home Information Pack.

2. Form CON29O – Optional enquiries of local authority (2007), which contains optional enquiries to be asked where relevant to a transaction. Replies to CON29O are 'authorised' documents for inclusion in a Home Information Pack. CON29O also includes commons registration enquiries.

56 *COMMERCIAL LANDLORDS ACCREDITATION SCHEME*

In July 2007, the British Property Federation launched the Commercial Landlords Accreditation Scheme which is open to all commercial landlords in England and Wales. The scheme builds upon the Code for Leasing Business Premises in England and Wales 2007 by offering members the opportunity to display the CLAS logo on their stationery and marketing materials, demonstrating that they are committed to the Code. The self-regulatory scheme will include a three-step complaints procedure and possible disciplinary action.

To achieve accreditation, landlords must commit to do all of the following:

1. Inform prospective tenants at the start of negotiations that they are a member of CLAS.

2. Provide prospective small business tenants with basic information on the risks involved in taking a lease (specifically the *Leasing Business Premises: Model Heads of Terms* and *Leasing Business Premises: Occupier Guide*).

3. Abide by the *Leasing Business Premises: Landlord Code*.

4. Explain to prospective tenants why any of the requirements in the 2007 Code cannot be complied with.

5. Have a written complaints procedure and a named complaints officer. The procedure should offer to deal with complaints within 28 days of receipt.

147

If a CLAS member breaks the scheme's rules, there is a three-step complaints process:

1. The landlord's internal complaints procedure.

2. A review by a CLAS case worker.

3. In serious cases and on appeals, a referral to the independent CLAS Standards Board, which will comprise equal numbers of landlord, occupier and independent representatives.

Further information is available at www.clascheme.org.uk/index.html

57 CONSULTATION ON RESIDENTIAL SERVICE CHARGES

On 25 July 2007, the Department for Communities and Local Government issued a consultation on possible amendments to sections 152 and 156 of the Commonhold and Leasehold Reform Act 2002. These sections were intended to address some of the problems faced by residential tenants in relation to service charges, but the provisions have not yet been implemented. Section 152 requires landlords to provide a statement of the service charge account to tenants within six months of the end of the accounting period. Section 156 requires landlords to hold service charge monies for separate groups of service charge payers in separate client accounts. Following a consultation on these provisions in 2004, the Government accepted that sections 152 and 156 would impose significant costs on landlords, which would be passed on to tenants. This consultation sets out proposals to amend sections 152 and 156 to address these concerns. The consultation is available at www.communities.gov.uk/publications/housing/statementsofaccount and closed on 4 October 2007.

On 16 January 2008, a summary of the responses received to the consultation was published and is available at www.communities.gov.uk/publications/housing/regularstatementresponse

In relation to the proposals relating to section 152:

- The majority of responses were in favour of the proposals to allow greater flexibility in how the information in the service charge account can be presented. The final content of the statement of account has still to be decided. However, the Government has recognised that there is a case for not insisting on the identification of improvements, or the individual items that represent 10% or more of total expenditure.

- Most responses were in favour of the proposals to modify the prescribed content of the statements of account to be provided by local authority landlords, to recognise the way in which local authorities are required to account for expenditure on their housing stock. The Government now intends to discuss the detailed requirements for the statements of account with the Social Sector Working Party.

- The majority of responses were in favour of the proposals to modify the prescribed content of the statements of account to be provided by registered social landlords. The Government will discuss with registered social landlords which is the most appropriate form of statement to be used in different circumstances.

- There were mixed responses to the proposal to introduce an exception from the requirement to provide an accountant's report where the service charges in the statement do not exceed £5,000. The Government is intending to proceed with the proposal, but has decided that the exemption should also be available where the information in the statement deals with the service charges for four or fewer dwellings.

In relation to the proposals relating to section 156:

- Most responses supported the proposal to allow a payee to hold a number of different service charge funds in the same account. The Government has stated that it is minded to proceed with this proposal.

- There were mixed views on the proposal to clarify that ground rent and administration charges must not be held in the same account as the service charge monies. The Government intends to proceed with this proposal. Combined cheques for service charges and ground rent/administration charges could either be paid into a separate account with the service charge element being transferred out to the relevant designated account on clearance of the cheque, or vice versa.

- The majority of responses were in favour of giving tenants the right to request all the statements of account required, in order to explain the balance of service charge monies held in the designated account into which that tenant's service charges are paid. The Government has confirmed that it is minded to proceed with this proposal.

The majority of responses also supported the proposal requiring an accountant's report under section 152 to consider all of the statements of account for service charges held in a single account. The Government has stated that it also intends to proceed with this proposal.

58 CONSULTATION ON LONGER TIME LIMITS FOR PROSECUTIONS FOR BREACHES OF BUILDING REGULATIONS

The Department for Communities and Local Government published consultation on 31 July 2007 on proposals to extend the period during which local authorities can bring a prosecution for breaches of Building Regulations from the current limit of six months to two years. The consultation is available at www.communities.gov.uk/publications/planningandbuilding/breachesconsultation and closed on 23 October 2007.

59 SDLT RETURNS FILED ONLINE

With effect from 4 August 2007, HM Revenue & Customs no longer issues a paper copy of the SDLT5 certificate for SDLT returns that are submitted online. An electronic SDLT5 will be issued, which should be printed off for submission to the Land Registry. In special circumstances, a paper copy of the SDLT5 certificate may be obtained from the HMRC Stamp Taxes Helpline.

60 GUIDANCE ON TALL BUILDINGS

The Commission for Architecture and the Built Environment and English Heritage have updated their joint guidance on tall buildings to reflect changes to the planning system and their experience of evaluating planning applications for tall buildings. The Guidance is available at www.cabe.org.uk/AssetLibrary/10173.pdf

61 SECOND LAND REGISTRY CONSULTATION ON E-CONVEYANCING LEGISLATION

In August 2007, the Land Registry issued a second consultation on legislation needed to implement the e-conveyancing system. The consultation paper, *E-conveyancing Secondary Legislation Part 2*, seeks views on:

1. The proposed Land Registration (Electronic Conveyancing) Rules 2008, which allow for the creation of electronic legal charges. This is the main focus of the consultation paper and section 5 sets out the proposals relating to the creation of electronic charges. The Rules only allow for the creation of an electronic legal charge:

   a) by an existing registered proprietor, or by someone who has applied to the Land Registry to be registered as the proprietor (limiting the use of electronic charges to re-mortgages and second charges);

   b) by individuals, not by companies; and

   c) over the whole of a registered estate in a single registered title.

   Although the legal charge would be created and lodged electronically, it would be processed manually within the Land Registry.

2. An extension to the facilities for lodging documents electronically. There are 17 Land Registry forms that can be lodged electronically using Land Registry Direct. The consultation paper proposes to move 13 of these forms from Land Registry Direct to the e-conveyancing service. The consultation paper also proposes to add forms that are not currently available through Land Registry Direct to the e-conveyancing service. These proposed forms include an electronic notice of discharge of a registered charge (E-DS1).

3. Enhancement of the Chain Matrix facility to allow paper contracts to be exchanged electronically. The Chain Matrix facility allows information about the progress of a conveyancing transaction to be shared with conveyancers, clients and estate agents. The Land Registry is working with the Law Society to create a new formula E to allow paper contracts to be exchanged electronically, using the Chain Matrix facility, rather than by telephone.

The consultation is available at http://econsultations.e-conveyancing. gov.uk/inovem/gf2.ti/f/52226/1146565.1/pdf/-/econ%20consultatio n%20FINAL.pdf and closed on 16 November 2007.

62 NEW GUIDANCE FOR LOCAL PLANNING AUTHORITIES ON VALIDATION OF PLANNING APPLICATIONS

In December 2007, the Department for Communities and Local Government published new guidance outlining new procedures for the validation of planning applications by local planning authorities. The new guidance replaces the interim guidance issued in 2005. It is intended to make the new validation requirements compulsory at the same time as the standard planning application form 1APP becomes mandatory. The implementation date for both the standard planning application form and the new validation procedures was 6 April 2008. The guidance is available at www.communities.gov.uk/publications/planningandbuilding/ validationplanningapplications

63 CONSULTATION ON TRANSFER OF PLANNING APPEALS TO INSPECTORS

On 13 August 2007, the Department for Communities and Local Government published a consultation paper on proposals to extend the range of cases that can be determined by planning inspectors. The paper envisages most types of planning and enforcement appeals being determined by inspectors; however, there would be limited exceptions where, after consideration of an inspector's report, the circumstances justify the Secretary of State determining the appeal. The consultation is available at www. communities.gov.uk/archived/publications/planningandbuilding/ transferplanningappeals and closed on 5 November 2007.

64 CONSULTATION ON OVERRIDING EASEMENTS AND OTHER RIGHTS

On 17 August 2007, the Department for Communities and Local Government published a consultation on a proposed amendment to section 237 of the Town and Country Planning Act 1990. Section 237 allows easements and rights affecting land acquired by a local authority to be overridden during construction works to that land, but not during the subsequent use of the land. The proposed amendment would allow easements and other rights to be overridden during the subsequent use of the land as well as during the construction phase. The consultation is available at www.communities.gov.uk/publications/planningandbuilding/ easementsconsultation and closed on 26 October 2007.

65 CONSULTATION ON TOLERATED TRESPASSERS

On 20 August 2007, the Department for Communities and Local Government published a consultation on tolerated trespassers, i.e. people who once occupied properties under residential tenancies but whose lettings have legally ended. The consultation seeks views on how to deal with the issues arising from a potentially large number of occupiers who have become tolerated trespassers and have lost their rights as tenants. The proposals include amending the Housing Act 1985 and the Housing Act 1988 to prevent the creation of future tolerated trespassers, and to reinstate the tenancies of tolerated trespassers, although possibly only for those who have complied with the terms of the possession order. The consultation is available at www.communities.gov.uk/publications/housing/toleratedtrespassers and closed on 2 November 2007.

66 LAND REGISTRY – PRACTICE GUIDE 14 – CHARITIES

In June 2007, the Land Registry published a new edition of LR Practice Guide 14 – Charities. The amendments result from the Charities Act 2006 which abolished the Charity Commissioners and created the Charity Commission. The Guide points out that the Land Registration Rules 2003 are to be amended to replace references to the Charity Commissioners. In the meantime, section 6(5) of the 2006 Act provides that references in existing legislation to the Charity Commissioners have effect as references to the Charity Commission. The Guide also advises conveyancers that applications to enter a standard restriction against a registered estate in Form F should now refer to the Charity Commission. A Form F restriction is used where the land is vested in the Official Custodian on trust for a non-exempt charity under section 18 of the Charities Act 1993. Transactions affecting the land must be authorised by a court order or the Charity Commission.

67 LAND REGISTRY – LASTING POWERS OF ATTORNEY

As from 1 October 2007, lasting powers of attorney replaced enduring powers of attorney. The Land Registry published the following revised practice guides to reflect the change:

- LR Practice Guide 8 – Execution of deeds: this guide advises on the execution of deeds that have to be submitted to the Land Registry.

- LR Practice Guide 9 – Powers of attorney and registered land: this guide explains the different types of power and explains what the Land Registry will check for when registering a document that has been signed by an attorney.

- LR Practice Guide 24 – Private trusts of land: this guide provides advice for anyone who is registering a transaction that involves trustees of land (other than public, ecclesiastical or charitable trustees).

68 LAND REGISTRY – ADDITIONAL GUIDANCE ON ADVERSE POSSESSION

The Land Registry has published a further guidance paper, *Additional Practice Affecting Practice Guide 5*, to clarify how it will treat adverse possession applications. The further guidance accompanies its existing guidance, *LR Practice Guide 05 – Adverse possession of unregistered land and transitional provisions for registered land in the Land Registration Act 2002*. The Land Registry has confirmed that, in its view, the decision of the European Court of Human Rights in *J A Pye (Oxford) Ltd and J A Pye (Oxford) Land Ltd v The United Kingdom* (Application No. 44302) does not affect current domestic case law. An application under paragraph 18 of Schedule 12 to the Land Registration Act 2002 must still show that its possession was inconsistent with the use, or intended use, of the land by the owner and not merely that it was without the owner's consent.

69 COMPANIES ACT 2006

Certain provisions of the Companies Act 2006 came into force on 1 October 2007. The following are relevant to conveyancers:

69.1 Right to inspect and require copies of records

Section 116 provides that the register and index of members' names must be open for inspection. The fees payable to inspect and copy company records are prescribed by the Companies (Fees for

155

Inspection and Copying of Company Records) Regulations 2007. Where a company receives a request under section 116, it must comply with that request within five days, or apply to the court, if it considers that a request is not for a proper purpose. If the court is satisfied that the inspection or copy sought is not for a proper purpose, it will direct that the company need not comply with the request.

It is an offence for a person making a section 116 request to knowingly or recklessly make a statement which is misleading, false or deceptive, or for a person in possession of information acquired from an inspection to disclose that information to a third party, whom the discloser knows or suspects will use the information for an improper purpose.

69.2 Loans to directors

Sections 197 to 214 of the 2006 Act replace sections 330 to 342 of the Companies Act 1985 and introduce a number of significant changes. The changes include the following:

- The abolition of the general prohibition on loans to directors is replaced by a requirement of shareholder approval for all companies.

- The abolition of the criminal penalty for breach of the provisions on loans.

- The introduction of a new exception for expenditure in connection with regulatory action or investigations.

- Restricting the exception for expenditure on defending legal or regulatory proceedings to proceedings in connection with any alleged negligence, default, breach of duty or breach of trust by the director in relation to the company or an associated company.

69.3 Directors

Part 10 of the 2006 Act aims to restate and amend Part X of the 1985 Act to:

a) simplify the overall structure;

b) deregulate where the existing provisions are unnecessary or excessive; and

c) reflect modern business practice.

Part 10 deals with the regulation of directors' conflicts of interest and details the requirements for:

- Disclosure to shareholders (for example, in the case of directors' service contracts and qualifying third party indemnity provisions).

- Shareholder approval (in the case of long-term service contracts, substantial property transactions, loans and payments for loss of office).

In relation to shareholder approval:

- Special provision is made for companies that are charities and they will require prior written consent of the Charity Commission in addition to shareholder approval.

- Where approval is given by written resolution, an accidental failure to send any required memorandum to every eligible member before the resolution is passed is to be disregarded (subject to any provision of the company's articles).

- Where approval is required under more than one provision, the requirements of each applicable provision must be met but a separate resolution is not required for the purposes of each provision.

- Where a long-term service contract, substantial property transaction, loan or payment for loss of office is entered into by a company and involves a director of the company's holding company, the transaction must be approved by both the company and the holding company (unless an exception applies).

- Approval is not required on the part of the member of a wholly-owned subsidiary or on the part of the members of a company that is not a UK-registered company.

69.4 Directors' duties

The 2006 Act aims to codify the duties of directors and includes a statutory statement of the duties owed by directors which replace many common law rules and equitable principles as they relate to directors.

The seven general duties of a director are:

1. To act within his powers.

2. To promote the success of the company for the benefit of its members as a whole. In doing this, the director must have regard to:

   a) the likely long-term consequences of the decision;

   b) the interests of the company's employees;

   c) the need to foster business relationships with the company's suppliers, customers and others;

   d) the impact of the company's operations on the community and the environment;

   e) the desirability of maintaining a reputation for high standards of business conduct; and

   f) the need to act fairly as between members of the company.

3. To exercise independent judgment.

4. To exercise reasonable care, skill and diligence.

5. To avoid conflicts of interest (this provision does not come into force until 1 October 2008).

6. Not to accept benefits from third parties (this provision does not come into force until 1 October 2008).

7. To declare to the other directors any interest in a proposed transaction or arrangement with the company (this provision does not come into force until 1 October 2008).

69.5 Substantial property transactions

These are arrangements by a company to acquire non-cash assets, including real property assets, from, or transfer such assets to, a director (or a person connected with a director) of the company or its holding company. Sections 190 to 196 of Part 10 of the 2006 Act replace sections 320 to 322 of the 1985 Act and propose a number of amendments to the rules on substantial property transactions. The most significant changes are:

a) the ability to make an agreement conditional on shareholder approval being given for the substantial property transaction; and

b) raising the *de minimis* threshold for the value of the non-cash assets to £5,000.

69.6 Connected persons

Sections 252 and 253 of the 2006 Act extend the definition of connected persons under section 346 of the 1985 Act to include:

- The director's civil partner.

- The director's children or step-children who are over 18 years old.

- Persons with whom the director lives as a partner in an enduring family relationship (unless that person is the director's grandparent or grandchild, sister, brother, aunt or uncle, nephew or niece).

- Children or step-children of the director's unmarried partner if they live with the director and have not attained the age of 18.

- The director's parents.

70 CARSBERG REVIEW OF RESIDENTIAL PROPERTY

Sir Bryan Carsberg, the former Director General of the Office of Fair Trading, was appointed in October 2007 to chair an independent review of the residential property sector. The review is sponsored by the National Association of Estate Agents, the Association of

Residential Lettings Agents and the Royal Institute of Chartered Surveyors. It will consider the standards, regulations and redress structures in the residential sector and, in particular, will:

1. Look at current practices in residential buying and selling and residential letting and renting, from the point of view of the professional adviser, the Government and the consumer.

2. Identify the issues in processes, regulatory frameworks and markets that prevent a consistency in approach, inhibit innovation and lead to consumer dissatisfaction.

The review is available at www.rics.org/NR/rdonlyres/DB467A4F-9750-4247-9F22-8E634853B148/0/Consultationfinalversion.pdf and responses were due by 7 January 2008.

71 VAT TREATMENT OF SERVICED BUILDING PLOTS

In October 2007, HM Revenue & Customs announced a change in the Value Added Tax treatment of land sold with the benefit of service connections. The disposal of this type of land is now treated as a single exempt supply of land for VAT purposes. Further information can be found in HM Revenue & Customs Brief 64/07 (October 2007), *VAT: Changes in the VAT treatment of serviced building plots*, which is available at www.hmrc.gov.uk/briefs/vat/brief6407.htm

72 CONSULTATION ON AMENDMENTS TO EIA REGULATIONS

On 19 October 2007, the Department for Communities and Local Government published a consultation paper on proposed amendments to the Town and Country Planning (Environmental Impact Assessment) (England and Wales) Regulations 1999. The amendments would allow for an environmental impact assessment to be required when reserved matters are considered in an outline planning application, where the effects of the development project were not fully identified or identifiable at the outline planning application stage. The proposals follow the European Commission's threat to bring legal proceedings against the UK Government for failing to comply with the May 2006 ruling of the European Court of Justice on the Environmental Impact Assessment Directive.

The consultation is available at www.communities.gov.uk/ publications/planningandbuilding/towncountryplanning and closed on 11 January 2008.

73 RESPONSES TO BUILDING REGULATIONS CONSULTATION

In July 2007, the Department for Communities and Local Government published a consultation on its proposal to lengthen the time limits for prosecution of breaches of the Building Regulations. The consultation closed on 23 October 2007 and a summary of the responses was published in November 2007 and is available at www.communities.gov.uk/publications/ planningandbuilding/longertime. The main proposals in the consultation, to implement longer time limits for local authorities to prosecute for breach of Building Regulations, were strongly supported by the majority of the respondents.

74 LAW SOCIETY ANTI-MONEY LAUNDERING PRACTICE NOTE

On 22 February 2008, the Law Society published a practice note to help solicitors comply with the Proceeds of Crime Act 2002, Terrorism Act 2000, Money Laundering Regulations 2007 and all amending legislation up to February 2008. The practice note is available at www.lawsociety.org.uk/productsandservices/ practicenotes/aml.page

75 LAND REGISTRY – CONSULTATION ON THE LAND REGISTRATION RULES 2003

In October 2007, the Land Registry issued a consultation paper, Review of Land Registration Rules 2003 consultation document, following an extensive internal review of the Land Registration

Rules 2003. The consultation was aimed primarily at conveyancers, lenders, financial institutions, their regulatory and representative bodies, and other property professionals. The consultation paper covers a considerable number of proposals on a wide variety of subjects. The consultation document predominantly considers amendments to existing rules and practice, although there are some proposals that, if adopted, would initiate entirely new practice.

The consultation paper is available at http://consultations. landregistry.gov.uk/inovem/consult.ti/RulesReview2003/ consultationHome and the consultation closed on 14 January 2008.

76 LAND REGISTRY – SUPPLEMENTARY CONSULTATION ON POSSESSORY TITLE REGISTERS

On 26 November 2007, the Land Registry published a short, supplementary consultation document on a proposal to remove the first proprietor entry on possessory title registers. The Land Registry feels that the original justification for the first proprietor entry is no longer relevant and that the change will involve no additional administrative burdens for customers.

The consultation paper is available at http://consultations. landregistry.gov.uk/inovem/gf2.ti/f/47490/1366469.1/pdf/-/Supple mentary%20consultation%20%20possessory%20titles.pdf and the consultation closed on 14 January 2008.

77 CONSULTATION ON DRAFT MAYOR OF LONDON ORDER

On 23 November 2007, the Department for Communities and Local Government published a consultation on the draft Mayor of London Order and a draft Circular on Strategic Planning in London. The draft Order contains detailed arrangements for the Mayor's new power to decide planning applications of potential strategic importance. It also proposes significant changes to the referral thresholds relating to applications for new housing developments, waste facilities and developments in the City of London. The draft Circular sets out the matters which the Mayor must consider before directing any changes to Local Development Schemes.

The consultation paper is available at www.communities.gov. uk/publications/planningandbuilding/golconsultation and the consultation closed on 14 February 2008.

78 *TREE PRESERVATION ORDERS: IMPROVING PROCEDURES*

On 27 November 2007, the Department for Communities and Local Government issued a consultation paper, *Tree Preservation Orders: Improving Procedures*. The consultation paper seeks views on four proposals to improve the tree preservation order system:

1. The introduction of a standard form for all applications to fell or prune trees subject to a tree preservation order.

2. A more streamlined method for processing tree preservation order appeals.

3. The transfer of all tree preservation order appeal administration from the Offices for the Regions to the Planning Inspectorate.

4. Revised requirements on local planning authorities regarding the circulation of newly-made tree preservation orders.

The consultation paper is available at www.communities.gov. uk/publications/planningandbuilding/tposconsultation and the consultation closed on 19 February 2008.

79 *CONSULTATION ON THE VALIDITY PERIOD FOR ENERGY PERFORMANCE CERTIFICATES*

On 13 December 2007, the Department for Communities and Local Government issued a consultation on the length of time for which energy performance certificates should be valid for private marketed sales of dwellings. The consultation paper takes the view that ten years – the maximum time for which an energy performance certificate can remain valid in accordance with the Energy Performance of Buildings Directive – is too long. The Government's opinion is that energy efficiency information that is ten years old is likely to be too out-of-date to be useful. Views are sought on the time limit that should apply to residential energy performance certificates on the basis of modelled examples based on the following periods:

- Three months

- One year

- Three years

- Five years

- Seven years

The consultation paper is available at www.communities.gov. uk/publications/planningandbuilding/validity and the consultation closed on 6 March 2008.

80 NEW GUIDANCE ON INFORMATION REQUIRED TO VALIDATE PLANNING APPLICATIONS

On 7 December 2007, the Government published final guidance on the information required to support a planning application in order to ensure that the application will be accepted as a valid application by the local planning authority. The Town and Country Planning (General Development Procedure) Order 1995 will be amended to bring into force, on 6 April 2008, requirements for the mandatory use of the standard planning application in Form 1APP and the mandatory information requirements, against which a planning application will be validated.

The final guidance provides that:

- Different levels of information and supporting document will be required to support different types of applications and scales.

- In all cases, the information required will be specified by the local planning authority.

- There will be a national core list of information that will be required in all cases. This list will include:

  i) the completed application form;

  ii) the correct fee (if required);

  iii) ownership certificates;

  iv) agricultural holdings certificate;

  v) design and access statement (where one is necessary);

  vi) the location plan and site plan;

  vii) other plans and drawings or information necessary to describe the subject of the application;

  viii) an environmental statement (where one is necessary).

- In addition to the national core list of information, there will be a local list of required information, compiled by each local planning authority from a list provided by central Government. Local planning authorities will be encouraged to consult on and adopt local lists, and to review the lists every three years. The local list may include all or any of the following:

  a) affordable housing statement;
  b) air quality assessment;
  c) biodiversity survey and report;
  d) daylight/sunlight assessment;
  e) economic statement;
  f) environmental statement;
  g) flood risk assessment;
  h) foul sewage and utilities assessment;
  i) heritage statement;
  j) land contamination assessment;
  k) landfill applications;
  l) landscaping details;
  m) lighting assessment;
  n) noise assessment;
  o) Open Space assessment;

p) planning statement;
q) site waste management plan;
r) statement of community involvement;
s) structural survey;
t) telecommunications development – supplementary information;
u) town centre uses – evidence to accompany applications;
v) transport assessment;
w) travel plans and parking provisions;
x) tree survey/arboricultural implications; or
y) ventilation/extraction statement.

• There is no statutory deadline for the adoption of a local list. If a local planning authority does not, however, adopt a local list, applicants will only be required to comply the information from the national list. It is intended that local authorities will provide local lists, as the combined use of the national and local list will give the authority and applicant more certainty when submitting applications and ensure that the information requested is proportionate to the type and scale of application being made.

• The Government expects that local planning authorities will only require the level of detail of required information that is appropriate for the scale of application. Local lists should take account of the Government's commitment to reduce the information requirements associated with planning applications. A local planning authority may still require additional information during the course of the application process and may impose conditions to require submission of detailed reports or other information.

The guidance also covers:

• The validation process, which includes the local planning authority targets for dealing with applications.

• The action a local planning authority should take if it considers an application to be invalid and the rights enabling applicants to appeal against a decision which finds an application to be invalid.

- Facilitation by local planning authorities of pre-application advice, particularly in relation to larger, more complex applications.

- Particular information requirements for particular types of application together with model local lists.

81 TAX INCENTIVES FOR DEVELOPMENT OF BROWNFIELD LAND

On 14 December 2007, HM Treasury published its proposals for reform of tax incentives for the development of brownfield land. The proposals include:

- Extending the existing land remediation tax relief to include the cost of developing long-term derelict land and the cost of removing Japanese knotweed.

- Phasing out the landfill tax exemption for contaminated waste.

The Government is expected to make a further announcement on its tax relief proposals in the Budget 2008.

The proposals are available at www.hm-treasury.gov.uk/media/6/9/consult_brownfieldresponse141207.pdf

82 CONSULTATION ON SDLT AVOIDANCE AND DISCLOSURE

On 17 December 2007, HM Treasury published a consultation paper on the reform of the tax treatment of residential property transactions effected through a special purpose vehicle. The consultation paper seeks views on 'fairer' ways of taxing transactions involving special purpose vehicles, to make the tax treatment closer to that of similar land transactions. The consultation also asks for comments on a possible extension of the SDLT disclosure rules to include residential property worth £1 million or more.

The consultation paper is available at www.hm-treasury.gov.uk/
consultations_and_legislation/stamp_duty/consult_stampdutyfairness.
cfm and the consultation closed on 8 February 2008.

83 *PLANNING POLICY STATEMENT ON CLIMATE CHANGE*

On 17 December 2007, the Department for Communities and Local
Government published a Planning Policy Statement on planning
and climate change, as a supplement to PPS 1 on Sustainable
Development. The new Planning Policy Statement sets out ways
in which the planning regime can contribute to reducing carbon
dioxide emissions and combating climate change. It includes
an important requirement (known as the 'Merton-plus' rule)
that new developments include a significant amount of on-site
or near-site renewable or low-carbon energy generation. The
Planning Policy Statement is available at www.communities.
gov.uk/planningandbuilding/planning/planningpolicyguidance/
planningpolicystatements/planningpolicystatements/
ppsclimatechange/

84 *CONSULTATION ON REVIEW OF CALL-IN DIRECTIONS*

On 7 January 2008, the Department for Communities and Local
Government published a consultation paper with its proposals
to reduce the number of planning applications that have to
be referred to the Secretary of State in England. It proposes to
withdraw all existing call-in directions and to issue one new
direction. The new direction will retain some of the current
requirements and will include new referral provisions relating to
World Heritage Sites.

The consultation paper is available at www.communities.gov.
uk/publications/planningandbuilding/callindirections and the
consultation closed on 31 March 2008.

85 SDLT: NOTIFICATION OF LEASES AND NOTIONAL LAND TRANSACTIONS

On 17 January 2008, HM Revenue & Customs announced the following in Issue 6 of *Stamp Duty Land Tax Technical News*:

- The wording of the Pre-Budget Report note, PBRN 21, was wrong. It has been corrected so that no SDLT return will be required for leases of seven years or more, provided that both the chargeable consideration is £40,000 or less and the annual rent is £1,000 or less.

- Where section 75A of the Finance Act 2003 applies, any SDLT paid on actual land transactions is deemed attributable to the notional land transaction. HM Revenue & Customs has confirmed that notional land transactions should be notified separately, by letter, to the Birmingham Stamp Office.

86 CONTRIBUTION OF ASSETS TO A PARTNERSHIP

On 24 January 2008, HM Revenue & Customs published *Revenue & Customs Brief 03/08* which sets out its practice with regard to the capital gains tax and corporation tax on chargeable gains treatment of a contribution of assets to a partnership. It confirms that HM Revenue & Customs considers that the concessionary relief set out in paragraph 4 of Statement of Practice D12 has been applied too widely. Therefore, in future, the disposal consideration will not be treated as equal to the disposing partner's indexed CGT base cost but will be calculated by reference to the fractional proportion of the actual consideration given by the partnership for the asset, or the fractional proportion of the market value of the asset (if the transfer is between connected persons or is made otherwise than on an arm's length basis). The fractional proportion will be equal to the fractional share of the asset that passes to the other partners. Apportionment of allowable costs will still be able to be made on a fractional basis. It has also been made clear that HM Revenue & Customs considers a sum credited to the partner's capital account as representing consideration for the disposal of the asset.

87 PERSONAL SEARCHES – NEW GUIDANCE AND CONSULTATION ON CHARGES

On 18 January 2008, the Department for Communities and Local Government published revised good practice guidance for local authorities and personal searchers. It replaces the 2005 Guidance and is intended to ensure that personal search companies are given equal, unrestricted access to local authority data and that the requisite information will be available for the compilation of Home Information Packs. The Guidance states that local authorities must give access to personal searchers, to enable them to view all the data required to compile a personal search, normally by the next working day.

The Guidance aims to:

a) ensure that local authorities make available all unrefined information to personal searchers so that they are not at a disadvantage;

b) promote good practice and relations between local authorities and personal searchers;

c) confirm that all requisite information should be made available to personal searchers;

d) assist local authorities in providing access to personal searchers whilst still being able to maintain their records;

e) explain local authorities' statutory duties in relation to property searches; and

f) ensure that local authorities do not act anti-competitively.

It includes the following recommendations for local authority good practice:

• Each local authority should provide an information note for personal searchers, including details of the available registers/ information, location and opening hours, any requirements for advance notice or appointments and the charges payable.

- Where practicable and if asked to do so, a local authority should provide a personal searcher with sight of the actual entry on the register.

- Any appointment system should be operated flexibly but on a first come, first served basis and all record-holding departments should operate the same opening hours.

- Appointments to view all the data required for a personal search should enable access to the records no later than the next working day, or within three working days in exceptional circumstances, for example, staff sickness.

- If the Local Land Charges Register is kept in electronic form, assistance should be given to personal searchers on how to operate the computer, at no extra charge. Personal searchers should not be required to search a manual record if this does not form part of the formal register.

- On written request and payment of the prescribed fee, the local authority must supply an office copy of any registration, or any document, map or plan filed in connection with a registration. Copies of other documents can be obtained on payment of a fee which covers the local authority's reasonable costs.

In relation to personal searchers, it recommends that:

- Personal searchers should give as much advance notice (where required) as possible of their visit and provide contact information and details of the property so that it can be identified.

- Personal searchers should be prepared to make an appointment, be on time and notify the local authority if unable to keep it.

- Payment of the fee should be made at the time the search is carried out.

- Personal searchers should be competent to carry out the search without assistance. Although local authorities must provide access, it is the duty of the searcher to identify and record the relevant information. Local authority staff do not have to provide anything more than factual clarification of what is in the public record.

- The report must make it clear that the search was compiled by the personal searcher, not by the local authority. If the personal searcher obtains an official LLC1 as part of the personal search, it should be made clear that only the LLC1 comprises an official search.

The guidance is available at www.communities.gov.uk/publications/housing/personalsearchesguidance.

On 18 January 2008, the Department for Communities and Local Government published a consultation paper on how charges should be set for personal searches. The paper proposes that local authority charges for providing access to the unrefined data needed to compile a search, should be set on a cost recovery basis.

The consultation aims to:

a) deliver a fair, open and transparent charging structure for property searches;

b) enable open access to all local authority data needed to compile a search; and

c) promote the use of IT.

The consultation paper seeks responses on the following key issues:

- Whether local authority charges for providing access to unrefined data should be based on cost recovery.

- Whether the current charging framework for local authority compiled searches should be changed.

- The proposals for monitoring local authority charges.

- Amending current legislation to clarify the provisions.

- Electronic delivery of property searches.

- The content of the draft guidance to local authorities on setting charges.

- The current and proposed fees for a personal search of the Local Land Charges Register.

The consultation is available at www.communities.gov.uk/ publications/housing/lachargesearchconsult and the consultation closed on 18 April 2008.

88 *LAND REGISTRY – CLARIFICATION OF POLICY ON SDLT CERTIFICATES*

In January 2008, the Land Registry issued a practice bulletin to clarify its requirements on evidence of Stamp Duty Land Tax compliance for transactions submitted for registration. The Land Registry requirements are set out in *LR Practice Guide 49 – Rejection of Applications for Registration*. The practice bulletin explains that concerns have been raised about the Land Registry's policy on rejecting applications where SDLT evidence is not provided. In particular, the requirement for 20 business days to have passed means that, in some circumstances, practitioners are unable to submit applications for registration within the priority period of their official searches. The bulletin provides some suggestions that may assist practitioners:

- An outline application may be used to protect some applications that cannot be protected by an official search.

- The Stamp Taxes Online Service enables conveyancers to obtain an electronic SDLT 5 as soon as the land transaction return has been submitted successfully.

The bulletin also confirms that the Land Registry has provided an assurance to the Law Society that it will not cancel a pending application if the delay in providing the SDLT 5 is as a result of a delay by HM Revenue & Customs and the applicant keeps the Land Registry informed of the position.

89 REVISED ARRANGEMENTS FOR ONLINE FILING OF SDLT RETURNS

On 1 February 2008, HM Revenue & Customs extended its online SDLT filing service to cover transactions involving more than 100 properties. While the process is only partially electronic, it is intended to make filing arrangements easier for these types of transactions.

Under the new process, the buyer (or the buyer's agent) completes an online return for the first 100 properties and submits a schedule to Birmingham Stamp Office for the remaining properties not included in the online return.

The schedule does not need to be in any particular form but must include:

a) the address, title number and National Land Property Gazette Unique Property Registration Number (UPRN) for each property referred to in the schedule;

b) the name of the (first) buyer;

c) a description of the transaction;

d) the effective date of the transaction; and

e) the agent's reference.

The Stamp Office allocates a reference number to the schedule. The format for this reference number is SDLTMP-9999999. The reference number is e-mailed to the person submitting the return and appears on the SDLT 5 certificate.

If the transaction is registrable at the Land Registry, a copy of the schedule must be sent with the application to register. The reference number allocated by the Stamp Office and the unique transaction reference number must be added to the schedule.

When processing applications for registration where the new SDLT procedure has been used, the Land Registry checks that the schedule includes the reference number supplied by HMRC and the properties listed on the schedule match those that are the subject of the Land Registry application.

90 RENT ARREARS: THE END OF DISTRESS

Under the Tribunal Courts and Enforcement Act 2007, distress will be abolished and replaced with a statutory procedure for the collection of commercial rent arrears. The Act will come into force at a later date, yet to be announced. Regulations dealing with the commencement date and the minimum level of rent capable of collection, etc. are awaited.

The main proposed changes are:

- Landlords will no longer be able to seize their tenants' goods themselves (although, in practice, most landlords use bailiffs now anyway). In the private sector, seizure by anyone other than a certificated bailiff will be a criminal offence. Government and local authority-appointed bailiffs will not need to be certificated but seizures by them will otherwise be subject to the same controls as for certificated bailiffs. Certificates will be issued by the courts and there will be detailed provisions dealing with who may apply for a certificate, complaints against certificate-holders, fees, etc.

- The term 'distress' and all the peculiarities that have grown up with it will be swept away. The new procedure will be called 'commercial rent arrears recovery' or 'CRAR'.

- CRAR will only be available where there are net arrears totalling at least the minimum amount set out in regulations (it is suggested this be one week's rent). One of the concerns with the current system is that it can be used maliciously to recover disproportionately small amounts of rent.

- Landlords will be required to give notice of their intention to use the remedy. The minimum notice period has yet to be set but is, again, expected to be one week. Currently, no prior notice is required. Of course, this may give tenants an opportunity to move their assets off-site.

- CRAR will only be available for commercial premises. Residential landlords will no longer be able to seize goods and will instead have to pursue their claims for rent arrears through the courts.

175

This change will affect fewer landlords than one might first think. 90% of distraint actions at the moment relate to commercial premises and many residential tenants, such as those holding under Assured Shorthold or Rent Act tenancies, are statutorily protected from distress.

• There has in the past been some doubt about whether landlords can distrain where there are arrears of service charge or insurance, as opposed to principal rent. The new system makes it clear that CRAR will only be available for principal rent, not for other sums reserved in the lease as 'rent'.

• A new, uniform fee structure will be introduced, making it clearer how much bailiffs are allowed to charge. Excessive fees are, apparently, the largest cause of complaints against bailiffs currently.

91 HOUSES IN MULTIPLE OCCUPATION: NEW REGULATIONS

New regulations which deal with the licensing regime that applies to blocks of self-contained flats came into force on 1 October 2007.

A converted block of flats is a House in Multiple Occupation (HMO) under section 257 of the Housing Act 2004 if:

a) the block is a building that has been converted into, and consists of, self-contained flats;

b) building works undertaken in connection with the conversion did not (and still do not) comply with the appropriate building standards; and

c) less than two-thirds of the self-contained flats are owner-occupied.

The Licensing and Management of Houses in Multiple Occupation (Additional Provisions) (England) Regulations 2007 (SI 2007/1903) impose duties on a person managing section 257 HMOs. The duties imposed relate to:

a) providing information to occupiers;

b) taking safety measures;

c) maintaining water supplies, drainage and other utilities;

d) maintaining common parts, fixtures, fittings and appliances;

e) maintaining living accommodation;

f) providing waste disposal facilities.

These duties are limited to the areas of the HMO over which the person managing has control. A failure by the manager to comply with these duties can result in an offence punishable by summary conviction with a fine not exceeding level 5 on the standard scale.

The Houses in Multiple Occupation (Certain Converted Blocks of Flats) (Modifications to the Housing Act 2004 and Transitional Provisions for section 257 HMOs) (England) Regulations 2007 (SI 2007/1904) modify certain provisions of the Housing Act 2004 in respect of a section 257 HMO. Examples of the provisions modified are:

- The definition of 'person having control'.

- The matters about which a local housing authority must satisfy itself when deciding whether or not to grant a licence.

- The licence conditions.

- The person in respect of whom a rent repayment order may be made.

- The circumstances in which a notice under section 21 of the Housing Act 1988 may be served.

92 LOCAL AUTHORITY REGISTER OF DEDICATED HIGHWAY LAND

Section 31(6) of the Highways Act 1980 allows land owners to protect their land against it being dedicated as a highway by depositing a map and a statement of what ways (if any) the land owner admits to be dedicated as highways with the local authority. From 1 October 2007, local authorities are required to maintain registers of such maps and statements. The registers, in both paper form and on the internet, must be available free of charge for public inspection.

93 SOLICITORS' CODE OF CONDUCT

The Solicitors' Code of Conduct 2007 came into force on 1 July 2007. Rule 3 sets out provisions for dealing with conflicts of interests. Conflicts between the duty of confidentiality and duty of disclosure owed by an individual or a firm to two or more clients are dealt with in rule 4 (confidentiality and disclosure). Sub-rules 3.01 to 3.03 deal with conflicts generally. Sub-rules 3.07 to 3.22 deal with conflicts in conveyancing. Contract races are dealt with by sub-rule 10.06.

94 ENVIRONMENT AGENCY PROPERTY SEARCH

The Environment Agency no longer supplies Property Search Reports. A report is now only available from a commercial reseller, e.g. Groundsure and Landmark.

95 TENANCY DEPOSIT SCHEMES

A deposit paid under an assured shorthold tenancy must now be dealt with in accordance with an authorised tenancy deposit scheme (Housing Act 2004, sections 212–215). A landlord or his agent who receives a deposit must comply with the requirements of the scheme within 14 days and must also, within 14 days, give to the tenant and to anyone other than the tenant who paid the deposit, details about how the deposit is protected, including:

a) the contact details of the tenancy deposit scheme selected;

b) the landlord or agent's contact details;

c) how to apply for the release of the deposit;

d) information explaining the purpose of the deposit;

e) what to do if there is a dispute about the deposit.

A deposit paid under an assured shorthold tenancy must be in money (Housing Act 2004, section 213(7), (8)).

Where a deposit has not been dealt with, or is not being held, in accordance with an authorised scheme, or where the required information has not been given by the landlord or his agent, the tenant may apply to the court. The court must either order repayment of the deposit or must order payment of the deposit to the administrator of an authorised scheme. The court must also order the landlord or his agent to pay to the applicant an amount equal to three times the deposit (Housing Act 2004, section 214(1)–(4)).

Where a deposit has been paid under an assured shorthold tenancy, unless the deposit has been dealt with and is being held under an authorised scheme, the landlord may not give notice requiring possession of the dwelling (Housing Act 2004, section 215).

There are two types of tenancy deposit protection scheme available for landlords and letting agents – insurance-based schemes and custodial schemes.

Under an insurance-based scheme, the tenant pays the deposit to the landlord and the landlord retains the deposit and pays a premium to the insurer. At the end of the tenancy:

- if an agreement is reached about how the deposit should be divided, the landlord or agent returns all or some of the deposit;

- if there is a dispute, the landlord must hand over the disputed amount to the scheme for safekeeping until the dispute is resolved;

- if for any reason the landlord fails to comply, the insurance arrangements will ensure the return of the deposit to the tenant if they are entitled to it.

There are two insurance-based scheme providers: Tenancy Deposit Solutions Ltd (www.mydeposits.co.uk) and the Tenancy Deposit Scheme (www.thedisputeservice.co.uk).

Under a custodial scheme, the tenant pays the deposit to the landlord or agent and the landlord or agent then pays the deposit into the scheme. At the end of the tenancy:

- if an agreement is reached about how the deposit should be divided, the scheme will return the deposit, divided in the way agreed by both parties;

- if there is a dispute, the scheme will hold the deposit until the dispute resolution service or courts decide what is fair.

The interest accrued by deposits in the custodial scheme will be used to pay for the running of the scheme and any surplus will be used to offer interest to the tenant, or landlord if the tenant is not entitled to it.

The Deposit Protection Service is the only custodial deposit protection scheme. It is free to use and open to all Landlords and Letting Agents. Further information can be found at www. depositprotection.com.

96 LAND REGISTRY COMPREHENSIVE LAND REGISTER

In November 2007, the Land Registry issued a consultation paper on the introduction of two new events that would trigger compulsory registration of title, namely:

- the appointment of a new trustee of unregistered land held in trust where the land vests in the new trustee by deed or other instrument in writing or by vesting order of the court; and

- the partitioning of unregistered land held in trust amongst the beneficiaries of the trust.

The consultation paper is available at www.consultations. landregistry.gov.uk and the consultation closed on 29 February 2008.

97 LAND REGISTRY IDENTITY CHECKS FOR APPLICANTS WHO ARE NOT LEGALLY REPRESENTED

As from 3 March 2008, the Land Registry requires evidence of identity when an application is made by a person who is not legally represented to register a transfer, lease, mortgage or discharge of a mortgage in paper form.

The evidence must be in Form ID1 (private individuals) or Form ID2 (corporate bodies). Further information is available in *Public Guide 20 – Identity checks*.

98 LASTING POWERS OF ATTORNEY

The Mental Capacity Act 2005 came into force on 1 October 2007. The new Court of Protection and the Office of the Public Guardian were established from that date. The Act also introduced lasting powers of attorney which have replaced enduring powers of attorney from 1 October 2007.

There are two different types of lasting powers of attorney:

1. A property and affairs lasting power of attorney is for decisions about finances, such as selling the Donor's house or managing their bank account.

2. A personal welfare lasting power of attorney is for decisions about both health and personal welfare, such as where to live, day-to-day care or having medical treatment.

An Attorney must act in the Donor's best interests and have regard to the Code of Practice which provides guidance on how the Mental Capacity Act 2005 works on a day-to-day basis.

A lasting power of attorney must be registered with the Office of the Public Guardian before it can be used. An unregistered lasting power of attorney will not give the Attorney any legal powers to make a decision for the Donor. The Donor can register the lasting power of attorney while they have capacity, or the Attorney can apply to register the lasting power of attorney at any time.

Further information, forms, guidance and the Code of Practice are available at www.publicguardian.gov.uk/index.htm

99 SRA CONSULTATION

On 26 April 2007, the Solicitors Regulation Authority issued a consultation on whether to retain or to amend the provisions in Rule 3 (3.07–3.15) of the Solicitors' Code of Conduct relating to conflict of interests and solicitors acting for seller and buyer in conveyancing, property selling and mortgage-related services.

The consultation is available at www.sra.org.uk/consultations/234. article and ended on 26 July 2007.

100 CML LENDERS' HANDBOOK – AMENDMENTS

Substantial amendments to the CML Lenders' Handbook were introduced on 1 June 2007. The following is a summary of the changes:

- Clause 1.13.2 – a new clause which has been inserted so that a firm cannot act if the partner or fee earner dealing with the transaction or a member of his immediate family is the seller unless the lender consents.

- Clause 3 – this clause has been separated out to include parts A and B. Part A relates to those working in practices regulated by the Solicitors Regulation Authority and Part B applies to licensed conveyancers.

- Clause 4 – this clause has been amended to ask conveyancers to deal with the home condition report in the same way as the Handbook asks the conveyancer to deal with a valuation.

- In clause 5.2, changes have been made to the searches and reports provisions to accommodate the implementation of the home information pack. Conveyancers are asked to 'ensure' that all the usual searches and enquiries have been carried out. Reference to mining searches has been deleted. Personal search requirements are no longer limited to local authority searches and Part 2 has been changed to allow lenders to set out their individual requirements.

- Clause 5.3 – all clauses have been amended in this section with the result that listed building consent and building regulation consent are now requirements.

- Clause 5.15 – a new clause relating to shared ownership and shared equity properties requiring conveyancers to check with the lender whether the lender lends on the relevant product and, if so, what that lender's requirements are.

- Clause 6.3 – introduces a new requirement to report any indirect incentive (cash or non cash) if the lender stipulates in Part 2. This covers the position where an incentive is given to a third party rather than direct to the borrower.

- Clause 6.5–6.5.1 requires the conveyancer to check that the lender lends on 'buy to let' properties and that the mortgage is for this purpose. Clause 6.5.4 states that where a property falls within the definition of a house in multiple occupation under the Housing Act 2002, the conveyancer should refer to Part 2 as to whether the lender will accept the property as security and, if so, what the lender's requirements are.

- Clause 6.6, relating to new properties let at completion was substantially amended. The list of warranty schemes has been deleted from Part 1 of the Handbook and lenders have to list acceptable schemes in Part 2.

- Clause 6.7 says that, where roads and sewers are not adopted and maintained by residents or a management company, it is acceptable to lenders so long as the conveyancer in his reasonable opinion is satisfied that appropriate arrangements for maintenance repairs and costs are in place.

- Clause 6.8 sees the deletion of the list of suggested easements.

- Clause 6.13 adds a Part 2 referral to allow flexibility in this requirement.

- Clause 14.1.1.2 is a new clause requiring registration of the charge at Companies House (when appropriate) has been added.

A minor amendment was made in July 2007 changing clause 6.6.4.6 to refer to a member of the Chartered Institute of Architectural Technologists (formally British Institute of Architectural Technologists) (MCIAT).

101 CLLS CERTIFICATE OF TITLE

The sixth edition of the City of London Law Society's certificate of title was published on 30 October 2007 and is available at www.citysolicitors.org.uk

Part D

HOME INFORMATION PACKS

1 THE DEFINITION OF A HOME INFORMATION PACK

A HIP is defined by section 148(2) of the Housing Act 2004 as 'a collection of documents relating to the property or the terms on which it is or may become available for sale'. The content of a HIP is prescribed by regulations made under section 163 of the Housing Act 2004 and the current regulations are the Home Information Pack (No. 2) Regulations 2007 ('the Regulations').

Procedural guidance on the Regulations has been produced by the Government and is available at www.homeinformationpack.gov. uk/pdf/DraftProceduralGuidanceforHIPRegs.pdf. General information on HIPs and links to relevant publications can also be found on the Home Information Pack website at www.homeinformationpack.gov. uk. The Law Society also provides information on HIPs on its website at www.hips.lawsociety.org.uk

Whilst the introduction of HIPs has changed some procedural aspects of conveyancing, the principal of caveat emptor remains unchanged. A HIP need only contain the documents and information specified in the Regulations, and this will not necessarily comprise all the relevant information that a buyer will need to complete a full investigation of a property. So, it is still the buyer's responsibility to investigate the property that he is buying.

2 PREPARING A HIP

A HIP must be prepared by either the estate agent or the seller (or on their behalf) and so conveyancers may prepare a HIP on behalf of a seller.

The preparation of a HIP does not fall within the Money Laundering Regulations 2007. This was confirmed by the Law Society when it published a letter from Ed Balls MP dated 27 June 2007, which clarified that the preparation of a HIP will not be subject to the draft Money Laundering Regulations 2007 as a HIP constitutes a preparatory stage in the marketing of a property and not assistance in the planning of a property transaction. The letter is available at www.lawsociety.org.uk/documents/downloads/dynamic/ letterfromedballsmlreg020707.pdf

Where a HIP is required, it must be available when the property is first put on the market for sale (whether or not through an estate agent). Certain required documents must be included in the HIP from the outset (see below); however, in certain circumstances, some required documents may be added up to 28 days after the first point of marketing.

When preparing a HIP, a conveyancer should:

- Before submitting a request for a search or other document, find out how long the person providing the information expects this to take. If the information cannot be supplied within 28 days the seller will have to delay putting the property on the market as there would not be 'reasonable grounds' to believe the document can be obtained within the necessary timescale.

- Keep a record of any requests for searches and other required documents.

- Note the date that is the expected date for the return of the search results/document(s). If there is a delay, then this should be followed up, and the index in the HIP should be amended to refer to the delay and the date that the search results and/or document(s) are expected.

- Arrange for the search results and/or document(s) to be included in the HIP (and the index updated) as soon as these are received.

If a HIP has been compiled by someone other than the seller, the seller must check it to make sure it is accurate. The seller should also check that the contents of the HIP comply with the Regulations to safeguard against possible enforcement action. If the content of a document in the HIP does not comply with the Regulations, the seller will not have to pay the penalty charge as long as he believes on reasonable grounds that the document does comply with that requirement.

When putting the HIP together, it is important to ensure that:

1. Each item in the HIP is either an original document, a true copy or (where required or authorised by the Regulations), an official copy. 'True copy' is not defined in the Regulations but is used in Regulations 5 and 6 in connection with the requirements for documents included in a HIP and copies provided to a prospective buyer (see below). Where a document included in a HIP contains a map, plan or drawing, any colours that are used to identify features on it must be reproduced with sufficient accuracy to enable them to be identified. The Guidance issued by the Government suggests that a true copy does not have to be an exact copy, but should be a copy reproduced with sufficient accuracy to enable the copy to be understood and the meaning of the document to be unaffected.

2. The documents appear in the correct order (see below).

3. Only documents that are required or authorised are included in the HIP. If the responsible person provides any other documents to the buyer at the same time as the HIP, these must be separated and clearly distinguished from the HIP.

Under section 156(8) of the Housing Act 2004, the responsible person may ask the potential buyer to pay the 'reasonable cost' of making and, if requested, sending the paper copy of the HIP or document. A seller is required to supply a copy of the energy documents free of charge.

All documents and copies included in a HIP must be legible and any maps, plans or drawings must be clear (there are specific exceptions to this requirement in Regulation 7).

The responsible person may provide an electronic copy of a HIP where the potential buyer consents to receiving it in that form (section 156(11), Housing Act 2004). This will avoid the need for photocopying.

There is no general requirement to update the documents in the HIP unless a further first point of marketing occurs. However, if the responsible person amends, obtains or creates a further version of a required document, this must be added to the HIP and the old version removed (Regulation 21). With authorised documents, a later version may be included in the HIP if the responsible person wishes to do so (Regulation 23). When a document (including a different version of a document) is added to or removed from a HIP, the index must be updated.

3   REQUIRED DOCUMENTS

The following documents specified in Regulation 8 are a compulsory component of a HIP:

Description of document	Timing for including document in the HIP	Age of document
An index to the HIP, complying with Schedule 1 to the Regulations (Regulation 8(a)).	First point of marketing (Regulation 14(1)(a)).	Most recent version (Regulation 15(3)).
Energy documents (Regulation 8(b) and (c)).	First point of marketing (Regulations 14(1)(b) and 14(1)(c)).This requirement is subject to the following Regulations (where applicable): • Regulation 20 if the predicted energy assessment is completely unobtainable. • Regulation 16 if the energy documents are unobtainable before the first point of marketing and the property is put on the market on or after 1 June 2008. • Regulation 34 if the energy documents are unobtainable before the first point of marketing and the property is put on the market before 1 June 2008.	Dated no more than 12 months before the first point of marketing (Regulation 15(2)).

Description of document	Timing for including document in the HIP	Age of document
A sale statement, complying with Schedule 3 to the Regulations (Regulation 8(d)).	First point of marketing (Regulation 14(1)(d)).	Most recent version (Regulation 15(3)).
Title documentation (Regulation 8(e) and (f)).	First point of marketing in the case of: • official copies of the register and title plan (for registered properties) (Regulation 14(1)(e)); • index map search (for unregistered properties) (Regulation 14(1)(f)). Other title documentation for unregistered properties must be included no later than 28 days from the first point of marketing (Regulation 14(2)) except to the extent any documents required to deduce unregistered title are completely unobtainable.	Dated no more than three months before the first point of marketing in the case of: • official copies of the register and title plan (for registered properties) (Regulation 15(1)(a)(i)); • index map search (for unregistered properties) (Regulation 15(1)(b)). Other title documentation for unregistered properties must be the most recent version (Regulation 15(3)).
Where applicable, commonhold documentation and information (Regulation 8(g)).	No later than 28 days from the first point of marketing (Regulation 14(2)) except to the extent any required commonhold documents are completely unobtainable.	Dated no more than three months before the first point of marketing in the case of official copies of: • the register and title plan relating to the common parts; • commonhold community statement (Regulation 15(1)(a)(ii)). Other title documentation for commonhold properties must be the most recent version (Regulation 15(3)).
Where applicable, leasehold documentation and information (Regulation 8(h)).	No later than 28 days from the first point of marketing (Regulation 14(2)) except to the extent any required leasehold documents are completely unobtainable.	Dated no more than three months before the first point of marketing in the case of official copies of the lease (if provided in this form) (Regulation 15(1)(a)(iii)). Other title documentation for leasehold properties must be the most recent version (Regulation 15(3)).

Description of document	Timing for including document in the HIP	Age of document
Where applicable, title documentation for sub-divided buildings (Regulation 8(i)).	No later than 28 days from the first point of marketing (Regulation 14(2)) except to the extent any required leases and licences are completely unobtainable.	Most recent version (Regulation 15(3)).
A search report recording results of local land charges register search (Regulation 8(j)).	No later than 28 days from the first point of marketing (Regulation 14(2)).	Dated no more than three months before the first point of marketing (Regulation 15(1)(c)).

3.1 HIP Index

The index must comply with the requirements set out in Schedule 1 to the Regulations and must:

1. Display prominently the title 'Home Information Pack Index'.

2. Contain the address or proposed address (which may include a plot number) of the property.

3. Contain a list of all the documents included in the HIP.

4. Be revised whenever a document is added to or removed from the pack.

5. Where a document is unobtainable:

   a) indicate that a document otherwise required by the Regulations is missing from the pack;

   b) specify which document it is; and

   c) give the reason why it is missing.

6. Where a document is temporarily unobtainable indicate:

   a) what steps are being taken to obtain the document; and

   b) the date by which the responsible person expects to obtain the document.

If there has been (or is likely to be) a further delay in obtaining the document, the index must specify the reason for any delay which has occurred to the original date and when the responsible person expects to obtain the document.

A home information pack index may also indicate where a particular pack document can be found in the HIP.

The index must be the first document in the HIP, followed by the applicable energy documents. The remaining documents can be included in any order.

3.2 Energy documents

For a property that is physically complete at the first point of marketing, an energy performance certificate and its accompanying recommendation report must be included in the HIP.

Where a property is marketed before it is physically complete, the HIP must include a predicted energy assessment compiled in accordance with Schedule 2 to the Regulations (unless the predicted energy assessment is completely unobtainable).

Schedule 2 provides that the predicted energy assessment must:

1. Display prominently the title 'Predicted Energy Assessment' and contain the statement prescribed by paragraph (b) of Schedule 2.

2. Contain the address or proposed address (which may include a plot number) of the property.

3. Provide the asset rating that is predicted for the property, which must be based on plans and specification rather than a visual inspection of the property. The asset rating must be expressed in the way that is approved under the building regulations.

4. Explain the predicted asset rating.

If the property is subsequently physically completed, the responsible person must obtain an EPC and recommendation report for the property and include these in the HIP no later than 14 days after the date the property becomes physically complete, and remove the predicted energy assessment from the HIP. The index will then need to be updated.

3.3 Sale statement

The sale statement must include the information set out in Schedule 3 to the HIPs No. 2 Regulations 2007 and must:

1. Display prominently the title, 'Sale Statement'.

2. Contain the address or proposed address (which may include a plot number) of the property.

3. State the tenure of the property; that is, whether the property interest is:

   a) a freehold estate; or

   b) a freehold estate in commonhold land; or

   c) a leasehold interest.

4. State whether at the first point of marketing the property interest is or includes the whole or part of:

   a) a registered estate; or

   b) an unregistered estate.

5. Contain the name of the seller. The seller must also state the capacity in which they are selling the property, for example as a personal representative or under a power of attorney.

6. State whether the property:

   a) is being sold entirely with vacant possession; or

   b) is a property that is subject to some element of occupation and is required to have a HIP by virtue of section 171(2) of the Housing Act 2004.

7. If section 171(2) applies, state the nature of any occupation.

Regulation 10 provides that where the sale involves the creation of a new commonhold or leasehold interest, the sale statement should be completed as if the interest had already been created.

3.4   Title documentation – registered land

If title to the property is registered, the HIP must include an official copy and title plan. Photocopies will not be adequate, but if the Land Registry supplied an official copy as a PDF, the Land Registry's view is that a printout of the PDF will be considered an official copy.

3.5   Title documentation – unregistered land

Where title to the property has not been registered, the HIP must contain the following:

1. An index map search.

2. 'Such other documents on which the seller can reasonably be expected to rely in order to deduce title to that estate for the purposes of its sale'.

3.6   Title documentation – required commonhold documents

As commonhold land is required to be registered under section 1 of the Commonhold and Leasehold Reform Act 2002, the requirements of Regulation 8(e) will apply and the HIP must therefore contain official copies of the register and title plan for the commonhold unit (see 5.1 below for details of other commonhold documents required under Regulation 8(g)). If the commonhold interest has not yet been registered, the provisions of Regulation 10(2) apply (see 7 below).

3.7   Title documentation – required leasehold documents

For details of leasehold documents required under Regulation 8(h), see below. If the sale involves the grant of a long lease, the provisions of Regulation 10(3) will modify these requirements (see 8 below).

3.8   Title documentation – required documents for sub-divided buildings

A HIP is not generally required for a property that is sold with vacant possession. However, section 171(2) of the Housing Act 2004 contains an exception to this where:

a) two or more dwellinghouses in a sub-divided building are marketed for sale (with any ancillary land) as a single property; and

b) any one or more of those dwellinghouses is not available for sale (with any ancillary land) as a separate residential property, and is available with vacant possession.

This would, for example, apply to a house with a 'granny annex' that is let separately but where the freehold to the whole property (including the granny annex) is sold together.

Where section 171(2) applies, the HIP must contain copies of all leases and licences to which the property is (or is expected to be) subject unless these have already been included under Regulation 8(h).

3.9   Local land charges search report

Regulation 8 provides that a HIP must contain one of the following:

a) an official certificate of search that complies with the Local Land Charges Act 1975; or

b) a personal search made under the right to inspect the register.

The provisions of Schedule 6 to the Regulations only apply to personal searches of the local land charges register.

3.10   Local authority enquiries search report

The local authority search must meet the specific requirements contained in Schedule 7 in addition to the general requirements for required searches. Schedule 7 specifies the wording of the local enquiries.

3.11   Drainage and water enquiries search report

Schedule 8 to the Regulations sets out the specific requirements for drainage and water search reports, including the wording of the enquiries. The general requirements for required searches also apply.

4 AUTHORISED DOCUMENTS

The responsible person does not have to include authorised documents in the HIP but the Government 'strongly recommends' that these are included where relevant.

Authorised documents may be included in a HIP at any time (Regulation 14(3)). An authorised document does not have to be particular age but must be the most recent version as at the first point of marketing (Regulation 15(3)).

The following documents and information are authorised under Regulation 9:

- A home condition report.

- Documentary evidence of any safety, building, repair or maintenance work which has been carried out in relation to the property since the date of any home condition report included in the HIP.

- Any warranty, policy or guarantee for defects in the design, building, or completion of the property, or its conversion for residential purposes, e.g. NHBC Buildmark warranty.

- Information about the design or standards to which a property has been or is being built.

- Alternative versions of any documents in the HIP, e.g. a translation, or in Braille or large print.

- A summary or explanation of any document in the HIP, including legal advice on the content of the HIP or any document in the HIP.

- Information identifying the property including a description, photograph, map, plan or drawing of the property.

- Information about a document in the HIP, about information contained within a document or about the HIP relating to its source or supply, or complaints or redress procedures arising from it.

- Official copy documents.

- Authorised commonhold documents.

- Authorised leasehold documents.

- Further search reports.

- Any documents referred to in a search report included in the pack under Regulation 8(j), (k), or (l) and paragraphs (m) or (n) of Regulation 9 of the Regulations.

4.1 Home condition report

It was originally intended that a home condition report would be a compulsory element of a HIP, but in July 2006, the Government announced that this would no longer be the case.

The requirements for home condition reports are to be found in Schedule 9 to the Regulations and include the terms on which the home condition report is made and its contents.

The basic requirement for a home condition report is that it must be:

a) made by a home inspector following an inspection of the property carried out in accordance with the provisions of one of the certification schemes, and using the standard format; and

b) entered onto the register of home condition reports.

A home inspector must be a member of a certification scheme. The current certification schemes are operated by:

- Buildings Research Establishment (www.bre.co.uk/index.jsp)

- Royal Institution of Chartered Surveyors (www.rics.org.uk)

- Surveyors and Valuers Accreditation Limited (www.sava.org.uk)

These schemes are there to make sure that home inspectors are fit and proper persons, are appropriately qualified to produce home condition reports, and have suitable indemnity insurance in place. The certification schemes must also make arrangements for handling any complaints about their members.

A home inspector is required to prepare home condition reports on the following terms:

1. A home condition report will be prepared with reasonable care and skill.

2. The home inspector will provide in the home condition report an objective opinion about the condition of the property based on his inspection.

3. The home inspector will identify in the home condition report such conditions within the property as appear to:

   a) be defects that are serious and/or require urgent attention;

   b) give rise to a need for repair or replacement; or

   c) give rise to further investigation.

If the seller decides to rectify any defects identified by the home inspector before putting the property on the market, it is advisable to obtain documentary evidence of the work which can then be included in the HIP as an authorised document under Regulation 9(b).

A responsible person may copy or issue a copy of the report for the purposes of:

a) including it in a HIP as an authorised document;

b) providing a copy of a HIP document to the seller; or

c) providing a copy to a potential buyer following a request for a HIP.

Any person may do one or more of the following for the purposes of a disclosure or other act authorised by Part 9 of the Regulations:

- Copy a report.

- Issue a copy of a report.

- Rent or lend a report.

- Communicate a report.

- Make an adaptation of a report or do any of the above in relation to an adaptation.

In addition, home inspectors must prepare home condition reports on terms that enable the following categories of person to enforce the provisions of the contract to prepare the report in their own right (whether or not that person is a party to such a contract):

- The seller.

- A potential or actual buyer of the property interest.

- A mortgage lender in respect of the property interest.

The Regulations do not prescribe the form a home condition report is to take. However, the certification schemes are responsible for ensuring that home inspectors use a standard form.

Home condition reports must contain the following information:

1. The name of the home inspector.

2. Whether the home inspector has any personal or business relationship with any person involved in the sale of the property.

3. The report reference number against which the report is registered so that a copy of the report can be obtained from the register (see below).

4. The name of the scheme that the home inspector is a member of and the membership number or identification code allocated to the home inspector by the scheme.

5. The name and address of the home inspector's employer, if applicable, or if the home inspector is self-employed, the name under which the home inspector trades.

6. The date of the inspection and the date on which the home condition report is completed.

7. The address of the property.

8. If it can be ascertained, the year in which the property was built, otherwise, an estimate of the year in which it was built should be included.

9. The number of storeys or levels in the property, and rooms on each storey or level of the property.

10. Car parking provision for residents and visitors to the property.

11. The mains utility services that are connected to the property and the condition of their visible parts.

12. If the property is – or forms part of a flat or maisonette:

    a) the number of storeys or levels of the building in which the flat or maisonette is situated;

    b) the number of flats and maisonettes in that building (or an estimate if the actual number cannot be ascertained);

    c) whether the building contains a lift; and

    d) the general condition of common parts and the building in which the flat or maisonette is situated.

13. Any risks to the health or safety of the property's occupants or visitors, so far as the home inspector can ascertain them.

14. The condition of the outside parts of the property, including any of the following that relate to the property:

    a) roof coverings;

    b) rainwater pipes and gutters;

    c) chimney stacks; and

    d) walls, doors and windows.

15. The condition of the inside parts of the property, including:

    a) roof structures accessible directly from the property;

    b) ceilings and floors;

    c) internal walls; and

    d) kitchen and bathroom fittings.

The home condition report should also state whether their appearance suggests that they have been materially affected by dampness.

16. The general condition of any outbuildings that form part of the property.

17. Whether any parts of the property to which the home inspector would normally expect to have access were not accessible on the day of the inspection.

18. Any additional provision required by the scheme of which the home inspector is a member and in which capacity the report is made.

Personal information (other than the name of the home inspector, the home inspector's employer and the address of the property) and information about security features at the property may not be included.

A home condition report must be entered onto a register and Part 9 of the Regulations sets out the requirements for the register. The register is intended to provide an independent means of checking that a home condition report is authentic and has not been altered. Landmark Information Group operates the register on behalf of the Government (see www.hcrregister.com/Welcome). Once a home condition report has been entered onto the register it may not be altered. However, a home condition report must be cancelled if it is inaccurate.

The Regulations provide for disclosure of a home condition report and restrict the following types of disclosure:

1. A primary disclosure, which includes:

    a) an inspection of the register or a home condition report entered on the register;

b) taking or giving an electronic or paper copy of the register or a home condition report entered on the register; or

c) giving information from the register or a home condition report entered on the register.

2. A secondary disclosure, which means disclosure of a home condition report or its contents where that information was obtained through a primary disclosure.

The keeper of the register may make a disclosure to:

a) the seller or their agent;

b) an actual or potential buyer or their agent;

c) mortgage lenders or automated valuation suppliers who use computer -based analytical methodologies and statistics to value a property without requiring a site visit;

d) a scheme or someone handling complaints against home inspectors;

e) enforcement officers.

Anyone may make either a primary or a secondary disclosure:

1. If the information is made anonymous.

2. If it is in connection with the prevention of crime.

3. If it is for the purpose of:

a) section 156 of the Housing Act 2004 (the duty to provide a copy of a HIP on request);

b) including it in a HIP;

c) copying a HIP in response to a request under section 156 of the Housing Act 2004; or

d) providing a copy of a HIP to the seller for checking under Regulation 24.

4. If it is in connection with legal proceedings or a court order.

Regulation 43 allows a seller to restrict disclosure so that the home condition report cannot be supplied to:

- Any person.

- A mortgage lender or an AVM supplier.

A home condition report may not be disclosed:

- If there is a condition imposed under section 157 of the Housing Act 2004 that prohibits that disclosure.

- Where the person who has been asked to make the disclosure suspects that this may result in an unauthorised disclosure.

- For commercial use by the keeper of the register (except as authorised by Part 9 of the Regulations).

An unauthorised disclosure of a home condition report is a criminal offence, punishable by a fine of up to £5,000.

4.2 Official copy documents

Official copies of documents referred to in the register may be included in the HIP. Where a document filed at the Land Registry is not legible, e.g. it has faded with age before being copied, if this is the only available copy, it may still be included in the HIP.

4.3 Further searches

Any search reports included in the HIP as authorised documents must be made in accordance with the general requirements contained in Part 1 of Schedule 6 to the Regulations. The matters to which authorised search reports relate are set out below but it must be noted that some of the searches below will not be suitable for inclusion in a HIP as the information is provided on an informal basis and the response will not satisfy the requirements of the Regulations. These searches are referred to as an illustration of the matters referred to in Regulation 9(m) of the Regulations.

4.3.1 *Information held by or derived from a local authority*

This will cover matters that are supplemental to those contained in the search reports required by the local land charges search or the enquiries of the local authority. The Guidance indicates that this is intended to refer to the optional enquiries of a local authority (CON29O). It may be appropriate to raise additional enquiries of the local authority relating to matters outside those dealt with by CON29R and CON29O. As there is now no reference to additional enquiries in CON29R, a check should be made with the local authority for the appropriate procedure.

4.3.2 *Common land or town or village greens*

This refers to a commons registration search which is now included in CON29O as Enquiry 22.

4.3.3 *Rights of access to, over or affecting the property interest*

It is suggested in the Guidance that this would include questions on rights of way affecting the property, e.g. enquiry 5 of CON29O – Optional enquiries of a local authority. These types of enquiries will be relevant for properties in rural areas. Other sources of information on rights of access over land include the registers maintained by county councils of applications to modify the map of all footpaths, bridleways and roads used as public paths that, in their opinion, are public rights of way (section 53, Wildlife and Countryside Act 1981), and maps showing land that is access land under the Countryside and Rights of Way Act 2000.

4.3.4 *Ground stability, the effects of mining or extractions or the effects of natural subsidence*

This includes the following searches:

- Coal mining and brine subsidence claims search.
- Tin, clay and limestone mining searches.
- Ground stability report on the risk of subsidence from manmade causes, such as coal mining, and from natural causes, such as clay shrinkage and soluble rocks.

4.3.5 Environmental hazards, including the risks of flooding or contamination from radon gas or any other substance

Some information about environmental matters can be obtained from replies to Form CON29R (2007), as enquiry 3.12 relates to contaminated land and enquiry 3.13 asks whether the property is in a Radon Affected Area.

CON29O (2007) also includes enquiries relating to environmental issues. Enquiry 18 asks the local authority to list any entries in the register of hazardous substances, maintained under section 28 of the Planning (Hazardous Substances) Act 1990. Enquiry 19 asks what outstanding statutory or informal notices have been issued by the local authority under the Environmental Protection Act 1990 or the Control of Pollution Act 1974.

4.3.6 Telecommunications, sewerage, drainage, water, gas or electrical services

Utility providers may be able to provide plans showing the route of any services and the location of other apparatus, details of any wayleave agreements that may affect the property, and information about connecting to utility supplies and services.

4.3.7 Transport services, including roads, waterways, trams and underground or over-ground railways

The local authority will reveal certain information relating to roads and railway proposals that may affect the property in CON29R (2007) and Enquiry 4 of CON29O (2007).

The following organisations also provide information about transport infrastructure that may be of interest to a prospective buyer:

- Highways Agency Roads Projects Search.

- Port of London Authority Property Related Search.

- British Waterways.

- Organisations responsible for overground and underground railways.

- Civil Aviation Authority Search.

4.3.8 Liabilities to repair or maintain buildings or land not within the property interest

This would include a chancel repair search.

4.4 Searches relating to other premises

A search report relating to other premises in the vicinity of the property may be included in the HIP as an authorised document if:

a) the type of search report is required or authorised in relation to the property; and

b) it would be of interest to potential buyers.

The Guidance suggests that this might be appropriate where the seller of a property in a rural or seafront location wants to show that there are no plans to develop adjacent land.

4.5 Additional relevant information

Regulation 9(p) permits the responsible person to include certain additional information in a HIP if it relates to matters described in Schedule 10 and would be of interest to potential buyers. This will cover a number of documents that would traditionally be provided by the seller in a conveyancing transaction including:

- Fixtures, fitting and contents form.

- Replies to pre-contract enquiries of the seller.

5   REQUIRED AND AUTHORISED DOCUMENTS FOR COMMONHOLD TRANSACTIONS

5.1   Required commonhold information

The following documents specified in Regulation 8 and Schedule 4 are compulsory components of a HIP where the property is commonhold (note that these documents are required in addition to other relevant required documents):

Description of document	Circumstances when document must be included	Age of document
Official copies of: • The register and title plan relating to the common parts. • The commonhold community statement referred to in that register.	Required in every instance where the property is commonhold (Regulation 8(g)(i), and paragraph 1(1)(a), Schedule 4).	Dated no more than three months before the first point of marketing (Regulation 15(1)(a)(ii)).
Any rules or regulations (in addition to those in the commonhold community statement) that may have been made for the purposes of managing the commonhold by any of the following (or their predecessors): • The commonhold association. • The managing agents that have been (or will be) appointed by the commonhold association to manage the commonhold. • Any other person that manages the commonhold or is likely to do so.	Required if these documents are: • in the seller's possession; • under his control. Items to which he can reasonably be expected to have access, taking into account the enquiries that it would be reasonable to make of: • the unit-holder (unless the seller is the unit-holder); and • the managers of the commonhold. (Regulation 8(g)(i), and paragraph 1(1)(b), Schedule 4).	Most recent version (Regulation 15(3)).

Description of document	Circumstances when document must be included	Age of document
Requests for payment or financial contribution towards the following (where relevant to the property) relating to the 12 months preceding the first point of marketing:· • Commonhold assessment. • Reserve funds. • Insurance against damage for the common parts, or for any person in respect of personal injury or death caused by or within the common parts, if requests for these amounts are made separately to the requests relating to commonhold assessment.	Required if these documents are: • in the seller's possession; • under his control; • items to which he can reasonably be expected to have access, taking into account the enquiries that it would be reasonable to make of the unit-holder (unless the seller is the unit-holder), and the managers of the commonhold. (Regulation 8(g)(i), and paragraph 1(1)(c), Schedule 4).	Most recent version (Regulation 15(3)).
The names and addresses of: • any managing agents that may have been (or will be) appointed by the commonhold association to manage the commonhold; and • any other person that manages the commonhold or is likely to do so. Any amendments that may be proposed to: • the commonhold community statement; or • any regulations or rules made by the managers of the commonhold. A summary of any works being undertaken or proposed, affecting the property or the common parts.	Required if this information is: • in the seller's possession; • under his control; • information to which he can reasonably be expected to have access, taking into account the enquiries that it would be reasonable to make of the unit-holder (unless the seller is the unit-holder), and the managers of the commonhold. (Regulation 8(g)(ii), and paragraph 2, Schedule 4).	Most recent version (Regulation 15(3)).

The responsible person must include all required commonhold documents in the HIP no later than 28 days from the first point of marketing (Regulation 14(2)), except to the extent that any are completely unobtainable.

5.2 Authorised commonhold information

Under Regulation 9(k) and paragraph 3 of Schedule 4 to the Regulations, information that relates to any of the following matters is authorised for inclusion in a HIP if this would be of interest to a potential buyer:

- The commonhold community statement.

- The rights or obligations of the unit-holder under the commonhold community statement or otherwise, including whether the unit-holder has complied with these obligations.

- The rights or obligations of the commonhold association under the commonhold community statement or otherwise, including whether the commonhold association has complied with these obligations.

- The commonhold association and any information that might affect the unit-holder's relationship with it.

- Any agent of the commonhold association or other manager of the property and any information that might affect the unit-holder's relationship with such persons.

- The membership of the commonhold association.

- The status or memorandum and articles of association of any company related to the management of the property or the commonhold. The seller could consider including a company search against the commonhold association to show that the commonhold association is in existence and remains registered; and there is no registered indication that the commonhold association is to be wound up. The buyer's conveyancer will need this if the *CML Lenders' Handbook* applies.

- Any commonhold assessment payable for the property, including whether payments for such assessment are outstanding. A commonhold unit information certificate will contain this information.

- Any reserve fund levy relating to the property or the commonhold, including whether payments for such levies are outstanding.

- Any planned or recent works relating to the property or the commonhold.

- Responsibility for insuring the property or the commonhold, including the terms of such insurance and whether payments relating to it are outstanding. Where the *CML Lenders' Handbook* applies, the buyer's conveyancer will need confirmation that the commonhold association has insured the common parts and that the insurance complies with the lender's requirements.

- Any lease or licence relating to the property.

Authorised commonhold information may be included in the HIP at any time, and does not have to be particular age but must be the most recent version as at the first point of marketing.

6 REQUIRED AND AUTHORISED DOCUMENTS FOR LEASEHOLD TRANSACTIONS

6.1 Required leasehold information

The following documents specified in Regulation 8 and Schedule 5 are a compulsory component of a HIP where the property is leasehold (note that these documents are required in addition to other relevant required documents):

Description of document	Circumstances when document must be included	Age of document
The lease in one of the following forms: • An official copy. • The original lease or a copy of it. Any copy must comply with Regulation 6. • An edited information document. This form is only permitted if, despite all reasonable efforts and enquiries by the responsible person, the lease can only be obtained in this form. It means the edited copy of a document lodged under rule 136(2)(b) or 138(4) of the Land Registration Rules 2003 where a document has been designated an exempt information document.	Required in every instance where the property is leasehold (Regulation 8(h), and paragraph 1(1)(a), Schedule 5).	If an official copy is provided, this must be dated no more than three months before the first point of marketing (Regulation 15(1)(a)(iii)).
Any rules or regulations that may have been made for the purposes of managing the property by any of the following (or their predecessors): • The landlord or proposed landlord. • The managing agents that have been (or will be) appointed by the landlord to manage the property. • Any other person that manages the property or is likely to do so.	Between 14 December 2007 and 1 June 2008 this information is not required but is authorised for inclusion under Regulation 9(l) (Regulation 10A). Required (before 14 December 2007 and on or after 1 June 2008) if these documents are: • in the seller's possession; • under his control; • documents to which he can reasonably be expected to have access, taking into account the enquiries that it would be reasonable to make of the leaseholder (unless the seller is the leaseholder), and the leasehold managers. (Regulation 8(h), and paragraph 1(1)(b), Schedule 5.)	Most recent version (Regulation 15(3)).

Description of document	Circumstances when document must be included	Age of document
Statements or summaries of service charges supplied in respect of the property under section 21 of the Landlord and Tenant Act 1985 or otherwise, and relating to the 36 months preceding the first point of marketing.	Between 14 December 2007 and 1 June 2008 this information is not required but is authorised for inclusion under Regulation 9(l) (Regulation 10A). Required (before 14 December 2007 and on or after 1 June 2008) if these documents are: • in the seller's possession; • under his control; • documents to which he can reasonably be expected to have access, taking into account the enquiries that it would be reasonable to make of the leaseholder (unless the seller is the leaseholder), and the leasehold managers. (Regulation 8(h), and paragraph 1(1)(c), Schedule 5.)	Most recent version (Regulation 15(3)).

Requests for payment or financial contribution towards the following (where relevant to the property) relating to the 12 months preceding the first point of marketing:
• Service charges.
• Ground rent.
• Insurance:
  • against damage for the building in which the property is situated; or
  • for any person in respect of personal injury or death caused by or within the building in which the property is situated;
if requests for these amounts are made separately to the requests relating to service charges.
	Between 14 December 2007 and 1 June 2008 this information is not required but is authorised for inclusion under Regulation 9(l) (Regulation 10A).
	
	Required (before 14 December 2007 and on or after 1 June 2008) if these documents are:
	
	• in the seller's possession;
	
	• under his control;
	
	• documents to which he can reasonably be expected to have access, taking into account the enquiries that it would be reasonable to make of the leaseholder (unless the seller is the leaseholder), and the leasehold managers. (Regulation 8(h), and paragraph 1(1)(d), Schedule 5.)
		Most recent version (Regulation 15(3)).

Description of document	Circumstances when document must be included	Age of document
The names and addresses of: • the landlord or proposed landlord; • any managing agents that may have been (or will be) appointed by the landlord to manage the property; and • any other person that manages the property or is likely to do so. Any amendments that may be proposed to: • the lease; or • any regulations or rules made by the leasehold managers. Where section 20 of the Landlord and Tenant Act 1985 applies to any 'qualifying works' or 'qualifying long term agreement' relating to the property, a summary of: • any such works or agreements where a relevant contribution (or any part of a relevant contribution) has not been paid by the first point of marketing; • the total or estimated costs of those agreements; • the expected remaining relevant contribution; • the date (or estimated date) that those works or agreements will be concluded; and • the date (or estimated date) that any remaining relevant contribution will be required to be paid. 'Relevant contribution' is defined in section 20(2) and is the amount that the leaseholder may be required to pay by way of service charge under the terms of the lease towards the costs of certain works.	Between 14 December 2007 and 1 June 2008, this information is not required but is authorised for inclusion under Regulation 9(l) (Regulation 10A). Required (before 14 December 2007 and on or after 1 June 2008) if these documents are: • in the seller's possession; • under his control; • information to which he can reasonably be expected to have access, taking into account the enquiries that it would be reasonable to make of the leaseholder (unless the seller is the leaseholder), and the leasehold managers. (Regulation 8(h), and paragraph 2, Schedule 5.)	Most recent version (Regulation 15(3)).

The responsible person must include all required leasehold documents in the HIP no later than 28 days from the first point of marketing except to the extent that any are completely unobtainable.

6.2 Authorised leasehold information

Information that relates to any of the following matters is authorised to be included in a HIP under Regulation 9(I) and paragraph 3 of Schedule 5 to the Regulations, if this would be of interest to a potential buyer:

- Any lease of the property, including those that are superior or inferior to the property interest.

- Any licence relating to the property.

- Any freehold estate to which the lease relates including any proposals to buy a freehold interest relating to the property.

- The rights or obligations of the lessee under the lease or otherwise, including whether the lessee has complied with such obligations.

- The rights or obligations of the lessor under the lease or otherwise, including whether the lessor has complied with such obligations.

- The lessor of the property and any information that might affect the lessee's relationship with the lessor.

- Any agent of the lessor or other manager of the property and any information that might affect the lessee's relationship with such persons.

- The membership or existence of any body of persons corporate or unincorporate which manages the property or building in which the property is situated.

- The status or memorandum and articles of association of any company related to the management of the property or building in which the property is situated.

- The rent payable for the property, including whether payments for such rent are outstanding.

- Any service charges payable in respect of the property, including whether payments for such charges are outstanding.

- Any reserve fund relating to the property for necessary works to it or the building in which the property is situated, including whether payments to such a fund are outstanding.

- Any planned or recent works to the property or the building in which the property is situated.

- Any responsibility for insuring the property or the building in which the property is situated, including the terms of such insurance and whether payments relating to it are outstanding.

With the exception of the lease itself, documents and information that are required documents under Regulation 8(h) are treated as authorised documents for properties put on the market between 14 December 2007 and 1 June 2008 (Regulation 10A).

Authorised leasehold information may be included in the HIP at any time and does not have to be particular age but must be the most recent version as at the first point of marketing.

7   THE CREATION OF A NEW COMMONHOLD INTEREST

The person completing the sale statement should do so as if the freehold interest in the commonhold unit had already been registered.

The requirement to provide title documentation in Regulation 8(e) and 8(f) is modified so that the HIP must include title information relating to the freehold interest out of which the commonhold unit will be created.

Paragraph 4 of Schedule 4 to the Regulations sets out the documents and information that are required in a HIP where the commonhold has not yet been created. The commonhold documents and information that are authorised for inclusion in a HIP are the same as for existing commonholds.

The required documents and information for the creation of a new commonhold interest are:

1. The terms of the commonhold community statement that will or – is expected to – apply in relation to the property interest once it has been registered as a freehold estate in commonhold land.

2. Estimates of the payment or financial contribution likely to be required towards the following within 12 months following completion of the sale of the property:

   a) commonhold assessment;

   b) reserve funds; and

   c) insurance against damage for the common parts or for any person in respect of personal injury or death caused by or within the common parts (if requests for these amounts are not to be included in contributions towards commonhold assessment).

Note that these required documents and information are required instead of those applicable to existing commonholds.

8   THE GRANT OF A LONG LEASEHOLD INTEREST

The person completing the sale statement should do so as if the leasehold interest had already been granted.

The required documents and information for the grant of a long leasehold interest are (but note that between 14 December 2007 and 1 June 2008 this information was not required but was authorised for inclusion under Regulation 9(l)):

1. The terms of the lease that will or is expected to be granted.

2. Estimates of the payment or financial contribution likely to be required towards the following within 12 months following completion of the sale of the property:

   a) service charges;

   b) ground rent; and

   c) insurance against damage for the building in which the property is situated or for any person in respect of personal injury or death caused by or within the building in which the property is situated (if requests for these amounts are not to be included in contributions towards service charges).

Note that these required documents and information are required instead of those applicable to existing leasehold interests.

9 NEW BUILDS

Other than requiring any HIP prepared for a property that is not physically complete to contain a predicted energy assessment, the Regulations do not treat new build properties differently to other properties.

However, the following requirements may be particularly relevant to new build properties:

- When completing the index and sale statement, the responsible person may use the plot number if the property does not yet have a postal address. The plot number may also be used in the predicted energy assessment.

- If the property will be marketed before it is physically complete, the HIP should include a predicted energy assessment instead of an EPC and recommendation report.

- The sale of a new build property may involve the creation of a new commonhold or the grant of a new long lease. Where this applies, Regulation 10 will modify what is required and authorised to be included in the HIP.

- The responsible person may consider including certain documents and information relating to the construction of the property in the HIP where this is authorised under Regulation 9, e.g. NHBC Buildmark warranty, and planning and building regulations documents referred to in the local authority search report.

10 EXCLUDED DOCUMENTS

No document, or information, other than a required document or an authorised document may be included in a HIP. There is a specific prohibition on home condition reports that were not prepared for the purpose of the sale of the property by the current seller and on advertising and marketing materials.

If documents that are neither required nor authorised documents are provided to a prospective buyer 'in close proximity' to documents in the HIP, these must be separated and clearly distinguished from the HIP.

11 UNOBTAINABLE DOCUMENTS

The Regulations make provision for documents that are unobtainable at the first point of marketing or are completely unobtainable.

11.1 Documents that are unobtainable at the first point of marketing

The Regulations allow marketing to start even if there is a delay in obtaining some of the required documents. There are separate provisions relating to unavailable energy documents (Regulations 16 and 34) and documents required within 28 days of the first point of marketing (Regulation 17).

11.1.1 Unavailable energy documents

Whilst the energy documents are a required component of a HIP, in certain circumstances the property can still be put on the market even if the energy documents for the property are not yet available. For this concession to apply, the responsible person must:

a) have made a request for the energy documents. If the first point of marketing is on or after 1 June 2008, the request must have been made at least 14 days before the date the property is put on the market;

b) have used all reasonable efforts to obtain the energy documents before the first point of marketing;

c) continue to use all reasonable efforts to obtain the energy documents once the property has been put on the market.

11.1.2 Documents required within 28 days of the first point of marketing

The documents that fall within this category are:

1. Documentation required to deduce title for unregistered properties, other than the index map search.

2. Commonhold documents and information.

3. Leasehold documents and information.

4. Title documentation for sub-divided buildings.

5. Required searches, which are:

   a) local land charges search report;

   b) local authority enquiries search report; and

   c) drainage and water enquiries search report.

However, certain conditions must be met if the responsible person wants to proceed with marketing without one or more of these documents being included in the HIP. The conditions are that:

- A request for the relevant document(s) was made before the date of the first point of marketing. The HIP must contain proof of that request.

- The responsible person believes on reasonable grounds that the document can be obtained no later than 28 days after the first point of marketing and uses all reasonable efforts to obtain it before then. If it is reasonable to expect the document to be available sooner, then the responsible person should use all reasonable efforts to obtain it in a shorter time.

- If the responsible person cannot obtain the document within the expected timescale, they should nevertheless continue to use all reasonable efforts to obtain the document.

- The responsible person includes the document in the HIP as soon as it becomes available.

- The index contains the information required for documents that are unavailable.

11.1.3 Requests for HIP documents

For the above provisions to apply, the responsible person must have made a request that is:

- Properly addressed to a person who usually provides or is likely to provide the document requested.

- Made in the usual form needed to obtain that document. The request must also contain the necessary information and payment (or an undertaking to make that payment).

A copy of the request should be kept, including details of when and how it was sent and to whom it was sent. This information will be needed to calculate the date when the request was deemed to have been delivered under Regulation 19.

Where a request has been made, the responsible person must include proof of the request in the HIP. This proof must be in writing and state:

- Which of the required documents it relates to.

- The date the request was deemed to have been delivered under Regulation 19.

- The name of the person to whom the request was sent.

- The date the responsible person believes the document is likely to become available.

- That the request complied with the requirements in Regulation 18(1).

11.2 Required documents that are completely unobtainable

The Regulations recognise that it may not be possible to obtain the following:

- Predicted energy assessment.

- Documents required to deduce unregistered title.

- Commonhold information.

- Leasehold information.

- Leases or licences for sub-divided buildings.

Regulation 20 provides that a HIP does not have to contain these documents if, following reasonable enquiries and efforts, the responsible person believes that the relevant document no longer exists in any form and cannot be obtained from or created by any person. Where this applies, the index must indicate that the document is missing from the HIP and the reason why. Note that the Guidance states that a document should not be considered unobtainable if it exists in electronic form, as a hard copy could be produced in those circumstances.

12 SEARCH REPORTS

12.1 Use of personal searches in HIPs

The Regulations allow personal searches to be used in HIPs if they meet the general requirements for search reports. The responsible person should bear in mind that some lenders do not accept personal searches and so including a personal search in a HIP may result in delays as a prospective buyer may need to commission their own search.

12.2 General provision on searches and search reports

The following information must be contained in search reports that are included in HIPs (both required and authorised search reports):

- The address of the premises that are the subject of the search.

- A statement of whether there is any personal or business relationship between the person(s) who conducted the search or prepared the search report and anyone involved in the sale of the property, e.g. a referral arrangement between the seller's estate agent or solicitor and the search provider.

- The enquiries that formed the basis of the search and the information sought.

- The results of the search unless the information cannot be obtained under any circumstances.

- The date on which the search was completed.

- A description of the records searched, and the name and address of the person who holds them.

- If the records searched are derived from other records, a description of those other records and the name and address of the person who holds them.

- A description of how any relevant documents can be obtained (if they are not already included in the HIP as an authorised document).

- The names and addresses of the parties to the arrangements for carrying out the search, and (if different) preparing the search report.

- The name of the person(s) liable for any negligent or incorrect entry in the records searched, any negligent or incorrect interpretation of the records searched, and any negligent or incorrect recording of that interpretation in the search report.

- A description of any complaints or redress procedures that may exist in relation to the report.

- The terms on which the report is made.

12.3 Terms for preparation of required search reports

The Regulations specify certain express terms that must be included in the contract to provide a search report that is a required document and may (but do not have to) be included in authorised searches:

- The search report will be prepared with reasonable skill and care.

- Any copyright in a search report does not prevent it being copied for the purpose of compiling a HIP.

- The seller, a potential or actual buyer of the property interest and a mortgage lender in respect of the property interest, must have contractual rights to enforce the contract to provide the search report.

- Financial compensation must be available to meet the liability towards third parties. This compensation must be backed by insurance.

- The amount of compensation must be equal to (or greater than) the value a potential or actual buyer reasonably believed to be the value of the property at the time the search report was completed. For this purpose, value is based on residential use.

It is possible to include additional terms, or terms that are more favourable to the seller, the buyer or the lender, provided that the terms listed above are not excluded or limited.

13 UPDATE

The Home Information Pack (Amendment) Regulations 2008 come into force on 31 March 2008. They amend the Home Information Pack (No. 2) Regulations 2007 in the following ways:

- To require that, in England, where a 'new' home is to be marketed, the HIP must include a sustainability certificate, which is a certified assessment of the home against the standards in the Code of Sustainable Homes. This new requirement will only apply to new homes being designed or constructed, or that have been constructed but never occupied, and not to existing properties that are being converted. Transitional measures mean that the new rules will only apply to those homes that are at the beginning of the construction process rather than to homes that are already in the process of being built.

- To extend, until 1 January 2009, the current arrangements in England and Wales under which personal search companies may use insurance to back up their searches where they are unable to access data in local authority records

Part E

FINANCE ACT 2007 AND PRE-BUDGET REPORT 2007

1 FINANCE ACT 2007: IMPLICATIONS FOR PROPERTY

The Finance Act 2007 received Royal Assent on 19 July 2007. It contains new tax rules and reliefs, amends existing legislation, and gives the Treasury the power to make regulations. It implements changes that were anticipated by the 2007 Budget and a few additional changes.

1.1 Corporation tax: deduction for expenditure on energy-saving items

The Income and Corporation Taxes Act 1988 is amended to allow a business that lets residential property to deduct the cost of acquiring and installing certain energy-saving items in a dwelling, or in a building containing a dwelling, when calculating its profits. These changes are yet to come into effect.

The relief is available if:

- The expenditure is incurred before 1 April 2015.

- The deduction is not prohibited by the 'wholly and exclusively' rule (section 74(1)(a) or (e) of the 1988 Act and as applied by section 21A), or would otherwise be prohibited by the 'capital prohibition' rule (section 74(1)(f) or (g) of the 1988 Act as applied by section 21A).

- No allowance under the Capital Allowances Act 2001 may be claimed in respect of the expenditure.

Where only part of any expenditure qualifies for the relief, a deduction is allowed for that part.

The definition of an 'energy-saving item' is as specified for the time being in regulations made by the Treasury. The Treasury has confirmed that these items will be loft insulation, cavity wall insulation, solid wall insulation, floor insulation, hot water system insulation and draught proofing.

There are restrictions on the relief so that no deduction is permitted if, when an item is installed:

- The dwelling is being constructed.

- The business does not have, or is in the process of acquiring, an interest or further interest in the building or land containing the dwelling.

- The business includes or consists of the commercial letting of furnished holiday accommodation, and the dwelling consists or forms part of furnished holiday accommodation for the relevant accounting period.

- Expenditure incurred more than six months before the business commenced a property business.

- Expenditure is not for the benefit of the dwelling.

The Treasury may make regulations to:

- Restrict the amount of expenditure which may be deducted.

- Exclude the relief in certain cases.

- Determine who is entitled to the relief if different people have different interests in the building containing the dwelling.

- Apportion deductions if an interest in land is owned jointly or in common, or if the property business is a partnership.

The relief can be apportioned to people required to pay income tax.

HM Revenue & Customs has confirmed that regulations will be made imposing a cap of £1,500 for each dwelling.

1.2 Income tax: extension of income tax deduction for expenditure on energy-saving items

The Income Tax (Trading and Other Income) Act 2005 is amended so that the Landlord's Energy Saving Allowance applies:

- To expenditure incurred on or after 6 April 2007 and up to 6 April 2015.

- Only to expenditure that benefits the dwelling.

- To an energy-saving item installed in a dwelling or anywhere in a building that contains a dwelling (rather than just in the dwelling itself) as long as it benefits the dwelling.

The Finance Act 2007 provides that the Treasury can make regulations pursuant to section 314 of the 2005 Act in relation to expenditure on or after 6 April 2007. The Treasury has made The Energy-Saving Items Regulations 2007, which have effect for expenditure incurred on or after 6 April 2007 and:

1. Confirm that 'energy-saving items' for the purposes of the 2005 Act are:

   a) hot water system insulation;

   b) draught proofing;

   c) solid wall insulation; and

   d) floor insulation.

2. Limit the expenditure to be taken into account in calculating the deduction to £1,500 for each dwellinghouse.

3. Apply where a dwellinghouse is subject to different estates and interests, in which case a just and reasonable apportionment of the relevant expenditure will be made.

4. Provide for apportionment where a part of the expenditure has been paid by a third party.

1.3 SDLT: relief for new zero-carbon homes

Amendments are made to the Finance Act 2003 so that regulations can be made to introduce a time-limited Stamp Duty Land Tax relief on the first acquisition of a new zero-carbon home. The 'first acquisition' of a dwelling is defined as an acquisition of a building that has been constructed for use as a single dwelling and has not been previously occupied.

The Stamp Duty Land Tax (Zero-Carbon Homes Relief) Regulations 2007 came into force on 7 December 2007. The Regulations have retrospective effect and apply to transactions on or after 1 October 2007.

If the 2007 Regulations apply to a land transaction, then the relief from SDLT can be claimed as set out in Regulation 4:

- If the chargeable consideration is not more than £500,000 and does not consist of or include rent, the transaction will be exempt from charge to SDLT.

- If the chargeable consideration includes rent and consideration other than rent, and the consideration other than rent is not more than £500,000, no SDLT will be charged in respect of the consideration other than rent.

- If the chargeable consideration does not include rent and is more than £500,000, or if the consideration other than rent is more than £500,000, the amount of tax chargeable will be reduced by £15,000.

HM Revenue & Customs may refuse relief if there are reasonable grounds for thinking that the dwelling is not a zero-carbon home, even if the dwelling has a certificate certifying that it is a zero-carbon home.

The 2007 Regulations will only apply to give relief from SDLT where the transaction is the first acquisition of a dwelling that is certified as a zero-carbon home and the acquisition is made on or after 1 October 2007 and before 1 October 2012.

In order to qualify as a zero-carbon home:

a) the home must meet the prescribed standards set out in the 2007 Regulations; and

b) the home must also be certificated as a zero-carbon home.

Regulation 5 defines a zero-carbon home by reference to various measurements calculated by an accredited assessor. In order to qualify as a zero-carbon home, the dwelling must satisfy each of the following aspects of efficiency:

1. It must have a heat loss parameter of no more than 0.8 Watts per square metre Kelvin. The heat loss parameter means 'the heat loss per unit of temperature difference per unit floor area determined by the internal dimensions of the surfaces bounding the dwelling, the thermal performance of the materials used in construction and the air permeability of the dwelling envelope', and it must be calculated in accordance with the approved methodology.

2. A dwelling carbon dioxide emission rate of no more than zero kilograms per square metre over the course of a year. The dwelling carbon dioxide emission rate means 'the annual carbon dioxide emissions per unit floor area for space heating, water heating, ventilation and lighting, less the emissions saved by energy generation technologies in or on the dwelling. The dwelling carbon dioxide emission rate must be no more than zero kilograms per square metre per year', and it must be calculated in accordance with the approved methodology.

3. Net carbon dioxide emissions not exceeding zero kilograms per square metre over the course of a year. The net carbon dioxide emissions means:

The annual carbon dioxide emissions per unit floor area for space heating, water heating, ventilation and lighting, and those associated with appliances and cooking	less	The carbon dioxide emissions saved by the use of energy generation technologies in or on the dwelling and additional 'allowable electricity'

For the purposes of the definition of net carbon dioxide emissions:

- 'Allowable electricity' means electricity that is generated from a zero-carbon energy source designed to serve the dwelling and which is conveyed to the dwelling or to a sub-station connected directly to the dwelling by cables used exclusively for the conveyance of electricity from that source.

- A 'zero-carbon energy source' includes wind, photovoltaic and hydro-electric power.

Net carbon dioxide emissions must be calculated in accordance with approved methodology.

If the accredited assessor is satisfied that the dwelling meets the requirements of Regulation 5, then a zero-carbon home certificate will be issued. This must contain the following information required by Regulation 6:

1. In relation to the building:

   a) the address of the building (including the postcode);

   b) the fact that the dwelling is a zero-carbon home within the meaning of the 2007 Regulations; and

   c) the unique identifying number from the energy performance certificate if an energy performance certificate has been produced.

2. In relation to the accredited assessor who issues the certificate:

   a) the full name of the accredited assessor;

   b) the name and address of the accredited assessor's employer or, if the assessor is self-employed, the name under which the assessor trades and the assessor's address; and

   c) the accreditation scheme, if any, to which the accredited assessor belongs.

3. The date on which the ZCH certificate was issued.

An 'accredited assessor' is a person who meets the requirements set out in Regulation 2. An accredited assessor is a person who is a member of an accredited scheme, approved by the Secretary of State in relation to newly erected dwellings under section 17A of the Building Regulations 2000 (as amended). Where no accreditation scheme has yet been approved, 'accredited assessor' refers to a person who is authorised to issue ratings (calculated by the Government's Standard Assessment Procedure for Energy Rating of Dwellings), by the holder of a licence granted by the Department for Environment, Food and Rural Affairs to certify that the ratings assessed under the Standard Assessment Procedure have been issued by a body authorised by the Secretary of State. There are slightly different requirements for Scotland and Northern Ireland.

The SDLT relief can only be claimed in a land transaction return or in an amendment of a land transaction return. Once a zero-carbon home has been built, the seller must obtain the zero-carbon home certificate from an accredited assessor and give it to the buyer so that he can then obtain the relief. This has to be done within the 'relevant time' as defined in Regulation 6(4) and it will depend on whether the first acquisition of the zero-carbon home happens before or after the 2007 Regulations came into force. If the first acquisition took place after the 2007 Regulations came into force, then the relevant time means on or before the date of the first acquisition. If the first acquisition takes place before the 2007 Regulations came into force, then the relevant time means 'as soon as reasonably practicable' following the coming into force of the 2007 Regulations.

Regulation 9 provides that no SDLT relief will be available where the first acquisition of one or more zero-carbon homes is one of a number of linked transactions.

1.4   SDLT and scheme transactions: anti-avoidance measures

The Finance Act 2003 is amended so that transactions within a scheme are prevented from being used to avoid SDLT. These 'scheme transactions' are to be disregarded for SDLT purposes. SDLT will be instead calculated on the 'notional land transaction', which brings about the acquisition of the property by the buyer from the seller.

This new rule will apply where:

- A seller disposes of a chargeable interest and a buyer acquires it, or a chargeable interest deriving from it.

- A number of transactions, including the disposal and acquisition, occur in connection with the disposal and acquisition.

- The total SDLT payable in respect of the scheme transactions is less than would be due in respect of a 'notional land transaction' effecting the acquisition of the chargeable interest by the buyer on its disposal by the seller.

A 'transaction' for the purpose of the new rule includes:

a) a non-land transaction;

b) an agreement, offer or undertaking not to take a specified action;

c) any arrangement whether or not it could otherwise be described as a transaction;

d) a transaction occurring after the buyer acquires the chargeable interest.

'Scheme transactions' may include the following:

- An acquisition by a buyer of a lease deriving from the freehold owned or previously owned by the seller.

- A sub-sale to a third party.

- A grant of lease to third party subject to a right to terminate.

- The exercise of a right to terminate a lease or to take some other action.

- An agreement not to exercise a right to terminate a lease or to take some other action.

- A variation of a right to terminate a lease or to take some other action.

The chargeable consideration for the 'notional land transaction' shall be the largest of, or the aggregate of, the amount:

a) paid as consideration for the scheme transactions.

b) received by the seller, or a person connected with the seller, within the meaning of section 839 of the Income and Corporation Taxes Act 1988, by way of consideration for the scheme transactions.

The effective date of the 'notional transaction' is:

- The last date of completion for the scheme transactions.

- If earlier, the last date on which a contract in respect of the scheme transactions is substantially performed.

These new anti-avoidance provisions do not apply to:

- Alternative property finance transaction under sections 71A to 73 of the Finance Act 2003. These apply where land is sold to a financial institution and then either re-sold or leased to an individual.

- Right to buy transactions and shared ownership leases for which SDLT relief is available under Schedule 9 to the Finance Act 2003.

When calculating the chargeable consideration for a notional transaction, consideration for a transaction that is incidental to the transfer of a chargeable interest from seller to buyer is ignored. A transaction is not incidental if it is any of the following:

a) a part of a process, or series of transactions, by which the transfer is effected;

b) a transfer that is conditional on completion of the transaction;

c) a scheme transaction as defined in the Stamp Duty Land Tax (Variation of the Finance Act 2003) Regulations 2006.

A transaction may be incidental if, and only so far as, it is undertaken relating to:

a) the construction of a building or property to which the chargeable interest relates, subject to otherwise being classed as not incidental under section 75B(2) of the Finance Act 2003;

b) the sale or supply of anything other than land, subject to not being part of a process or series of transactions and not being a scheme transaction defined in the 2006 Regulations;

c) a loan to the buyer secured by a mortgage, or other provision of finance, enabling the buyer or another person to pay for part of a process, or series of transactions, by which the chargeable interest transfers from seller to buyer, subject to otherwise being classed as not incidental under section 75B (2) of the Finance Act 2003.

The Finance Act 2007 contains provisions relating to the various transactions that are incidental, or not incidental, and these include transfers of shares and securities, and partnerships. An interest in a property-investment partnership is a chargeable interest if it relates to land owned by the partnership.

The anti-avoidance measures are retrospective and affect disposals and acquisitions where the disposal occurred or occurs on or after 6 December 2006.

There are detailed supplemental provisions in section 75C of the Finance Act 2003 relating to scheme transactions. However, these have no effect where a disposal of a chargeable interest occurred before 19 July 2007 if that provision would cause a person to be liable for a higher amount of tax than would have been charged in accordance with the 2006 Regulations.

1.5 SDLT: anti-avoidance and partnerships

The Finance Act 2007 amends Schedules 15 and 16 to the Finance Act 2003, and contains provisions relating to Stamp Duty Land Tax in respect of property owned and dealt with by partnerships, trusts and property investment partnerships.

1.6 SDLT: alternative finance arrangements

The Finance Act 2007 contains provisions relating to exempt interests in relation to alternative finance arrangements, which are arrangements between individuals and financial institutions whereby land is sold to a financial institution who re-sells the land to the individual who grants the financial institution a legal charge over the property.

1.7 SDLT: exchanges of property between connected persons

Section 47(1) of the Finance Act 2003 is amended so that each transaction in an exchange of properties is, for SDLT purposes, to be treated independently of the other. The effect is that an exchange between the same seller and buyer, or persons connected with them, is not a 'linked transaction' and the rate of SDLT will not be determined on an aggregate basis. This provision applies to transactions where the effective date occurs on or after 19 July 2007.

A 'connected person' is defined as '(1) husband, wife, civil partner, (2) brother, sister, ancestor or descendant, (3) brother-in-law, sister-in-law and other combinations of (1) and (2)'.

1.8 SDLT: relief for shared ownership trusts

A shared ownership trust is designed to allow people to acquire shares in commonhold property that has been created pursuant to the Commonhold and Leasehold Reform Act 2002. The Finance Act 2007 amends Schedule 9 to the Finance Act 2003 so that an SDLT relief similar to that benefiting a shared owner under a shared ownership lease applies to shared ownership trusts of commonhold social housing.

'Shared ownership trust' is defined as a trust of land within section 1 of the Trusts of Land and Appointments of Trustees Act 1996 which meets the following conditions:

1. The trust property must be a dwelling in England or Wales.

2. The social landlord must be a 'qualifying body' as defined in schedule 9 to the Finance Act 2003.

3. The terms of the shared ownership trust must:

   a) give the buyer exclusive use of the property as his only or main residence;

   b) require that the buyer make an initial capital payment to the social landlord;

c) require that the buyer make additional payments to the social landlord as compensation under section 13(6)(a) of the Trusts of Land and Appointment of Trustees Act 1996;

d) enable the buyer to make additional 'equity-acquisition' payments to the social landlord;

e) determine the initial beneficial interests of the buyer and the social landlord by reference to the 'initial capital' paid by the buyer;

f) specify a sum (relating to the market value of the property) by reference to which the initial capital payment was made; and

g) provide for the buyer's interest in the property to increase (and the social landlord's interest to decrease) as 'equity-acquisition' payments are made.

A 'dwelling' includes:

- A building that is being constructed or adapted for use as a dwelling.

- Land to be used for the purpose of the construction of a dwelling.

- Land that is, or is to become, the garden or grounds of a dwelling.

At the initial payment stage, a buyer may make a market value election, whereby it elects to pay SDLT on the market value of the dwelling, rather than on any rent-equivalent payments. This election must be included in the land transaction return for the declaration of the shared ownership trust or any amendment of it. A market value election cannot be revoked. The chargeable consideration for the declaration of the shared ownership trust will be the market value of the dwelling by reference to which the initial capital was calculated. Rent-equivalent payments are to be disregarded.

Any additional 'equity acquisition' payment that increases the buyer's interest in the property is exempt from SDLT if:

a) a market value election has been made;

b) the SDLT due in respect of the declaration of trust (initial acquisition) has been paid; and

c) the buyer's interest does not exceed 80% of the total interest.

The final transfer to the buyer is exempt from SDLT if both of the following apply:

- The buyer has made a market value election.
- Any SDLT relating to the declaration of the shared ownership trust has been paid.

If no market value election is made:

- The initial capital payment is treated as chargeable consideration other than rent.
- Any rent-equivalent additional payment is treated for SDLT purposes as a payment of rent.

The new SDLT relief will apply to shared ownership trusts provided by qualifying bodies that have an effective date on or after 19 July 2007.

1.9 SDLT: shared ownership leases

The Finance Act 2007 amends paragraph 2 of Schedule 9 to the Finance Act 2003 to provide that where a market value election is made under Schedule 9 to the Finance Act 2003, the rent due under the shared ownership lease is to be disregarded for SDLT purposes. This applies to all transactions that occur on or after 19 July 2007.

1.10 SDLT: surplus school land

The Finance Act 2007 repeals sections 79 and 79A of the School Standards and Framework Act 1998 which provided for stamp duty and SDLT relief for transfers of surplus school land between foundations, trustees, boards of governors and local education authorities. This repeal in relation to stamp duty took effect for instruments executed on or after 19 July 2007, and in relation to SDLT took effect for land transactions where the effective date occurred on or after 19 July 2007.

1.11 VAT: rules on partial non-business use amended

The Finance Act 2007 makes two changes relating to *Lennartz* accounting and surrenders for no consideration.

Lennartz accounting provides that a business acquiring land and buildings that will only partly be used for business purposes, can allocate the asset wholly to business purposes, recover all of the input tax up front and account for the cost of irrecoverable VAT on any non-business use over the economic life of the asset. Legislation introduced in 2003 to prevent *Lennartz* accounting on land and buildings was subsequently rendered ineffective by the European Court of Justice in *Charles and Charles-Tijmens* (Taxation) [2005] EUECJ C-434/03 (14 July 2005) and *Wollny* (Taxation) [2006] EUECJ C-72/05 (14 September 2006). The European Court of Justice ruled that an EC member state could introduce legislation to make the period over which *Lennartz* accounting is possible, the same as the period for adjusting for VAT on capital items used to make taxable and exempt supplies and this would reduce the *Lennartz* accounting period from twenty to ten years.

The Finance Act 2007 implements the following changes:

- To reflect the decision in *Wollny*, it repeals the provision in Schedule 4 to the Value Added Tax Act 1994, to prevent *Lennartz* accounting on land and buildings.

- It amends paragraph 7 of Schedule 6 to the 1994 Act to allow HM Revenue & Customs to make new regulations for calculating the VAT charges for non-business use of an asset on which input VAT has been deducted.

- The regulations will be able to make transitional provisions.

In relation to surrenders for no consideration, paragraph 9 of Schedule 4 to the 1994 Act is amended so that the word 'grant', in respect of deemed supply, is to include a surrender. So, a surrender for no consideration will now be treated in the same way as a grant of a new interest, or assignment of an existing interest, for no consideration. This provision applies to surrenders occurring on or after 21 March 2007.

1.12 VAT: transfers of going concerns

Sections 49 and 94(6), and Schedules 1 and 4 to the Value Added Tax Act 1994 which deal with the transfer of records, information and registrations on a transfer of a going concern are amended. The amendments are:

- A transfer of a going concern will include the transfer of part of a business.

- Where a business, or part of a business, is transferred as a going concern, the buyer is no longer automatically required to preserve the business records.

- The obligation to retain records will generally remain with the seller.

- Where the VAT registration of the seller is also transferred, HM Revenue & Customs may make regulations requiring the buyer, rather than the seller, to retain the business records unless HM Revenue & Customs directs otherwise at the seller's request.

- If the seller is required to retain and preserve the business records, it must make available to the buyer information necessary for the buyer to comply with the 1994 Act.

- If the seller is required to retain the business records, HM Revenue & Customs may disclose to the buyer information it holds that is needed by the buyer to comply with the 1994 Act.

These changes affect transfers made pursuant to contracts entered into on or after 1 September 2007.

1.13 Capital allowances: industrial and agricultural buildings allowances

The Government intends to withdraw industrial building allowances and agricultural building allowances over the next four years. In the meantime, the rate of writing down allowances for both types of building will be reduced to 3% from April 2008, 2% from April 2009, and 1% from April 2010. The writing down allowances will be withdrawn from 1 April 2011.

The Finance Act 2007 effectively withdraws balancing adjustments, and recalculation of writing down allowances for qualifying industrial and agricultural building expenditure. This change is backdated to 21 March 2007.

These changes do not affect the following:

1. Qualifying enterprise zone expenditure.

2. A Pre-Commencement Date Contract, which is any written contract entered into before 21 March 2007 where:

   a) the contract is unconditional or any conditions were satisfied before 21 March 2007;

   b) none of its terms remain to be agreed on or after 21 March 2007; and

   c) it has not been significantly varied after 21 March 2007.

The withdrawal of balancing adjustments does not apply to a balancing event that occurs before 1 April 2011, and that is pursuant to a Pre-Commencement Date Contract.

The change to writing down allowances relates to a balancing event taking place after 21 March 2007 and a buyer of an existing industrial building will step into the seller's shoes in acquiring the seller's unrelieved qualifying expenditure rather than the unrelieved qualifying expenditure being recalculated. This excludes a balancing event which is pursuant to a Pre-Commencement Date Contract and occurs prior to 1 April 2011.

No balancing adjustment may be made for agricultural buildings under Part 4 of the Capital Allowances Act 2001 after 21 March 2007.

Section 376 of the Capital Allowances Act 2001 is amended so that a buyer of an agricultural building will take on the residue of qualifying expenditure that applied before the sale. This does not apply to a balancing event that is pursuant to a Pre-Commencement Date Contract and occurs before 1 April 2011.

1.14 Capital allowances: temporary increase in first year capital allowances for small enterprises

The Finance Act 2007 increases the amount of first year allowances to 50% for a further year. First year allowances bring forward the time over which tax relief is available for capital spending so that a larger proportion of the investment cost may qualify for tax relief against taxable profits for the period during which the investment is made. This applies to small businesses only and the 40% rate remains unchanged for medium-sized businesses.

The relief applies to expenditure during a twelve-month period from the following dates:

- 1 April 2007, if the small enterprise is within the charge to corporation tax.

- 6 April 2007, if the small enterprise is within the charge to income tax.

1.15 Service charge income

The relief for registered social landlords from the special trust tax rate of 40% on income arising from service charges and sinking funds held on trust, so that the rate payable on income arising from these funds is 20%, is extended to private sector landlords. This applies to UK dwellings for the tax year 2007–2008 and subsequent tax years.

2   *2007 PRE-BUDGET REPORT*

The 2007 Pre-Budget Report and Comprehensive Spending Review was delivered by the Chancellor on 9 October 2007. It is available at www.hm-treasury.gov.uk/pbr_csr/pbr_csr07_index.cfm. Whilst it covered a mixture of tax matters, the following matters will be of particular interest to conveyancers.

2.1 SDLT: notification thresholds for land transactions

It was announced that changes will be introduced in the 2008 Budget to remove the requirement to notify HM Revenue & Customs about certain land transactions where the chargeable consideration is under £40,000. This will ease the administrative burden on HM Revenue & Customs when processing land transaction returns where the chargeable consideration is very low.

The changes will involve the introduction of a threshold for non-residential property and a raising of the threshold for residential property. There will no longer be any need to notify HM Revenue & Customs about a land transaction that involves residential or non-residential land and is for a chargeable consideration of less than £40,000.

A lease will have to be notified if it is for a term of seven years or more, any chargeable consideration is more than £40,000 and the annual rent is more than £1,000.

Linked transactions involving both commercial or residential property will not need to be notified to HM Revenue & Customs if the chargeable consideration of the linked transactions is less than £40,000.

2.2 SDLT: partnerships

The Finance Bill 2008 will amend the Finance Act 2007 so that a transfer of an interest in property within an investment partnership will not give rise to a charge to SDLT. This change will apply retrospectively to transactions that occurred on or after 19 July 2007.

2.3 SDLT: high value residential property transactions

It was announced that there will be a consultation in relation to extending the disclosure regime to high value residential property transactions as the Government believes that the use of special purpose vehicles to reduce SDLT liability on high value residential property transactions is unfair to those who pay SDLT on this type of transaction in the UK.

2.4 VAT: reduced rates to encourage occupation of empty homes

From 1 January 2008, VAT will be payable at a reduced rate of 5% on renovations and alterations to residential properties that have been empty for at least two years.

2.5 VAT: simplification

A joint HM Revenue & Customs and HM Treasury review was announced with the aim of simplifying certain aspects of VAT.

2.6 Public Service Agreements

30 new Public Service Agreements were announced. Public Service Agreements were originally introduced in the 1998 Comprehensive Spending Review, which set around 600 performance targets for around 35 areas of Government. The following Public Service Agreements are of particular relevance to conveyancers:

- PSA 20: Increase in long-term housing supply and affordability.

- PSA 22: Deliver a successful Olympic Games.

- PSA 27: Lead the global effort to avoid dangerous climate change.

- PSA 28: Secure a healthy natural environment.

These Public Service Agreements are available at www.hm-treasury. gov.uk/pbr_csr/psa/pbr_csr07_psaindex.cfm

Part F

ENERGY PERFORMANCE OF BUILDINGS

1 BACKGROUND

One of the ways in which the EU and the Government propose to tackle climate change and reduce emissions is through greater energy efficiency, including efficiency in buildings. The building sector is thought to account for approximately 40% of the EU's total energy consumption and 50% of the UK's total carbon dioxide emissions (with residential buildings accounting for approximately 27% of the UK's total carbon dioxide emissions).

The Energy Performance of Buildings Directive (2009/91/EC) aims to promote improved energy performance of buildings (both commercial and residential) in the EU. Its principal requirements are as follows:

- Member states must set minimum energy performance requirements for buildings.

- New buildings, and large buildings which are subject to major renovations, must meet these minimum energy performance requirements.

- A feasibility assessment of alternative heating and energy supply systems must be carried out before construction of a new large building (i.e. a building with a total useful floor area of more than 1,000 square metres).

- Energy performance certificates must be made available to prospective buyers and tenants whenever a building is constructed, sold or rented.

- Display energy certificates must be displayed in large buildings occupied by public authorities and by institutions providing public services.

- Boilers and air-conditioning systems in buildings must be inspected on a regular basis.

- The issuing of energy performance certificates and display energy certificates, and the inspection of boilers and air-conditioning systems, must be carried out by independent experts.

The Directive required member states to implement it by 4 January 2006. Member states were given a further three years in which to bring some of the provisions into force, to allow time for sufficient energy assessors to be trained. The Government failed to meet the deadline of 4 January 2006 for putting in place all the necessary regulations, but the Directive has now been implemented in England and Wales, in two stages:

1. Building and Approved Inspectors (Amendment) Regulations 2006, which implement Articles 3 to 6 of the Directive relating to minimum energy performance requirements, by amending the Building Regulations 2000. The 2006 Regulations came into force on 6 April 2006.

2. Energy Performance of Buildings (Certificates and Inspectors) (England and Wales) Regulations 2007 which implement Articles 7, 9 and 10 of the Directive, which relate to energy certificates, inspection of air-conditioning systems and independent experts.

Article 8 of the Directive, which relates to the inspection of boilers, is being implemented by the provision of advice to users on the replacement of boilers and other modifications to heating systems.

The Energy Performance of Buildings (Certificates and Inspectors) (England and Wales) Regulations 2007 have been amended by:

- The Energy Performance of Buildings (Certificates and Inspections) (England and Wales) (Amendment) Regulations 2007 to take account of the delay in introducing Home Information Packs.

- The Energy Performance of Buildings (Certificates and Inspections) (England and Wales) (Amendment No. 2) Regulations 2007 to delay the introductions of EPCs and DECs for some categories of property.

The Energy Performance of Buildings (Certificates and Inspectors) (England and Wales) Regulations 2007 contain four main requirements:

1. Energy performance certificates and recommendations for improvement of the energy performance of the building are to be produced whenever a building is constructed, sold or rented out.

2. Display energy certificates are to be displayed in larger buildings occupied by public authorities and by institutions providing public services to a large number of people. Advisory reports containing recommendations for improvement of the energy performance of such buildings must also be obtained.

3. Air-conditioning systems with an output of more than 12kW must be inspected at regular intervals.

4. The energy assessors who produce energy performance certificates and display energy certificates and inspect air-conditioning systems must be accredited.

2   ENERGY PERFORMANCE CERTIFICATES

2.1   What is an energy performance certificate?

An energy performance certificate is a certificate containing information about the energy efficiency of a building. The Department for Communities and Local Government has developed a model form of energy performance certificate for use by energy assessors on the sales of dwellings and this is available at www.communities.gov.uk/documents/planningandbuilding/pdf/319282

The Energy Performance of Buildings (Certificates and Inspectors) (England and Wales) Regulations 2007 do not prescribe the form of an energy performance certificate, but Regulation 11 requires an energy performance certificate to include the following information:

- The asset rating of the building.

- The asset rating indicates the energy performance of the building's fabric and its services, calculated using standardised energy usage patterns. The asset rating is expressed on a scale from A to G, similar to the energy efficiency labels on domestic appliances, and allows prospective buyers or tenants to compare the energy performance of buildings. A rating indicates that the building is very energy efficient, with G being the lowest rating.

- For homes, an energy performance certificate includes the energy efficiency rating (on the A–G scale) and an environmental impact rating, which indicates the level of carbon dioxide emissions from the property.

- A reference value. This is a benchmark against which the asset rating for a building can be judged. The DCLG model form of energy performance certificate states that the benchmark asset rating for an average dwelling in England and Wales is E.

- The reference number under which the energy performance certificate is registered.

- The address of the building.

- An estimate of the total useful floor area of the building. The 2007 Regulations do not specify how the floor area of a building should be measured but guidance issued by the DCLG defines the total useful floor area as the total of all enclosed spaces measured to the internal face of the external walls. This is comparable to the definition of 'gross internal area' in the RICS Code of Measuring Practice.

- The name of the energy assessor who issued the energy performance certificate together with the name and address of their employer, or, if the energy assessor is self-employed, the name under which they trade and their address.

- The date on which the energy performance certificate was issued.

- The name of the approved accreditation scheme of which the energy assessor is a member.

An EPC must not contain any information that identifies a living individual (other than the energy assessor and their employer) in order to protect the privacy of owners and occupiers, particularly from unsolicited marketing.

2.2 Blocks of flats and multi-let buildings

There are special requirements for energy performance certificates in relation to flats, buildings that are multi-let and mixed-use properties. The DCLG Guidance states that, in general terms, the energy performance certificate should reflect the extent of the space being offered for sale or rent.

In relation to flats, every dwelling must have its own energy performance certificate. An energy performance certificate can be produced for each flat based on an energy assessment of a representative flat in the same block.

If a building is made up of separate commercial units but has a common heating system, either one energy performance certificate can be prepared for the whole building, or an energy performance certificate can be prepared for the part of the building that is being offered for sale or rent. In such cases, the energy performance certificate can be based on an energy assessment of a representative unit in the same block.

In a mixed-use building with a common heating system, the commercial areas of the building can be assessed on a common energy performance certificate.

If a building is made up of separate commercial units that do not share a common heating system, an energy performance certificate is required for each part of the building that is being offered for sale or rent. In such cases, the energy performance certificate can be based on an energy assessment of a representative unit in the same block.

Where a building has common parts that are solely or mainly for access to the individual units, the energy use of the common parts is allocated to each unit (based on the floor area of each unit as a proportion of the floor area of all of the units).

2.3 Recommendation reports

When a seller or landlord is required to provide an energy performance certificate, it must be accompanied by a recommendation report containing suggestions for the improvement of the energy performance of the building, which is issued by the energy assessor who issued the energy performance certificate.

The recommendation report contains two categories of recommendation:

1. Cost-effective alterations to the building that would improve energy performance.

2. Measures that require a higher level of expenditure, including installation of renewable energy systems, which could be adopted to improve the building's energy performance.

2.4 When a building is sold or rented out

When a building is to be sold or rented out, the seller or landlord must provide any prospective buyer or tenant with a valid energy performance certificate and a recommendation report, free of charge, at the earliest opportunity. Either the seller or the landlord can provide a copy of a valid energy performance certificate and an electronic copy is permissible if the recipient consents to receiving the certificate electronically.

The obligation to provide an energy performance certificate is triggered by whichever of these events occurs first:

- The seller or landlord provides written information about the building to a person who has requested information.

- A prospective buyer or tenant views the building.

- A contract is entered into to sell or rent out the building.

The seller or landlord must ensure that the ultimate buyer or tenant has received a valid energy performance certificate.

The obligation to provide an energy performance certificate does not apply if the seller or landlord has reasonable grounds to believe that a prospective buyer or tenant:

a) is unlikely to have sufficient funds to buy or rent the building;

b) is not genuinely interested in buying or renting that type of property;

c) is not someone to whom the seller or landlord would be prepared to sell or rent out the building.

The Guidance confirms that selling includes the assignment of a lease and renting out includes the grant of a sublease. In the case of an assignment, the assignor should provide the energy performance certificate to the proposed assignee. Where a tenant proposes to sublet its property, it may either negotiate with the head landlord to obtain an energy performance certificate for the whole building, as long as there is a common heating system, or obtain an energy performance certificate for the part of the building that is being sublet.

The Guidance gives the following examples of transactions that are not considered to be selling or renting out:

- Lease renewals or extensions.

- Compulsory purchase orders.

- Lease surrenders.

Neither the 2007 Regulations nor the Guidance clarify whether granting a licence to occupy a property amounts to renting out for the purposes of the energy performance certificate requirements.

Where the Housing Act 2004 imposes a duty to provide a HIP for a building, the asset rating of the building must be included in any marketing particulars (including any marketing particulars on the internet). Alternatively, a copy of an energy performance certificate for the building may be attached to the marketing particulars.

2.6 On construction of a building

The 2007 Regulations amend the Building Regulations 2000 to require a developer to produce an energy performance certificate when a building is erected or converted into fewer or more units and the services (e.g. the heating, hot water or air-conditioning systems) in the building are modified. This requirement replaces the requirement to produce an energy rating for new dwellings.

Unless an energy performance certificate and recommendation report have been given to the owner of the building by the developer, the building control inspector cannot issue a completion certificate for the works.

Certain buildings are not subject to the Building Regulations 2000, but are still within the scope of the 2007 Regulations. The person who carries out the construction work must give the owner of the building an energy performance certificate and recommendation report within five days of completing the construction work.

2.7 Off-plan sales and lettings

The 2007 Regulations do not require an energy performance certificate to be provided for off-plan sales or lettings before the construction of the building has been completed. However, the Home Information Pack (No. 2) Regulations 2007 do contain obligations relating to new-build properties. Where a property is marketed before it is physically complete, if a HIP is required, the HIP must include a Predicted Energy Assessment. Once the building has been constructed, the Predicted Energy Assessment will be replaced by an energy performance certificate. Schedule 2 to the Home Information Pack (No. 2) Regulations 2007 specifies what information must be included in a Predicted Energy Assessment.

2.8 Buildings which do not require an energy performance certificate

The 2007 Regulations define a building as 'a roofed construction having walls, for which energy is used to condition the indoor climate', which includes buildings that have fixed heating, mechanical ventilation or air conditioning. However, buildings that only have hot water or electric lighting do not fall within the 2007 Regulations and do not require an energy performance certificate.

Regulation 4 of the 2007 Regulations states that an energy performance certificate is not required on construction, sale or rent of any of the following types of building:

- Buildings which are used primarily or solely as places of worship.

- Temporary buildings with a planned time of use of two years or less.

- Industrial sites and workshops with low energy demand. The Guidance states that this exemption covers buildings whose purpose is to accommodate industrial activities in spaces where the air is not fully heated or cooled. This may include foundries, forges, food and drink-packing plants, storage and warehouses. Such buildings may have local heating or cooling appliances to serve people at workstations.

- Non-residential agricultural buildings with low energy demand. The Guidance states that this exemption covers buildings that are heated for a few days each year to enable plants to germinate but are otherwise unheated.

- Stand-alone buildings with a total useful floor area of less than 50m^2, which are not dwellings.

The obligations to provide an energy performance certificate and to include the asset rating in marketing particulars do not apply to buildings that are to be demolished. The Guidance states that where a building is to be demolished, the seller or landlord must be able to show that:

a) the building is being sold or rented with vacant possession;

b) the building is suitable for demolition and the site is suitable for redevelopment; and

c) they have reasonable grounds to believe that a prospective buyer or tenant intends to demolish the building. Evidence of this intention would include an application for planning permission.

2.9 How long is an energy performance certificate valid?

The general rule is that an energy performance certificate is valid for ten years from the date on which it was issued. A valid energy performance certificate will be revoked if a new energy performance certificate is issued for the building.

If a HIP is required in relation to a sale or letting of a building, any energy performance certificate provided to prospective buyers or tenants cannot be more than 12 months old when the building is first marketed.

2.10 Information needed to produce an energy performance certificate

The Guidance states that an energy assessor will require the following information to produce an energy performance certificate:

- Details of the individual spaces or zones in use within a building and their dimensions.

- The activities conducted within the zones, e.g. retail space, office space, kitchen or storage.

- The heating and ventilation services for each zone, including details of the type of system, metering, controls and fuel used.

- The lighting and controls used for each zone.

- The construction of the fabric of the building and the thermal efficiency of the materials used.

If plans for the building are not available, the energy assessor will need to survey the building.

2.11 Timetable for implementation

For residential properties, energy performance certificates will be required:

- From 6 April 2008, for all homes when built.

- From 1 October 2008, for all residential property, when rented to new tenants, and for all sales including sales not covered by HIPs.

For commercial properties, energy performance certificates will be required:

- From 6 April 2008, for commercial buildings with a total floor area of more than 10,000m² when built, sold or rented.
- From 1 July 2008, for commercial buildings with a total floor area greater than 2,500m² when built, sold or rented.
- From 1 October 2008, for all remaining commercial buildings when built, sold or rented.

3 DISPLAY ENERGY CERTIFICATES

From 1 October 2008, occupiers of certain buildings will have to display a display energy certificate in a prominent place to allow members of the public to compare the energy performance of public buildings and to promote improved energy use.

3.1 Buildings which require a display energy certificate

The requirement to display a display energy certificate only applies to 'buildings with a total useful floor area over 1,000m² occupied by public authorities and by institutions providing public services to a large number of persons and therefore frequently visited by those persons'.

3.2 Information to be included in a display energy certificate

The 2007 Regulations do not prescribe the form of a display energy certificate, but Regulation 17 requires a display energy certificate to include the following information:

- The asset rating of the building, which indicates the energy performance of the building's fabric and its services and will be expressed on a scale from A to G.
- The operational rating of the building. This is an indication of the amount of energy consumed at the building over a period of 12 months and will be assessed from meter readings for the services provided to the building. If the occupier has displayed display

253

energy certificates in the previous two years, the operational rating for the building in those two years must be shown in the current display energy certificate.

- A reference value which is a benchmark against which the asset rating for a building can be judged.

- The reference number under which the display energy certificate is registered.

- The address of the building.

- An estimate of the total useful floor area of the building. The 2007 Regulations do not specify how the floor area of a building should be calculated. The Guidance defines the total useful floor area as the total of all enclosed spaces measured to the internal face of the external walls. This is comparable to the definition of 'gross internal area' in the RICS Code of Measuring Practice.

- The name of the energy assessor who issued the display energy certificate, together with the name and address of their employer. If the energy assessor is self-employed, the name under which they trade and their address.

- The date on which the display energy certificate was issued.

- The nominated date. This must fall within three months of the end of the period over which the operational rating is calculated and is chosen by the energy assessor. A display energy certificate is valid for 12 months from the nominated date.

- The name of the approved accreditation scheme of which the energy assessor is a member. A display energy certificate must be produced by an energy assessor who is accredited to produce display energy certificates for that category of building.

3.3   Exceptions for new occupiers

Regulation 18 of the 2007 Regulations contains some exceptions for new occupiers of buildings where a display energy certificate is required:

- During an occupier's first 15 months of occupation, the operational rating does not have to be included on the display energy certificate.

- If the occupier was not given an energy performance certificate when they took occupation of the building, the asset rating does not have to be shown on the display energy certificate.

- Until 4 January 2009, if both of the two circumstances set out above applies then the occupier does not have to display a display energy certificate nor obtain an advisory report.

- On 4 January 2009, if an occupier has been in occupation for less than 15 months and they do not have an energy performance certificate, the operational rating for the display energy certificate can be calculated over the period they have occupied the building.

3.4 Advisory reports

As well as displaying a display energy certificate, occupiers must also obtain an advisory report containing recommendations for improving the energy performance of the building. The advisory report is valid for seven years from the date it was issued and must be issued by an energy assessor who has assessed the building.

4 INSPECTION OF AIR-CONDITIONING SYSTEMS

Part 4 of the 2007 Regulations imposes an obligation on those who have control of air-conditioning systems (with a maximum calorific output of more than 12kW) to ensure that the system is inspected at least every five years by an energy assessor.

The energy assessor must provide a written report of the inspection as soon as practicable after the inspection. The report must include:

- An assessment of the air-conditioning efficiency of the system.

- An assessment of the size of the system compared to the cooling requirements of the building.

- Appropriate advice on possible improvements to the system (including replacement of the system and alternative solutions).

The requirement to have an air-conditioning system inspected has been introduced in stages from 1 January 2008:

1. If the system was put into service after 1 January 2008, the first inspection must take place within five years of the system being put into service.

2. If the system was in service before 1 January 2008, the date of the first inspection depends on the output of the system:

   i) systems with an output of more than 250kW must be inspected before 4 January 2009;

   ii) systems with an output of more than 12kW must be inspected before 4 January 2011.

5   ENERGY ASSESSORS

Any energy assessor who issues an energy performance certificate or display energy certificate, or inspects an air-conditioning system, must be a member of an approved accreditation scheme. The approval of an accreditation scheme can be limited by reference to:

a) the categories of building for which members may produce certificates; and

b) the types of air-conditioning systems members may inspect.

Accreditation schemes must ensure that energy assessors are properly qualified to carry out energy assessments in an independent and accurate manner. They must also provide a standard form of energy performance certificate, recommendation report, display energy certificate and advisory report, which energy assessors should follow when preparing the different types of document.

The following 12 accreditation schemes have been approved:

- BESCA/HVCA (www.besca.org.uk)
- BRE (www.bre.co.uk/accreditation)

- Chartered Institute of Architectural Technologists (www.ciat.org.uk)
- Chartered Institute of Building Services Engineers (www.cibse.org)
- Elmhurst (www.elmhurstenergy.co.uk)
- EPC Limited (www.epc-solutions.co.uk)
- HI Certification (www.hicertification.co.uk)
- Knauf Insulation(www.knauf.co.uk)
- NAPIT (www.napit.org.uk)
- National Energy Services (http://www.nher.co.uk)
- Northgate (www.northgate-ispublicservices.com)
- Quidos (www.quidos.co.uk)
- Royal Institution of Chartered Surveyors (www.rics.org/hips)
- Stroma (www.stroma.com)

6 REGISTRATION OF CERTIFICATES

The Government is required to maintain registers of energy performance certificates, display energy certificates, recommendation reports and advisory reports. The responsibility for registering a document lies with the energy assessor who issued the document. Once a document has been registered it cannot be altered and must be stored on the register for at least 20 years. Landmark Information Group operates the register on behalf of the Government.

The aims of the register are:

- To allow owners and occupiers to obtain additional copies of the energy performance certificate for their property.
- To enable prospective purchasers, tenants and enforcement bodies to check that any energy performance certificate provided to them is valid.

- To enable accreditation scheme operators to carry out quality checks on the energy performance certificates produced by their energy assessors.

- To allow the Government to use the data to improve energy performance benchmarks and for statistical and research purposes.

- To allow the DCLG to monitor compliance with the 2007 Regulations.

Registered energy performance certificates are given a reference number, which must be quoted before a copy of the energy performance certificate will be provided. It is a criminal offence to unlawfully disclose an energy performance certificate, punishable by a fine of up to £5,000.

7   ENFORCEMENT

The local weights and measures authority is responsible for enforcement which will normally be carried out by Trading Standards Officers issuing penalty charge notices to those who fail to comply. The level of the penalty charge varies according to the type of property. The penalty for failing to comply with the 2007 Regulations when selling or renting out a dwelling is currently set at £200, whilst the penalty for failing to provide an energy performance certificate when selling or renting out commercial property is, in most cases, 12.5% of the rateable value of the building, with a minimum penalty of £500 and a maximum penalty of £5,000.

The Guidance advises that a penalty charge notice will not be issued in the following circumstances:

1. On the sale or rent of a property where a request for an energy performance certificate was made at least 14 days before it was required but, despite all reasonable efforts, it is not in the possession of the seller or landlord. Evidence of the request for an energy performance certificate will be needed to rely on this exemption.

2. On the renting out of a property:

   a) where a prospective tenant was seeking to rent the building in an emergency that required their urgent relocation;

   b) where the landlord did not have a valid energy performance certificate at the time of the letting;

   c) where there was insufficient time for the landlord to be reasonably expected to have obtained an energy performance certificate before renting out the building; and

   d) where the landlord has given a valid energy performance certificate to the tenant as soon as reasonably practicable after the building was rented out.

The Guidance states that enforcement officers can request a copy of an energy performance certificate from a duty-holder up to six months after the energy performance certificate was required, and so the duty-holder should keep a record of the reference number for the energy performance certificate to allow further copies to be requested in the future.

Part G

REFERENCE SECTION

---

1   PUBLICATIONS

1.1   Public Rights of Way and Access to Land
Author: Angela Sydenham
Publisher: Jordan Publishing Ltd

1.2   Dilapidations on the End of a Tenancy
Author: Jeremy Moody
Publisher: Central Association of Agricultural Valuers

1.3   Conveyancer's Factfinder
Publisher: Jordan Publishing Ltd

1.4   Directory of Local Authorities: 2007
Publisher: Sweet & Maxwell

1.5   Stack v Dowden: A Special Bulletin
Authors: David Burrows and Nicholas Orr
Publisher: Jordan Publishing Ltd

1.6   Complex Conveyancing
Author: Lord Brennan
Publisher: Tottel Publishing

1.7   Conveyancing Handbook
Authors: Frances Silverman, Annette Goss, Peter Reekie
Publisher: The Law Society

1.8   Residential Conveyancing Manual
Author: Susan Alterman
Publisher: Callow Publishing Ltd

1.9   Conveyancing Tables: 2007
Author: P M Callow
Publisher: Callow Publishing Ltd

1.10 Land Licences
Authors: L Blohm and J Sharples
Publisher: Jordan Publishing Ltd

2 ARTICLES

2.1 An unworkable position
Publication: Property Law Journal P.L.J. (2007) No. 184 Pages 7–9
Author: Michael Hunter
Topic: The implications of the Government's adoption, in its 2006 pre-Budget report, of a Stamp Duty Land Tax anti-avoidance measure, under the Finance Act 2003 section 75A, affecting partnerships, leases and subsales.

2.2 The potential for misuse
Publication: Property Law Journal P.L.J. (2007) No. 184 Pages 10–11
Author: Andrew Olins
Topic: The steps that a developer was forced to take when a potential purchaser, whom it suspected of mortgage fraud or money laundering, lodged priority searches against the properties in response to the developer's cancellation of reservations, thus preventing the developer from concluding transactions with new purchasers.

2.3 Leases as contracts
Publication: Property Law Journal P.L.J. (2007) No. 184 Pages 16–17
Authors: Malcolm Dowden and Catherine Hooker
Topic: The Court of Appeal ruling in *Reichman v Beveridge* on whether a commercial landlord, rather than claiming for rent arrears after a company vacated the premises and stopped paying rent, was under a duty to mitigate its loss by either forfeiting the lease or putting a new tenant in place.

2.4 Unjust enrichment and proprietary estoppel: two sides of the same coin?
Publication: Lloyd's Maritime and Commercial Law Quarterly L.M.C.L.Q. (2007) No. 1 February Pages 14–18
Author: Kelvin F.K. Low

Topic: The Privy Council judgment in *Blue Haven Enterprises Ltd v Tully* on a dispute between two intending purchasers of the same land, where one was allowed to take possession and develop the land but after the work was complete the land was transferred to the other.

2.5 A centre of revolution
Publication: Estates Gazette E.G. (2007) No. 0709 Pages 194–196
Authors: Antony Phillips and David Jackson
Topic: A review of case law illustrating the increasing use of human rights arguments in property and planning disputes.

2.6 How to get what you're owed
Publication: Estates Gazette E.G. (2007) No. 0709 Pages 198–199
Author: Emma Humphreys
Topic: An overview of the options available to landlords seeking to recover rent arrears.

2.7 A stairlift fraught with problems
Publication: Estates Gazette E.G. (2007) No. 0709 Page 201
Author: Sandi Murdoch
Topic: The Court of Appeal ruling in *Richmond Court (Swansea) Ltd v Williams* on whether a residential landlord had discriminated against an elderly disabled tenant, contrary to the Disability Discrimination Act 1995 sections 22(3)(a) and 24, by refusing consent for the installation of a stairlift to the common parts of a block of flats.

2.8 Expensive quandary
Publication: Estates Gazette E.G. (2007) No. 0710 Pages 174–176
Authors: Peter Levaggi and David Marsden
Topic: The steps that landlords can take in the event that an insolvent tenant goes into administration under the regime introduced by the Enterprise Act 2002.

2.9 Unconscionable behaviour
Publication: Estates Gazette E.G. (2007) No. 0710 Page 181
Author: Sandi Murdoch
Topic: The Chancery Division ruling in *Bexley LBC v Maison Maurice Ltd* on whether the local authority was estopped from denying that a property owner possessed a permanent right of access to the highway on the ground.

2.10 Quick pennies and slow pounds
Publication: Property Law Journal P.L.J. (2007) No. 185 Pages 11–13
Author: Kate Andrews
Topic: The Court of Appeal ruling in *Thomas v Ken Thomas Ltd* on whether a commercial landlord had waived his right to forfeit the lease for arrears of rent by accepting rent payments arranged by a third party after the tenant entered into a company voluntary arrangement.

2.11 Over-stepping the line
Publication: Property Law Journal P.L.J. (2007) No. 185 Pages 15–17
Author: Richard Marshall
Topic: The Court of Appeal ruling in *Haycocks v Neville* on whether the trial judge was entitled to reject the parties' disputed methods for determining a boundary between two properties in favour of her own interpretation.

2.12 Medieval law, modern problem
Publication: Property Law Journal P.L.J. (2007) No. 185 Pages 19–21
Author: Frances Richards
Topic: The origins of chancel repair liability and the need for reform of this area of law.

2.13 Landowners face a snake in the grass
Publication: Estates Gazette E.G. (2007) No. 0711 Page 155
Author: Julian Boswall
Topic: The effect of the Commons Act 2006 section 15 on the registration of land as a village green.

2.14 Landlords must seize the day
Publication: Estates Gazette E.G. (2007) No. 0711 Pages 156–157
Authors: Emma Humphreys and Patricia Mellody
Topic: Further advice on the options available to landlords seeking to recover rent arrears.

2.15 Protecting a claim to a beneficial interest
Publication: Family Law Fam. Law (2007) No. 37 March Pages 227–230
Author: Alex Ralton

Topic: Ways to protect a client's claim to a beneficial interest in registered land.

2.16 HM Land Registry's index
Publication: Family Law Fam. Law (2007) No. 37 March Page 252
Author: Ian Coules
Topic: How to use the Index of Proprietors Names searching facility whereby a search can be made of properties registered at the Land Registry by using the name of the spouse.

2.17 Drive-way robbery?
Publication: Solicitors Journal S.J. (2007) Vol. 151 No. 12 Page 389
Author: Andrew Butler
Topic: A review of conflicting authorities on easements and how to determine whether building work proposed by the owner of a servient tenement will interfere with the right of way of the dominant owner.

2.18 The pivot point in the quarrel
Publication: Estates Gazette E.G. (2007) No. 0712 Page 153
Author: Sandi Murdoch
Topic: The Court of Appeal ruling in *Haycocks v Neville* on the location of a pivot point in the gardens of two neighbouring properties which would determine the boundary between the properties.

2.19 Tenant settles for a relaxing break
Publication: Property Law Journal P.L.J. (2007) No. 186 Pages 6–8
Author: Tim Reid
Topic: The Court of Appeal ruling in *Legal & General Assurance Society Ltd v Expeditors International (UK) Ltd* on whether a commercial landlord had waived its right to rely on the conditions of a break clause.

2.20 Code green
Publication: Property Law Journal P.L.J. (2007) No. 186 Pages 12–13
Authors: Greg Richards and Mark Silcock
Topic: The Code for Sustainable Homes – A Step-Change in Sustainable Home Building Practice.

2.21 **Further illuminations**
Publication: Property Law Journal P.L.J. (2007) No. 186 Pages 15–18
Author: Bryan Johnston
Topic: Current judicial thinking on the right to light.

2.22 **Historically speaking...**
Publication: Property Law Journal P.L.J. (2007) No. 186 Pages 23–24
Author: Rosemary Herbert
Topic: The history of chancel repair liability.

2.23 **Budget 2007 – property**
Publication: Tax Journal Tax J. (2007) No. 879 Pages 11–12
Author: Charles Beer
Topic: The 2007 Budget proposals on the tax treatment of real property.

2.24 **Tenancy deposit protection**
Publication: Legal Action (2007) April Pages 31–32
Author: Jacky Peacock
Topic: The requirement to protect deposits paid by tenants to landlords in connection with an assured shorthold tenancy with effect from 6 April 2007.

2.25 **A good opportunity**
Publication: Estates Gazette E.G. (2007) No. 0714 Pages 94–95
Author: Chris Edwards
Topic: The RICS Code of Practice: Service Charges in Commercial Property.

2.26 **The winning OSCAR**
Publication: Estates Gazette E.G. (2007) No. 0714 Pages 96–97
Author: David Griffin and Gavin Blackwell
Topic: The RICS Code of Practice: Service Charges in Commercial Property.

2.27 **All bark and no bite**
Publication: Estates Gazette E.G. (2007) No. 0714 Pages 98–99
Author: Stephen Jourdan
Topic: The RICS Code of Practice: Service Charges in Commercial Property.

2.28 Statutory demands
Publication: Estates Gazette E.G. (2007) No. 0714 Pages 100–101
Author: James Driscoll
Topic: The operation of tenancy deposit schemes for assured
shorthold tenancies.

2.29 The problem with infringements
Publication: Estates Gazette E.G. (2007) No. 0714 Page 103
Author: Sandi Murdoch
Topic: The Chancery Division ruling in *Tamares (Vincent Square)*
Ltd v Fairpoint Properties (Vincent Square) Ltd on the appropriate
measure of damages to be awarded to an occupier whose right to
light had been infringed.

2.30 Speed of light
Publication: Solicitors Journal S.J. (2007) Vol. 151 No. 13 Pages
417, 419
Authors: Matthew Baker and Keith Shaw
Topic: The assessment of damages for developers' infringements of
rights to light where the infringement is not serious enough for an
injunction.

2.31 Renting protection
Publication: Solicitors Journal S.J. (2007) Vol. 151 No. 14 Pages
451–452
Author: James Driscoll
Topic: The three tenancy deposit schemes for assured shorthold
tenancies set up under the Housing Act 2004.

2.32 It's up for promotion
Publication: Estates Gazette E.G. (2007) No. 0713 Pages 246–248
Authors: Geoff Le Pard and Clare Maunder
Topic: The Code for Leasing Business Premises in England and
Wales and its aims, scope and key provision.

2.33 Keeping track of the legal rules
Publication: Estates Gazette E.G. (2007) No. 0713 Page 253
Author: Sandi Murdoch
Topic: The need to inspect land to check whether any use is being
made of it which could amount to an easement.

2.34 The right form at the right moment
Publication: Estates Gazette E.G. (2007) No. 0715 Page 145
Author: Sandi Murdoch
Topic: The Court of Appeal ruling in *Scottish & Newcastle Plc v Raguz (No. 3)* on whether a landlord was under an obligation to serve a notice for rent arrears under the Landlord and Tenant (Covenants) Act 1995 section 17 within six months of the review date even though the tenant was not in default at that time because the rent review was still outstanding.

2.35 A question of morality...
Publication: Property Law Journal P.L.J. (2007) No. 187 Pages 3–6
Author: Janet Keeley
Topic: A solicitor's moral duty to warn clients of the hazards of engaging in litigation over boundary disputes.

2.36 An administrative nightmare for landlords
Publication: Property Law Journal P.L.J. (2007) No. 187 Pages 11–13
Author: John Martin
Topic: The Court of Appeal ruling in *Scottish & Newcastle Plc v Raguz (No. 3)* on the correct form of notice to be served under the Landlord and Tenant (Covenants) Act 1995 section 17 in the event that a rent review is pending.

2.37 Over-reaching and unauthorised disposition of registered land
Publication: Conveyancer and Property Lawyer Conv. (2007) March/April Pages 120–132
Author: Nicola Jackson
Topic: Whether equitable interests, charges and powers over registered land will be over-reached where the disposition of the land is unauthorised.

2.38 Prescriptive easements in England and legal 'climate change'
Publication: Conveyancer and Property Lawyer Conv. (2007) March/April Pages 133–147
Author: Fiona R. Burns
Topic: The potential demise of the prescriptive easement.

2.39 Prescriptive easements: acquisition, abandonment and leasehold land

Publication: Conveyancer and Property Lawyer Conv. (2007) March/April Pages 161–168

Author: Ed.

Topic: The Court of Appeal decision in *Williams v Sandy Lane (Chester) Ltd* on whether a prescriptive right of way could arise in circumstance where a tenancy existed over part of the servient land.

2.40 Rights to light: radical consequences of an orthodox decision

Publication: Conveyancer and Property Lawyer Conv. (2007) March/April Pages 175–183

Author: Paul Chynoweth

Topic: The Chancery Division and the Court of Appeal decisions in *Regan v Paul Properties DPF No. 1 Ltd* on right to light.

2.41 Leasehold enfranchisement – tenant's personal signature and notices

Publication: Landlord & Tenant Review L. & T. Review (2007) Vol. 11 No. 2 Pages 38–40

Author: Margarita Madjirska

Topic: Whether the initial notice under which a tenant claims the right to enfranchise must be signed by the tenant in person or whether it is sufficient for it to be signed by a solicitor or an attorney acting on his behalf.

2.42 Duty to mitigate in leasehold law

Publication: Landlord & Tenant Review L. & T. Review (2007) Vol. 11 No. 2 Pages 41–45

Author: Mark Pawlowski

Topic: The rights and duties of landlords where premises are abandoned by a tenant who has defaulted on the rent.

2.43 Deemed withdrawal in the 1993 Act: confusion reigns?

Publication: Landlord & Tenant Review L. & T. Review (2007) Vol. 11 No. 2 Pages 46–49

Author: Gary Cowen

Topic: A tenant's right, under the Leasehold Reform, Housing and Urban Development Act 1993, to acquire a new lease of his/her flat.

2.44 **Service charges – issues of jurisdiction and definition**
Publication: Landlord & Tenant Review L. & T. Review (2007) Vol.
11 No. 2 Pages 50–53
Author: Robert Wood
Topic: The Court of Appeal decision in *Oakfern Properties Ltd
v Ruddy* on whether the Leasehold Valuation Tribunal had
jurisdiction to hear a claim brought by a subtenant against the
freeholder in relation to building maintenance charges levied
on the head tenant by the freeholder, and passed down to the
subtenant.

2.45 **That sinking feeling**
Publication: Solicitors Journal S.J. (2007) Vol. 151 No. 15 Page 494
Author: John Martin
Topic: The problems which may arise for tenants regarding the
payment of service charges under a business tenancy which the
landlord pays into either a sinking fund or a reserve fund.

2.46 **An unfortunate set of circumstances**
Publication: Estates Gazette E.G. (2007) No. 0716 Page 189
Author: Sandi Murdoch
Topic: The Court of Appeal ruling in *Scottish & Newcastle Plc v
Raguz (No. 3)* on whether a former tenant was able to recover
payments from its immediate assignee where the landlord had
failed to comply with the procedure for issuing default notices
under the Landlord and Tenant (Covenants) Act 1995 section 17.

2.47 **Budget and Finance Bill 2007 – SDLT**
Publication: Tax Journal Tax J. (2007) No. 882 Pages 11–12
Author: Patrick Cannon
Topic: The Finance Bill 2007 reforms to Stamp Duty Land Tax.

2.48 **Does Raguz have wider application?**
Publication: Property Law Journal P.L.J. (2007) No. 188 Pages 2–5
Author: Natalie Johnston
Topic: Whether the Court of Appeal ruling in *Scottish & Newcastle
Plc v Raguz (No. 3)* will have implications for service charge
balancing charges.

2.49 A boost in the Budget
Publication: Property Law Journal P.L.J. (2007) No. 188 Pages 6–8
Author: Laurence Target
Topic: Reductions in Stamp Duty Land Tax and shared ownership trusts.

2.50 New lease of life?
Publication: Property Law Journal P.L.J. (2007) No. 188 Pages 9–12
Author: Nick Darby
Topic: The Code for Leasing Business Tenancies with focus on the Landlord Code.

2.51 Further obstacles for development
Publication: Property Law Journal P.L.J. (2007) No. 188 Pages 13–17
Author: David Shakesby
Topic: Changes to the law on town and village greens.

2.52 An option with a surprising result
Publication: Property Law Journal P.L.J. (2007) No. 188 Pages 18–20
Author: Nick Lloyd
Topic: The Chancery Division ruling in *Rennie v Westbury Homes (Holdings) Ltd* on whether a developer's option period had been extended.

2.53 A new lease of life
Publication: Law Society's Gazette L.S.G. (2007) Vol. 104 No. 17 Pages 20–21
Author: Grania Langdon-Down
Topic: The introduction of tenant deposit protection schemes and home information packs, and the publication of an updated code of practice for commercial leases.

2.54 It's all over
Publication: Taxation Tax. (2007) Vol. 159 No. 4104 Pages 463–465
Author: Stephanie Churchill
Topic: The capital gains tax treatment of a former matrimonial home on divorce.

2.55 The judicious application of the broad sword
Publication: Trusts and Estates Law & Tax Journal T.E.L. & T.J. (2007) No. 85 April Pages 4, 6–8
Author: Michael O'Sullivan
Topic: The decision in *Re Horley Town Football Club* on the validity of a gift of land to an unincorporated sports club to hold in trust and use as a football ground.

2.56 HIPs – can they stand up?
Publication: Solicitors Journal S.J. (2007) Vol. 151 No. 17 Pages 548, 551, 553–554
Author: Miles Geffin
Topic: The requirement to provide home information packs from 1 June 2007.

2.57 Essential timekeeping
Publication: Estates Gazette E.G. (2007) No. 0719 Pages 160–161
Author: Peta Dollar
Topic: The principle of time of the essence under contract law.

2.58 Not always an accurate picture
Publication: Estates Gazette E.G. (2007) No. 0719 Page 163
Author: Sandi Murdoch
Topic: The Chancery Division ruling in *Business Environment Bow Lane Ltd v Deanwater Estates Ltd* on whether an assurance that a tenant would not be responsible for disrepair at the end of the lease term amounted to a collateral contract.

2.59 Living over the shop
Publication: Property Law Journal P.L.J. (2007) No. 189 Pages 2–5
Authors: Mark Shelton and Lynn James
Topic: Determining which security of tenure regime is applicable to mixed use premises on termination of the lease.

2.60 Putting the client's welfare first where capacity is an issue
Publication: Law Society's Gazette L.S.G. (2007) Vol. 104 No. 20 Page 22
Author: Frances Mayne
Topic: The Mental Capacity Act 2005.

2.61 **Making sixth sense of the latest title**
Publication: Law Society's Gazette L.S.G. (2007) Vol. 104 No. 20
Page 34
Author: Warren Gordon
Topic: The changes introduced in the sixth edition of the *City of London Law Society's Land Law Committee Long Form Certificate of Title*.

2.62 **Key area of the law is under review**
Publication: Estates Gazette E.G. (2007) No. 0720 Pages 288–289
Author: Katherine Campbell
Topic: The Law Commission's proposals on the law of forfeiture.

2.63 **Technical objections will not prevail**
Publication: Estates Gazette E.G. (2007) No. 0720 Page 293
Author: Sandi Murdoch
Topic: The decision in *Rennie v Westbury Homes (Holdings) Ltd* on whether the purported exercise of the right to extend an option to purchase was valid or not.

2.64 **Stack v Dowden – the implications**
Publication: Property Law Journal P.L.J. (2007) No. 190 Pages 22–24
Author: William Selby-Lowndes
Topic: The House of Lords decision in *Stack v Dowden* that a family home was not held on trust for cohabitants as tenants in common in equal shares.

2.65 **Information meltdown**
Publication: New Law Journal N.L.J. (2007) Vol. 157 No. 7274
Page 723
Author: Mark Riddick
Topic: The introduction of home information packs will be hindered by the failure to reform the local authority search market.

2.66 **Presuming too much?**
Publication: Solicitors Journal S.J. (2007) Vol. 151 No. 20 Pages 660–661

Author: James Freeman

Topic: Examines, in the light of the House of Lords ruling in *Stack v Dowden*, the legal framework by which the courts resolve property disputes between unmarried cohabiting couples on the breakdown of their relationship.

2.67 A wake-up call for landlords

Publication: Estates Gazette E.G. (2007) No. 0721 Pages 122–124

Authors: Katie Bradford and Simon Hartley

Topic: The Chancery Division ruling in *Prudential Assurance Co Ltd v PRG Powerhouse Ltd* on whether a tenant was permitted to use a company voluntary arrangement to reduce its liability for future rent and to prevent a landlord from bringing a claim under a parent company guarantee.

2.68 The right notice served at the right time

Publication: Estates Gazette E.G. (2007) No. 0721 Page 125

Authors: David Haines and Olivier Kalfon

Topic: When a landlord of commercial premises should serve notice under the Landlord and Tenant (Covenants) Act 1995 section 17 where a rent review is still in progress but the review date has passed.

2.69 Curbing fraudulent behaviour

Publication: Estates Gazette E.G. (2007) No. 0722 Page 156

Author: Simon Edwards

Topic: The implications of the Fraud Act 2006 for the property industry.

2.70 Authorised guarantee agreements

Publication: Property Law Journal P.L.J. (2007) No. 191 Pages 18–21

Author: John Martin

Topic: The drafting of authorised guarantee agreements in the light of the Code for Leasing Business Premises in England and Wales 2007.

2.71 A question of interpretation

Publication: Property Law Journal P.L.J. (2007) No. 191 Pages 22–24

Authors: Emma Humphreys and Malcolm Dowden

Topic: The differing interpretations by the Court of Appeal of the term 'let as a dwelling' in *Patel v Pirabakaran* and *Phaik Seang Tan v Sitkowski*.

2.72   How green is my law?
Publication: Law Society's Gazette L.S.G. (2007) Vol. 104 No. 23
Page 36
Author: Katie Paxton-Doggett
Topic: The provisions of the Commons Act 2006 section 15 on the
registration of town or village greens.

2.73   New commercial property code
Publication: Solicitors Journal S.J. (2007) Vol. 151 No. 22 Pages
734, 736
Author: Nick Darby
Topic: The Code for Leasing Business Premises.

2.74   Problem shared is not a problem halved
Publication: Law Society's Gazette L.S.G. (2007) Vol. 104 No. 24
Page 30
Author: Julie Exton
Topic: Discusses, by reference to the House of Lords decision
in *Stack v Dowden*, the beneficial interests of cohabitees in
property.

2.75   True intentions
Publication: New Law Journal N.L.J. (2007) Vol. 157 No. 7277
Pages 841–842
Authors: Elizabeth Fitzgerald and Greville Healey
Topic: The Court of Appeal ruling in *KPMG v Network Rail
Infrastructure Ltd* on whether the court at first instance was
correct to conclude the intention of the parties to a lease to order
rectification due to mutual mistake, where vital words were missed
from the contract.

2.76   Soul searches
Publication: New Law Journal N.L.J. (2007) Vol. 157 No. 7277
Page 844
Author: Matt Le Breton
Topic: The establishment of chancel repair liabilities and the
difficulties of gaining information from the Church of England and
its dioceses.

2.77 **The code for leasing business premises 2007**
Publication: Landlord & Tenant Review L. & T. Review (2007) Vol. 11
No. 3 Pages 69–71
Author: Nick Darby
Topic: The Code for Leasing Business Premises.

2.78 **Easements: give and take in recent case law**
Publication: Landlord & Tenant Review L. & T. Review (2007) Vol. 11
No. 3 Pages 75–78
Author: John Summers
Topic: The two Court of Appeal judgments in *Jones v Cleanthi* and
Williams v Sandy Lane (Chester) Ltd relating to easements.

2.79 **Rent reviews, default notices and indemnities**
Publication: Landlord & Tenant Review L. & T. Review (2007) Vol. 11
No. 3 Pages 79-82
Author: E.J. Slessenger
Topic: The Court of Appeal decision in *Scottish & Newcastle Plc v
Raguz (No. 3)*.

2.80 **Rights of parking and the ouster principle after Batchelor v
Marlow**
Publication: Conveyancer and Property Lawyer Conv. (2007) May/June
Pages 223-234
Author: Alexander Hill-Smith
Topic: The validity of easements of parking by reference to the
'ouster principle'.

2.81 **The pitfalls of rent increases**
Publication: Property Law Journal P.L.J. (2007) No. 192 Pages 7–10
Author: Yetunde Dania
Topic: Rent increases for assured and assured shorthold tenancies.

2.82 **A code with teeth?**
Publication: Property Law Journal P.L.J. (2007) No. 192 Pages 11–13
Author: Matthew Williams
Topic: The RICS Code of Practice, Service Charges in Commercial
Property and whether it will be beneficial for both landlords and
tenants.

2.83 **Stack v Dowden revisited**
Publication: Family Law Journal Fam. L.J. (2007) No. 67 June
Pages 7–10
Author: Elissa Da Costa
Topic: The impact on cohabitation and the law of the *Stack v Dowden* case.

2.84 **A common VAT trap in property transactions**
Publication: Tax Journal Tax J. (2007) No. 891 Pages 15–16
Author: Michael Conlon
Topic: The provisions of the Value Added Tax Act 1994 Schedule 10 paragraph.8 on the party upon whom the burden of input tax falls where the benefit of the consideration involved in the grant of interests or rights over land does not fall to the person making the grant.

2.85 **A limit to a landlord's liability**
Publication: Estates Gazette E.G. (2007) No. 0725 Page 181
Author: Sandi Murdoch
Topic: The Court of Appeal ruling in *Alker v Collingwood Housing Association* on the extent of a landlord's liability under section 4 of the Defective Premises Act 1972.

2.86 **What are the options?**
Publication: Property Law Journal P.L.J. (2007) No. 193 Pages 13–15
Author: Sheonagh Richards
Topic: The issues which landowners need to take into consideration before agreeing to grant a developer an option to buy.

2.87 **A lacuna closed**
Publication: Property Law Journal P.L.J. (2007) No. 193 Pages 16–17
Author: Siobhan Cross
Topic: The Court of Appeal ruling in *Lay v Drexler* which filled a lacuna in the Regulatory Reform (Business Tenancies) (England and Wales) Order 2003 which exposed landlords to the risk of liability for a tenant's costs in proceedings for the grant of a new lease where the tenant decided against renewal and requested the court to dismiss proceedings.

2.88 **The tip of the iceberg**
Publication: Property Law Journal P.L.J. (2007) No. 201 Pages 5–7
Author: Robert Adam
Topic: Directive 2002/91 and the requirements introduced by the Energy Performance of Buildings (Certificates and Inspections) (England and Wales) Regulations 2007.

2.89 **Insurance**
Publication: Property Law Journal P.L.J. (2007) No. 201 Pages 16–20
Author: Edward Bannister
Topic: Insurance provisions in commercial leases.

2.90 **Shared intentions**
Publication: New Law Journal N.L.J. (2007) Vol. 157 No. 7279 Pages 922–923
Author: Elizabeth Hicks and Sital Amin
Topic: The approach which should be taken to the distribution of wealth between cohabitees upon relationship breakdown where no express trust is in place following *Stack v Dowden*.

2.91 **An independent personal service**
Publication: Solicitors Journal S.J. (2007) Vol. 151 No. 25 Pages 824, 826, 828
Author: Janet Baker
Topic: Developments which will benefit conveyancers carrying out searches for clients.

2.92 **Building an alternative to HIPs**
Publication: Law Society's Gazette L.S.G. (2007) Vol. 104 No. 28 Page 14
Author: Paul Marsh
Topic: Proposals submitted to the Government by the Law Society for the improvement of conveyancing procedures and systems, with reference to the Law Society's conveyancing TransAction protocol.

2.93 **Signposting your intent to the public**
Publication: Solicitors Journal S.J. (2007) Vol. 151 No. 27 Pages 912–913
Author: J.J. Pearlman

Topic: The House of Lords ruling in *R. (on the application of Godmanchester Town Council) v Secretary of State for the Environment, Food and Rural Affairs* on the correct test for determining whether a landowner had sufficiently demonstrated that there was no intention for a way over land to be dedicated as a public right of way within the meaning of section 31(1) of the Highways Act 1980.

2.94 A charity performance
Publication: Estates Gazette E.G. (2007) No. 0729 Pages 134–136
Author: James McCallum
Topic: The importance of a good understanding of the Charities Act 1993 section 36 by valuers dealing with dispositions of land by charities.

2.95 How to gain a qualified entry
Publication: Estates Gazette E.G. (2007) No. 0729 Page 137
Authors: Cathy Braddish and Jonathan Klein
Topic: Whether the Access to Neighbouring Land Act 1992 will assist where a neighbour is refusing to allow a builder access to his land to perform construction works.

2.96 Safe as houses?
Publication: Law Society's Gazette L.S.G. (2007) Vol. 104 No. 30 Pages 26–27
Author: Grania Langdon-Down
Topic: The need for solicitors to take precautions against inadvertently assisting in mortgage fraud.

2.97 Tinkering really won't do the trick
Publication: Estates Gazette E.G. (2007) No. 0730 Pages 125–126
Author: Andrew Francis
Topic: Problems with the law of easements and covenants which the Law Commission is likely to tackle in its forthcoming review of the law.

2.98 Shedding some light
Publication: Estates Gazette E.G. (2007) No. 0731 Pages 76–77
Authors: Emma Humphreys and Andrew Francis
Topic: An overview of the law on rights to light.

2.99   Level Properties Ltd v Balls Brothers Ltd
Publication: Conveyancer and Property Lawyer Conv. (2007) July/
August Pages 379–385
Author: Editor
Topic: The Chancery Division decision in *Level Properties Ltd v Balls
Brothers Ltd*, which considered the extent to which an expert's
interpretation of a lease bound the parties to a rent review.

2.100 Beneficial entitlement – no longer doing justice?
Publication: Conveyancer and Property Lawyer Conv. (2007) July/
August Pages 354–364
Author: Mark Pawlowski
Topic: The House of Lords ruling in *Stack v Dowden* on the size of
each legal owner's share of the equity in the family home in the
event of the relationship breakdown of an unmarried couple.

2.101 HIPS – what next?
Publication: New Law Journal N.L.J. (2007) Vol. 157 No. 7286
Page 1183
Author: Peter Ambrose
Topic: The proposals for home information packs and when they
will be required.

2.102 A code that lacks strength
Publication: Solicitors Journal S.J. (2007) Vol. 151 No. 32 Pages
1080–1081
Author: John Martin
Topic: Whether landlords joining the British Property Federation
Landlords Accreditation Scheme will be able to opt out of
requirements under the Landlord Code in the Code for Leasing
Business Premises in England and Wales 2007.

2.103 The new CLLS certificate of title
Publication: Landlord & Tenant Review L. & T. Review (2007) Vol.
11 No. 4 Pages 101–103
Author: Jacqueline Button
Topic: Changes to the process for disclosures on title and leasehold
matters introduced by the Sixth Edition of the City of London Law
Society Land Law Committee Long Form Certificate of Title.

2.104 Co-owners, the transfer, the intent and Stack
Publication: Family Law Fam. Law (2007) No. 37 August Pages 712–715
Author: Alex Ralton
Topic: The implications of *Stack v Dowden* for unmarried couples who co-own property.

2.105 Extinguishment of easements
Publication: Property Law Journal P.L.J. (2007) No. 194 Pages 3–7
Author: Tristan Ward
Topic: The Court of Appeal ruling in *Wall v Collins* on whether a leasehold easement which benefited the freehold survived the merger of the lease.

2.106 Patch me if you can
Publication: Property Law Journal P.L.J. (2007) No. 194 Pages 11–13
Author: Mark Pawlowski
Topic: The circumstances in which repair works may be more appropriate than replacement where a landlord is attempting to claim under a repair covenant.

2.107 A warning to objectors in the Lands Tribunal
Publication: Property Law Journal P.L.J. (2007) No. 194 Pages 18–21
Author: Andrew Olins
Topic: The Lands Tribunal decision in *Jones v Stuart* on whether the defendant's conduct, before and after the issue of proceedings for the modification of restrictive covenants under the Law of Property Act 1925 section 84, had been so unreasonable.

2.108 New lease ... new rent
Publication: Property Law Journal P.L.J. (2007) No. 194 Pages 22–24
Authors: Matthew Baker and Keith Shaw
Topic: The Court of Appeal ruling in *Trans-World Investments Ltd v Dadarwalla* on the factors which the court should take into account when determining a reasonable rent on the renewal of a business tenancy under the Landlord and Tenant Act 1954 section 34 where insufficient comparable properties exist.

2.109 Distress signals
Publication: Law Society's Gazette L.S.G. (2007) Vol. 104 No. 34
Page 30
Author: Peter Glover
Topic: The House of Lords decision in *Farley v Skinner (No. 2)* on
the contract between a surveyor and a house purchaser.

2.110 Be prepared – and benefit
Publication: Estates Gazette E.G. (2007) No. 0736 Pages 292, 294–295
Authors: Tim Dixon, Miles Keeping and Claire Roberts
Topic: Energy performance and sustainability.

2.111 Duty calls: but to whom?
Publication: Estates Gazette E.G. (2007) No. 0736 Page 295
Author: Allyson Colby
Topic: Considers who may be responsible for providing energy
performance certificates.

2.112 Landlords must pay the price
Publication: Estates Gazette E.G. (2007) No. 0736 Pages 296–297
Authors: Malcolm Dowden and Andrew Garvey
Topic: The implications of the Energy Performance of Buildings
(Certificates and Inspections) (England and Wales) Regulations
2007 for landlords and tenants of commercial properties.

2.113 Values under a novel regime
Publication: Estates Gazette E.G. (2007) No. 0736 Pages 298–299
Author: Philip Freedman and Simon Edwards
Topic: The implications for landlords of the duty to provide energy
performance certificates to prospective tenants.

2.114 Say what you mean
Publication: New Law Journal N.L.J. (2007) Vol. 157 No. 7288
Pages 1263–1264
Author: Natalie Johnston
Topic: The Court of Appeal decision in *Business Environment Bow
Lane Ltd v Deanwater Estates Ltd* on whether a letter sent to a
tenant after the surrender of a business lease and the conclusion
of a shorter lease of part of the property, informing the tenant that
a terminal schedule of dilapidations would not be served at the
end of the term, created a collateral contract to the original lease.

2.115 Bring it into sharper focus
Publication: Estates Gazette E.G. (2007) No. 0737 Pages 224, 226
Authors: Patrick Stell and Keith Firn
Topic: The draft *RICS Guidance Note on Dilapidations, 5th Edition*.

2.116 Shut out of Europe
Publication: Estates Gazette E.G. (2007) No. 0737 Pages 228–229
Author: Oliver Radley-Gardner and Jonathan Small
Topic: The European Court of Human Rights Grand Chamber
judgment in *JA Pye (Oxford) Ltd v United Kingdom (44302/02)* on
the law on adverse possession of registered land.

2.117 The courts' rights will always prevail
Publication: Estates Gazette E.G. (2007) No. 0737 Page 233
Author: Sandi Murdoch
Topic: The Chancery Division ruling in *Aribisala v St James Homes
(Grosvenor Dock) Ltd* and the court's jurisdiction to order the return of
a deposit paid upon exchange of a contract for the sale of leasehold
properties under the Law of Property Act 1925 section 49(2).

2.118 Grave consequences
Publication: Estates Gazette E.G. (2007) No. 0735 Pages 134–135
Author: Christine Wilson
Topic: The rule against perpetuities in commercial property
transactions.

2.119 EPCs and DECs considered
Publication: Property Law Journal P.L.J. (2007) No. 195 Pages 6–11
Author: Ben Tarrant
Topic: The implications of energy performance certificates and
display energy certificates for new and existing commercial
properties.

2.120 Return of deposits
Publication: Property Law Journal P.L.J. (2007) No. 195 Pages 12–13
Author: Laurie Heller
Topic: The attitude of the courts towards their discretionary
jurisdiction, under the Law of Property Act 1925 section 49(2), to
order repayment of a deposit under a contract for sale of land.

2.121 Occupation and the renewal of business tenancies: fact, fiction and legal abstraction
Publication: Journal of Business Law J.B.L. (2007) October Pages 759–777
Author: Michael Haley
Topic: The policy objectives of the Landlord and Tenant Act 1954 Part II and why the concept of occupation is crucial to its operation.

2.122 Bears and bulls in the property market
Publication: Solicitors Journal S.J. (2007) Vol. 151 No. 35 Pages 1180,1182
Author: Nicola Laver
Topic: The proceedings of the 2007 National Conveyancing Congress.

2.123 Full circle in the Pye litigation
Publication: Property Law Journal P.L.J. (2007) No. 196 Pages 2–5
Author: Andrew Francis
Topic: The European Court of Human Rights Grand Chamber decision in *JA Pye (Oxford) Ltd v United Kingdom (44302/02)* on the compatibility of the law on adverse possession under the Limitation Act 1980 and the Land Registration Act 1925 section 75 with the European Convention on Human Rights 1950 Protocol 1 Art.1.

2.124 Transfers of part: drafting tactics
Publication: Property Law Journal P.L.J. (2007) No. 196 Pages 6–9
Author: Laurie Heller
Topic: The pitfalls of conducting transactions involving the transfer of part of a property without paying adequate regard to existing easements.

2.125 Whose consent is it anyway?
Publication: Property Law Journal P.L.J. (2007) No. 196 Pages 11–13
Author: Paul Tonkin
Topic: The Chancery Division ruling in *City Inn (Jersey) Ltd v Ten Trinity Square Ltd* on a restrictive covenant involving the requirement to obtain consent for development.

2.126 An end to relief?
Publication: Property Law Journal P.L.J. (2007) No. 196 Pages 18–20
Author: Kate Andrews
Topic: The Rating (Empty Properties) Act 2007.

2.127 Forfeiture – and its future?
Publication: Property Law Journal P.L.J. (2007) No. 196 Pages 22–24
Author: Jeremy Steele
Topic: The law on forfeiture in the light of the Law Commission proposals for reform.

2.128 The local authority as applicant for the modification or discharge of a restrictive covenant
Publication: Journal of Planning & Environment Law J.P.L. (2007) November Pages 1564–1569
Author: Clive Moys
Topic: The situations in which a local authority may seek to discharge or modify a restrictive covenant over land which it owns.

2.129 There's no need to go the whole hog
Publication: Estates Gazette E.G. (2007) No. 1740 Page 267
Author: Sandi Murdoch
Topic: Whether, where a tenant was in breach of repair covenants, it was reasonable of the landlord to replace the whole roof and charge the tenant for the cost of doing so, or whether a patch repair would have been sufficient to achieve the required standard of repair.

2.130 What's exceptional?
Publication: New Law Journal N.L.J. (2007) Vol. 157 No. 7291 Pages 1374–1375
Author: Sarah Greer
Topic: The factors which the court needs to consider when deciding whether to grant an application for the sale of a property where the owner becomes bankrupt.

2.131 Developers need a nudge in the right direction
Publication: Estates Gazette E.G. (2007) No. 0742 Page 292
Author: Guy Fetherstonhaugh
Topic: The reasons why commonhold has had limited success and the proposals for a government consultation aimed at improving take-up.

2.132 Dedication and vigilance
Publication: Property Law Journal P.L.J. (2007) No. 197 Pages 17–20
Authors: Sarah Wex and Matthew Stokes
Topic: The House of Lords decision in *R. (on the application of Godmanchester Town Council) v Secretary of State for the Environment, Food and Rural Affairs* on the steps a landowner must take to prevent public right of ways being created over their land under section 31 of the Highways Act 1980.

2.133 Beneficial entitlement after Stack
Publication: Property Law Journal P.L.J. (2007) No. 197 Pages 22–24
Author: Mark Pawlowski
Topic: A review of the approach adopted in *Stack v Dowden* to determination of beneficial interests in a property purchased in the joint names of cohabitees.

2.134 The never-ending story – co-ownership after Stack v Dowden
Publication: Conveyancer and Property Lawyer Conv. (2007) September/October Pages 456–461
Author: Martin Dixon
Topic: Cases decided since the House of Lords judgment in *Stack v Dowden* involving a dispute about beneficial ownership of a home shared, or jointly owned, by the parties.

2.135 A risky environment
Publication: New Law Journal N.L.J. (2007) Vol. 157 No. 7294 Page 1499
Author: James Sherwood Rogers
Topic: The lack of information on environmental risks when acting for a buyer.

2.136 The law's an apse
Publication: New Law Journal N.L.J. (2007) Vol. 157 No. 7294 Pages 1500–1501
Author: James Naylor
Topic: The abolition of chancel repair liability.

2.137 Cohabitants and joint ownership: the implications of Stack v Dowden
Publication: Family Law Fam. Law (2007) No. 37 October Pages 924–929
Author: Rebecca Probert
Topic: The House of Lords decision in *Stack v Dowden* on joint ownership of property by cohabiting couples.

2.138 Bankruptcy and the family home: Part 1
Publication: Insolvency Law & Practice I.L. & P. (2007) Vol. 23 No. 5 Pages 141–145
Author: Philippa Daniels
Topic: Case law on the competing interests of a bankrupt's family and the trustees in bankruptcy in respect of the bankrupt's family home.

2.139 A balancing act
Publication: Property Law Journal P.L.J. (2007) No. 198 Pages 10–14
Author: Trevor Ivory and Paul Maile
Topic: New development and adequate flood protection measures.

2.140 What's my option?
Publication: Taxation Tax. (2007) Vol. 160 No. 4131 Pages 476–479
Author: Neil Warren
Topic: The option to tax supplies of commercial property for VAT purposes.

2.141 A shadow of doubt
Publication: Estates Gazette E.G. (2007) No. 0744 Pages 176–177
Author: Keith Shaw
Topic: The law on the award of damages in lieu of an injunction for breach of covenant.

2.142 A not so long-lived enjoyment
Publication: Estates Gazette E.G. (2007) No. 0744 Page 179
Author: Sandi Murdoch
Topic: The Chancery Division ruling in *RHJ Ltd v FT Patten (Holdings) Ltd* on whether a reservation in a lease providing a landlord with a right to build on adjoining land prevented a property owner from acquiring a right to light under the Prescription Act 1832.

2.143 E-conveyancing – what comes next?
Publication: Solicitors Journal S.J. (2007) Vol. 151 No. 41 Pages 1380, 1382
Author: Janet Baker
Topic: Forthcoming changes for conveyancers as a result of e-conveyancing.

2.144 SDLT and developments
Publication: Tax Journal Tax J. (2007) No. 909 Pages 9–10
Author: Alison Morris
Topic: The application of Stamp Duty Land Tax to land development transactions.

2.145 Prescribing the course of action
Publication: Estates Gazette E.G. (2007) No. 0745 Page 157
Author: Richard Webber
Topic: The meaning of 'best endeavours' and 'reasonable endeavours' in relation to contracts for the sale of land.

2.146 Keep out and stay off my land
Publication: Estates Gazette E.G. (2007) No. 0745 Page 160
Author: Allyson Colby
Topic: Applications to register land as town or village greens.

2.147 What's on paper is not always proof
Publication: Estates Gazette E.G. (2007) No. 0745 Page 161
Author: Sandi Murdoch
Topic: The Chancery Division ruling in *Derbyshire CC v Fallon* on whether an adjudicator had been wrong to conclude that the land register should not be altered where it had been established that the boundary indicated on the filed plan was inaccurate.

2.148 An anomalous situation
Publication: Estates Gazette E.G. (2007) No. 0746 Page 169
Author: Robert Highmore and Tony Beswetherick
Topic: Changes to the law relating to squatters introduced by the Land Registration Act 2002.

2.149 The answer lies in the wording
Publication: Estates Gazette E.G. (2007) No. 0746 Page 175
Author: Sandi Murdoch

Topic: The Chancery Division ruling in *City Inn (Jersey) Ltd v Ten Trinity Square Ltd* on whether a restrictive covenant benefiting the transferor's neighbouring properties, which required consent to be obtained from the transferor before alterations or additions to the property were carried out, extended to the transferor's successors in title.

2.150 The personal touch
Publication: Law Society's Gazette L.S.G. (2007) Vol. 104 No. 45 Page 12
Author: Fiona Hoyle
Topic: Solicitors' requirements in relation to personal local searches.

2.151 Further modernisation
Publication: Property Law Journal P.L.J. (2007) No. 199 Pages 14–17
Author: David Shakesby
Topic: Changes to the law on the management of commons and village greens introduced under the Commons Act 2006 on 1 October 2007.

2.152 Side road orders: new private means of access – problems of maintenance
Publication: Journal of Planning & Environment Law J.P.L. (2007) December Pages 1661–1664
Author: Michael Orlik
Topic: The legal issues associated with the use of side road orders to stop up a minor road under the Highways Act 1980 and substitute a private means of access to premises previously enjoying direct access to a highway.

2.153 SDLT: property development issues
Publication: Tax Journal Tax J. (2007) No. 911 Pages 13–15
Author: Roger Thomas
Topic: The application of Stamp Duty Land Tax to land development transactions.

2.154 Issues to be reckoned with
Publication: Estates Gazette E.G. (2007) No. 0747 Pages 164–165
Author: Peta Dollar

Topic: An overview of the ways in which rents due before and after completion of a sale of commercial leasehold property can be apportioned between buyer and seller.

2.155 Time to ease out a thorn in the developer's side
Publication: Estates Gazette E.G. (2007) No. 0747 Page 166
Author: Guy Fetherstonhaugh
Topic: The need for a reform of the law of easements.

2.156 Following the line of liabilities
Publication: Estates Gazette E.G. (2007) No. 0747 Page 167
Author: Sandi Murdoch
Topic: The Court of Appeal ruling in *Lyndendown Ltd v Vitamol Ltd* on the appropriate level of damages for a tenant's breach of a repairing covenant under section 18 of the Landlord and Tenant Act 1927.

2.157 Can HIPs save the planet?
Publication: New Law Journal N.L.J. (2007) Vol. 157 No. 7298 Pages 1634–1635
Author: David Marsden
Topic: The impact home information packs on the conveyancing market.

2.158 HIPs: the first 100 days
Publication: Solicitors Journal S.J. (2007) Vol. 151 No. 46 Pages 1554, 1556
Author: Fiona Barron
Topic: The impact of home information packs 100 days after their introduction.

2.159 This is not your land
Publication: Solicitors Journal S.J. (2007) Vol. 151 No. 46 Pages 1562–1563
Authors: Jonathan Steinert and Abigail Cohen
Topic: The Chancery Division ruling in *Anderson Antiques (UK) Ltd v Anderson Wharf (Hull) Ltd* on the liability for the improper entry of unilateral notices.

2.160 Not for the back burner
Publication: Estates Gazette E.G. (2007) No. 0749 Pages 98–99
Author: Peta Dollar

Topic: An overview of boilerplate clauses under contracts for the sale and purchase of commercial property.

2.161 There's something in the air
Publication: Estates Gazette E.G. (2007) No. 0750 Page 102
Author: Sukhi Rai (Wragge & Co LLP)
Topic: The legal and practical considerations for developers wishing to build into the airspace.

2.162 Damage limitation
Publication: Estates Gazette E.G. (2007) No. 0750 Pages 104–105
Authors: Ian Dias and Jason Hunter
Topic: The advantages and disadvantages of incorporating schedules of condition into leases.

2.163 The performance of a lifetime on the cards?
Publication: Solicitors Journal S.J. (2007) Vol. 151 No. 47 Pages 12, 14, 16
Author: Sandra Banks
Topic: The need for commercial buildings that are being sold or rented out to display an energy certificate.

2.164 Property interest in a burial plot
Publication: Conveyancer and Property Lawyer Conv. (2007) November/December Pages 517–543
Author: Remigus N. Nwabueze
Topic: The different approaches to the issue of the existence of proprietary rights in burial plots.

2.165 The tip of the iceberg
Publication: Property Law Journal P.L.J. (2007) No. 201 Pages 5–7
Author: Robert Adam
Topic: The Energy Performance of Buildings (Certificates and Inspections) (England and Wales) Regulations 2007.

2.166 Death, severance and survivorship
Publication: Family Law Fam. Law (2007) No. 37 December Pages 1082–1088
Author: John Wilson
Topic: Issues arising in relation to severance, survivorship and beneficial joint tenancies.

2.167 Who owns what?
Publication: Solicitors Journal S.J. (2008) Vol. 152 No. 1 Pages 8–9
Authors: Andrew Davies and Sue Haylock
Topic: The property rights of cohabiting couples on the breakdown of their relationship.

2.168 Don't get carried away
Publication: Estates Gazette E.G. (2008) No. 0801 Pages 130–131
Author: Lisa Bevan
Topic: An overview of lockout agreements used in the sale of residential properties.

2.169 A dearth of judicial guidance put right
Publication: Estates Gazette E.G. (2008) No. 0801 Page 133
Author: Sandi Murdoch
Topic: The Court of Appeal ruling in *Lawntown Ltd v Camenzuli* giving guidance on applications to the county courts for discharge or modification of restrictive covenants under section 610 of the Housing Act 1985 so that a single dwellinghouse can be converted into two or more dwellings where planning permission has been obtained.

2.170 Playing the chance card
Publication: Taxation Tax. (2008) Vol. 161 No. 4141 Pages 60–63
Author: Keith Gordon
Topic: Whether a taxpayer with two residences, who intends to sell one of them, can elect to qualify for main residence relief from capital gains tax if the two-year time limit has expired.

2.171 Check out the vicinity
Publication: Estates Gazette E.G. (2008) No. 0803 Pages 170–171
Authors: Roger Cohen and Jonathan Seitler
Topic: The importance for developers of being able to identify to whom obligations may be owed in respect of neighbouring land.

2.172 Illuminating times ahead if change can be embraced
Publication: Estates Gazette E.G. (2008) No. 0803 Page 176
Author: Guy Fetherstonhaugh
Topic: The repeal of section 3 of the Prescription Act 1832.

2.173 Not a question of gain, but of loss
Publication: Estates Gazette E.G. (2008) No. 0803 Page 177
Author: Sandi Murdoch
Topic: The Court of Appeal ruling in *Winter v Traditional & Contemporary Contracts Ltd* on the grounds on which compensation for the modification of restrictive covenants could be ordered.

2.174 Return to seller
Publication: Property Law Journal P.L.J. (2007) No. 202 Pages 8–10
Author: Simon East
Topic: The Chancery Division ruling in *Aribisala v St James Homes (Grosvenor Dock) Ltd* and the repayment of a deposit made under a contract for the sale of land.

2.175 Car-parking rights re-evaluated
Publication: Property Law Journal P.L.J. (2007) No. 202 Pages 17–20
Author: Sarah Allen
Topic: The House of Lords ruling in the Scottish case of *Moncrieff v Jamieson* on whether a servitude right of access to the dominant tenement included an implied right to park on the servient land.

2.176 A potentially burdensome risk
Publication: Estates Gazette E.G. (2008) No. 0804 Page 163
Author: Teresa Edmund
Topic: The Court of Appeal decision in *Scottish & Newcastle Plc v Raguz (No. 3)* on the circumstances in which a landlord is required to serve notices under section 17 of the Landlord and Tenant (Covenants) Act 1995.

2.177 Intention, fairness and the presumption of resulting trust after Stack v Dowden
Publication: Modern Law Review M.L.R. (2008) Vol. 71 No. 1 Pages 120-131
Author: Nick Piska
Topic: The House of Lords ruling in *Stack v Dowden* on the the determination of cohabitees' beneficial interests in the jointly owned former family home where there was no express declaration of their beneficial interests at the time the property was purchased.

2.178 A tale from north of the border
Publication: Estates Gazette E.G. (2008) No. 0805 Page 165
Author: Sandi Murdoch
Topic: The House of Lords ruling in the Scottish case of *Moncrieff v Jamieson*.

2.179 Don't be a village idiot
Publication: Property Law Journal P.L.J. (2008) No. 203 Pages 16–18
Authors: Francis Giacon and Jane Dockeray
Topic: The grounds on which an application to register land as a village green will satisfy the requirements of the Commons Act 2006.

2.180 Whose consent is required?
Publication: Property Law Journal P.L.J. (2008) No. 203 Pages 19–21
Author: Jayne Elkins
Topic: The Chancery Division ruling in *City Inn (Jersey) Ltd v Ten Trinity Square Ltd* and the Queen's Bench Division judgment in *Mahon v Sims* on the persons from whom consent must be obtained where a restrictive covenant prevents works from being carried out without approval.

2.181 Picking up the pieces
Publication: Law Society's Gazette L.S.G. (2008) Vol. 105 No. 06 Pages 23–24
Author: Catherine Baksi
Topic: The potential delays in the conveyancing process resulting from home information pack requirements on inclusion of documentation.

2.182 Ultimate Leisure Ltd v Tindle
Publication: Landlord & Tenant Review L. & T. Review (2007) Vol. 12 No. 1 Pages 13–15
Author: Peter Dodge
Topic: The Court of Appeal decision in *Ultimate Leisure Ltd v Tindle* and option agreements.

2.183 Parking lots
Publication: New Law Journal N.L.J. (2008) Vol. 158 No. 7308 Page 239
Author: Alec Samuels

Topic: Whether a right to park on a servient tenement existed as an easement where the dominant tenement had a right of way through the servient land.

2.184 No place like (a second) home
Publication: New Law Journal N.L.J. (2008) Vol. 158 No. 7308 Page 251
Author: Michael Waterworth
Topic: Capital gains tax planning for owners of more than one home.

2.185 Once a house, always a house?
Publication: Solicitors Journal S.J. (2008) Vol. 152 No. 7 Pages 18, 20
Author: Damian Greenish
Topic: The House of Lords ruling in *Boss Holdings Ltd v Grosvenor West End Properties Ltd* on whether a property was a 'house' that was 'designed or adapted for living in' within the meaning of the Leasehold Reform Act 1967.

2.186 A question of design
Publication: Estates Gazette E.G. (2008) No. 0807 Pages 136–137
Author: David Conway
Topic: The House of Lords ruling in *Boss Holdings Ltd v Grosvenor West End Properties Ltd* on the right to enfranchise under the Leasehold Reform Act 1967.

2.187 When in doubt, play it safe with deeds of variation
Publication: Estates Gazette E.G. (2008) No. 0807 Page 140
Author: Guy Fetherstonhaugh
Topic: The difficulties which can occur where a property transaction is effected but is not registered at the Land Registry.

2.188 Can I have my money back?
Publication: Property Law Journal P.L.J. (2008) No. 204 Pages 2–4
Authors: Craig Bowes and Keith Shaw
Topic: The Chancery Division ruling in *Midill (97PL) Ltd v Park Lane Estates Ltd* on whether it was appropriate for the court to order the return of a deposit under section 49(2) of the Law of Property Act 1925.

3 WEBSITES

3.1 PARLIAMENT

3.1.1 www.parliament.uk
UK Parliamentary site

3.1.2 www.parliament.uk/about_commons/about_commons.cfm
House of Commons

3.1.3 www.parliament.uk/about_lords/about_lords.cfm
House of Lords

3.2 LEGISLATION

3.2.1 www.hmso.gov.uk/acts.htm
UK Acts of Parliament

3.2.2. www.hmso.gov.uk/stat.htm
UK Statutory Instruments

3.2.3 www.hmso.gov.uk
HM Stationery Office

3.3 GOVERNMENT DEPARTMENTS

3.3.1 www.direct.gov.uk
Website of the UK Government

3.3.2 www.homeoffice.gov.uk
Home Office

3.3.3 www.hmrc.gov.uk
HM Revenue & Customs

3.3.4 www.hmrc.gov.uk/so/index.htm
Stamp Taxes

3.3.5 www.dca.gov.uk
Department for Constitutional Affairs

3.3.6 www.insolvency.gov.uk
The Insolvency Service

3.3.7 www.treasury.gov.uk
HM Treasury

8.3.8 **www.communities.gov.uk**
Department of Communities and Local Government

8.3.9 **www.defra.gov.uk**
Department for Environment Food and Rural Affairs

8.3.10 **www.charity-commission.gov.uk**
The Charity Commission

8.3.11 **www.lawcom.gov.uk**
The Law Commission

8.3.12 **www.courtservice.gov.uk**
The Court Service

8.3.13 **www.officialsolicitor.gov.uk**
Official Solicitor

8.3.14 **www.berr.gov.uk**
Department for Business, Enterprise and Regulatory Reform

8.3.15 **www.homeinformationpack.gov.uk**
The Government's Home Information Pack website

8.4 **LAND REGISTRATION**

8.4.1 **www.landreg.gov.uk**
HM Land Registry

8.4.2 **www.landreg.gov.uk/e-conveyancing**
HM Land Registry's e-conveyancing website

8.4.3 **www.landreg.gov.uk/legislation**
HM Land Registry's Land Registration Act website

8.4.4 **www.landregistrydirect.gov.uk**
Land Registry Direct

8.4.5 **www.landregisteronline.gov.uk**
Online service aimed at the general public.

8.4.6 **www.landregistry.gov.uk/strategy**
HM Land Registry strategy

8.5 **PUBLISHERS**

8.5.1 **www.oup.co.uk/law**
Oxford University Press

3.5.2 www.cavendishpublishing.com
Routledge-Cavendish

3.5.3 www.butterworths.com
Butterworths

3.5.4 www.smlawpub.co.uk
Sweet & Maxwell

3.5.5 www.shaws.co.uk
Shaw & Sons Ltd

3.5.6 www.jordans.co.uk
Jordans

3.6 ONLINE LEGAL RESEARCH SERVICES

3.6.1 www.butterworths.com
Butterworths LexisNexis Direct

3.6.2 www.westlaw.co.uk
Westlaw

3.6.3 www.bailii.org
British and Irish Legal Information Institute

3.6.4 www.justis.com
Justis

3.6.5 www.lawtel.com
Lawtel

3.6.6 www.egi.co.uk
Estates Gazette EGi

3.6.7 www.icclaw.com
The International Centre for Commercial Law

3.6.8 www.propertylawuk.net
Property Law website

3.7 PROFESSIONAL BODIES

3.7.1 www.lawsociety.org.uk
The Law Society

3.7.2 www.cml.org.uk
Council of Mortgage Lenders

3.7.3 www.rics.org.uk
Royal Institution of Chartered Surveyors

3.7.4 www.conveyancers.org.uk
The Society of Licensed Conveyancers

3.7.5 www.theclc.gov.uk
The Council of Licensed Conveyancers

3.7.6 www.bpf.propertymall.com
British Property Federation

3.7.7 www.nhbc.co.uk
NHBC

3.7.8 www.sava.org.uk
Independent standard setting body for property practitioners

3.7.9 www.legalcomplaints.org.uk
Legal Complaints Service

3.7.10 www.sra.org.uk
Solicitors Regulation Authority

3.7.11 www.olso.org
Legal Services Ombudsman

3.7.12 www.olscc.gov.uk
Office of the Legal Services Complaints Commissioner

3.8   LEGAL PORTALS

3.8.1 www.venables.co.uk
Legal resources pages

3.8.2 www.infolaw.co.uk
UK legal gateway site

3.8.3 www.online-law.co.uk
Online law

3.8.4 www.lawontheweb.co.uk
Legal resources

3.9   CONVEYANCING SEARCHES AND ENQUIRIES

3.9.1 www.homecheck.co.uk
Free report service for buyers

3.9.2 www.nlis.org.uk
National Land Information Service

3.9.3 www.searchflow.co.uk; www.tmsearch.co.uk; www. jordansproperty.co.uk
The licence holders providing access to the NLIS hub.

3.9.4 www.coal.gov.uk
Coal Authority

3.9.5 www.countrywidelegal.co.uk
Countrywide Legal Indemnities

3.9.6 www.home-envirosearch.com
Envirosearch

3.9.7 www.landmarkinfo.co.uk
Landmark Information Group

3.9.8 www.drainageandwater.co.uk
Drainage & Water searches

3.9.9 property.practicallaw.com/0-103-2123
Commercial Property Standard Enquiries

3.9.10 www.nwpropertysolutions.co.uk
Northumbrian Water

3.9.11 www.safe-move.co.uk
Yorkshire Water

3.9.12 www.geodesys.com
Anglian Water

3.9.13 www.severntrentsearches.com
Severn Trent Water

3.9.14 www.twpropertyinsight.co.uk
Thames Water

3.9.15 www.southernwater.co.uk
Southern Water

3.9.16 www.wessexwater.co.uk
Wessex Water

3.9.17 www.swwater.co.uk
South West Water

3.9.18 www.unitedutilities.com
United Utilities

3.9.19 www.dwrcymru.com
Welsh Water

3.9.20 www.stlgroup.co.uk
ChancelCheck

3.9.21 www.crasearches.co.uk
Conveyancing Report Agency

3.9.22 www.onesearchdirect.co.uk
Onesearch Direct

3.9.23 www.psgonline.co.uk
Property Search Group

3.10 MISCELLANEOUS

3.10.1 www.timesonline.co.uk
The Times

3.10.2 www.streetmap.co.uk
UK street maps

3.10.3 www.commercialleasecodeew.co.uk
Code of Practice for Commercial Leases

3.10.4 www.splintacampaign.co.uk
SPLINTA (Sellers' Pack Law Is Not The Answer)

3.10.5 www.solicitors-online.com
Law Society's Directory

3.10.6 www.lawgazette.co.uk
Law Society's Gazette

3.10.7 webjcli.ncl.ac.uk
Web Journal of Current Legal Issues

3.10.8 www.lease-advice.org
The Leasehold Advisory Service

3.10.9   **www.thelawyer.co.uk**
The Lawyer

3.10.10   **www.planningadvice.co.uk**
Free planning law service

3.10.11   **www.shelter.org.uk**
Shelter

3.10.12   **www.nfrl.org.uk**
National Federation of Residential Landlords

3.10.13   **www.landlordlaw.co.uk**
Information and resources for landlords and tenants

3.10.14   **www.lease-advice.org**
The Leasehold Advisory Service

3.10.15   **www.planningportal.gov.uk**
The planning portal

3.10.16   **www.copso.org.uk**
The Council of Property Search Organisations

3.10.17   **www.pla.org.uk**
Property Litigation Association

3.10.18   **www.thedisputeservice.co.uk**
The Tenancy Deposit Scheme

3.10.19   **www.mydeposits.co.uk**
Tenancy Deposit Solutions

3.10.20   **www.depositprotection.com**
The Deposit Protection Service

3.10.21   **www.landstribunal.gov.uk**
Lands Tribunal

3.10.22   **www.hipag.co.uk**
HIPAG – The Independent HIP Group

4 LAND REGISTRATION RULES 2003 – TABLE OF LAND REGISTRY FORMS

HM Land Registry form Code	Form
ACD	Application for approval of a standard form of charge deed and allocation of official Land Registry reference
ADV1	Application for registration of a person in averse possession under Schedule 6 of the Land Registration Act 2002
ADV2	Application to be registered as a person to be notified of an application for adverse possession
AN1	Application to enter an agreed notice
AP1	Application to change the register
AS1	Assent of whole of registered title(s)
AS2	Assent of charge
AS3	Assent of part of registered title(s) by personal representative
CC	Entry of a note of consolidation of charges
CCD	Application to cancel a caution against dealings
CCT	Application to cancel a caution against dealings
CH1	Legal charge of a registered estate
CH2	Application to enter an obligation to make further advances
CH3	Application to note agreed maximum amount of security
CI	Certificate of inspection of title plan
CIT	Application in connection with court proceedings insolvency and tax liability
CM1	Application to register a freehold estate in commonhold land
CM2	Application for the freehold estate to cease to be registered as a freehold estate in commonhold land during the transitional period

CM3	Application for the registration of an amended commonhold community statement and/or altered memorandum and articles of association
CM4	Application to add land to a commonhold registration
CM5	Application for the termination of a commonhold registration
CM6	Application for the registration of a successor commonhold association
CN1	Application to cancel a notice (other than a unilateral notice)
COE	Notification of change of extent of a commonhold unit over which there is a registered charge
CON1	Consent to the registration of land as commonhold land
CON2	Consent to an application for the freehold estate to cease to be registered as a freehold estate in commonhold land during the transitional period
COV	Application for registration with unit-holders
CS	Continuation Sheet for use with application and disposal forms
CT1	Caution against first registration
DB	Application to determine the exact line of a boundary
DI	Disclosable overriding interests
DJP	Application to remove from the register the name of the deceased joint proprietor
DL	List of documents
DS1	Cancellation of entries relating to a charge
DS2	Application to cancel entries relating to a registered charge
DS2E	Application to cancel entries relating to a registered charge
DS3	Release of part of the land from a registered charge
EX1	Application for the registrar to designate a document as an exempt information document
EX1A	Reasons for exemption in support of an application to designate a document as an exempt information document

EX2	Application for official copy of an exempt information document
EX3	Application to remove the designation of a document as an exempt information document
FR1	First registration application
HC1	Application for copies of historical edition(s) of the register/title plan held in electronic form
ID1	Evidence of identity for a private individual
ID2	Evidence of identity for a corporate body
HR1	Application for registration of a notice of home rights
HR2	Application for renewal of registration in respect of home rights
HR3	Application by mortgagee for official search in respect of home rights
HR4	Cancellation of a home rights notice
ID1	Evidence of identity for a private individual
ID2	Evidence of identity for a corporate body
ID3	Evidence of identity. For use with Forms RP2 or FR1 only
K001	Application for registration of a Land Charge
K002	Application for registration of a Land Charge of Class F
K003	Application for registration of a Pending Action
K004	Application for registration of a Writ or Order
K005	Application for registration of a Deed of Arrangement
K006	Application for registration of a Priority Notice
K007	Application for the renewal of a registration
K008	Application for the renewal of a registration of a Land Charge of Class F
K009	Application for the rectification of an entry in the register
K010	Continuation of an application
K011	Application to cancel an entry in the Land Charges Register (other than class F)
K012	Application for cancellation of an entry in the register under special directions of The Registrar

K013	Application for cancellation of a Land Charge of Class F
K015	Application for an official search (Not applicable to registered land)
K016	Application for an official search (Bankruptcy Only)
K019	Application for an office copy of an entry in the register
K020	Application for a certificate of the cancellation of an entry in the register
K14	Declaration in support of an application for registration or rectification
NAP	Notice to the registrar in respect of an adverse possession application
OC1	Application for official copies of register/plan or certificate in Form CI
OC2	Application for official copies of documents only
OS1	Application by purchaser for official search without priority
OS2	Application by purchaser for official search without priority of part of land in a registered title or a pending first registration application
OS3	Application for official search without priority of the land in a registered title
PIC	Application for a personal inspection under s.66 of the Land Registration Act 2002
PN1	Application for a search in the index of Proprietor's name
PRD1	Request for missing documents
PRD2	Notice to produce a document s.75 of the Land Registration Act 2002 and the Land Registration Rules 2003
RD1	Request for the return of original documents
RX1	Application to enter a restriction
RX2	Application for an order that a restriction be disapplied or modified
RX3	Application to cancel a restriction
RX4	Application to withdraw a restriction

SC	Application for noting the overriding priority of a statutory charge
SIF	Application for an official search of the index of relating franchises and manors
SIM	Application for an official search of the index map
SR1	Notice of surrender of development right(s)
TP1	Transfer of part of registered titles
TP2	Transfer of part of registered title(s) under power of sale
TP3	Transfer of portfolio of titles
TR1	Transfer of whole of registered title
TR2	Transfer of whole of registered title(s) under power of sale
TR3	Transfer of Charge
TR4	Transfer of a portfolio of whole titles
TR5	Transfer of portfolio of whole titles
UN1	Application to enter a unilateral notice
UN2	Application to remove a unilateral notice
UN3	Application to be registered as beneficiary of an existing unilateral notice
UN4	Application for the cancellation of a unilateral notice
UT1	Application of upgrading of title
WCT	Application to withdraw a caution
LRf-AF1	Annotated forms (AN1, RX1, UN1)
Lease clauses	Prescribed clauses contained in Schedule 1A to the Land Registration Rules 2003

5   TABLE OF LAND REGISTRY PRACTICE GUIDES

LRPG001 First Registrations (01/11/2006)

LRPG002 First registration of title where deeds have been lost or destroyed (01/03/2003)

LRPG003 Cautions against first registration (01/10/2005)

LRPG004 Adverse possession of registered land under the new provisions of the Land Registration Act 2002 (01/03/2003)

LRPG041-S6 Developing estates – registration services: Supplement 6
    – Voluntary application to note overriding interests
    (01/03/2003)

LRPG042 Upgrading the class of title (01/11/2006)

LRPG043 Applications in connection with court proceedings,
    insolvency and tax liability (28/04/2006)

LRPG044 Fax facilities (01/03/2003)

LRPG045 Receiving and replying to notices by e-mail (01/10/2003)

LRPG046 Land Registry forms (01/12/2005)

LRPG047 Transfers of public housing estates (01/08/2003)

LRPG048 Implied covenants (01/10/2005)

LRPG049 Rejection of applicationsfor registration (01/12/2005)

LRPG050 Requisition and cancellation procedures (01/12/2005)

LRPG051 Areas served by Land Registry Offices (22/06/2007)

LRPG052 Easements claimed by prescription (01/10/2006)

LRPG053 Scheme Titles (01/03/2003)

LRPG054 Acquisition of land by general vesting declaration under
    the Compulsory Purchase (Vesting Declarations) Act 1981
    (01/04/2004)

LRPG055 Address for service (01/03/2003)

LRPG056 Formal apportionment and redemption of a rent or a
    rentcharge that affects a registered estate (01/04/2004)

LRPG057 Exempting documents from the general right to inspect
    and copy (07/08/2006)

LRPG058 Land Registry's Welsh Language Scheme – register format
    (01/06/2005)

LRPG059 Receiving and replying to requisitions by email
    (12/08/2004)

LRPG060 Commonhold (07/08/2006)

LRPG060 Commonhold – Addendum (30/08/2006)

LRPG061 Telephone Services (credit accountholders only)
    (09/08/2007)

LRPG062 Easements (01/03/2005)

6	**LAND REGISTRY OFFICES**

6.1   Land Registry Head Office
32 Lincoln's Inn Fields
London
WC2A 3PH
DX 1098 London/Chancery Lane WC2
Tel: 020 7917 8888
Fax: 020 7955 0110

6.2   Birkenhead (Old Market)
Old Market House
Hamilton Street
Birkenhead
Merseyside
CH41 5FL
Tel: 0151 473 1110
Fax: 0151 473 0251
DX 14300 Birkenhead (3)

6.3   Birkenhead (Rosebrae)
Rosebrae Court
Woodside Ferry Approach
Birkenhead
Merseyside
CH41 6DU
Tel: 0151 472 6666
Fax: 0151 472 6789
DX 24270 Birkenhead (4)

6.4 **Coventry**
Leigh Court
Torrington Avenue
Tile Hill
Coventry
CV4 9XZ
Tel: 024 7686 0860
Fax: 02476860021
DX 18900 Coventry (3)

6.5 **Croydon**
Trafalgar House
1 Bedford Park
Croydon
CR0 2AQ
Tel: 020 8781 9103
Fax: 020 8781 9110
DX 2699 Croydon (3)

6.6 **Durham (Southfield)**
Southfield House
Southfield Way
Durham
DH1 5TR
Tel: 0191 301 3500
Fax: 0191 301 0020
DX 60200 Durham (3)

6.7 **Durham (Boldon)**
Boldon House
Wheatlands Way
Pity Me
Durham
DH1 5GJ
Tel: 0191 301 2345
Fax: 0191 301 2300
DX 60860 Durham (6)

.8   Gloucester
Twyver House
Bruton Way
Gloucester
GL1 1DQ
Tel: 01452 511111
Fax: 01452510050
DX 7599 Gloucester (3)

.9   Harrow
Lyon House
Lyon Road
Harrow
Middlesex
HA1 2EU
Tel: 020 8235 1181
Fax: 020 8862 0176
DX 4299 Harrow (4)

.10   Kingston upon Hull
Earle House
Colonial Street
Hull
HU2 8JN
Tel: 01482 223244
Fax: 01482224278
DX 26700 Hull (4)

.11   Lancashire
Wrea Brook Court
Lytham Road
Warton
Lancashire
PR4 1TE
Tel: 01772 836700
Fax: 01772 836970
DX No: 721560 Lytham St Annes (6)

6.12 Leicester
Westbridge Place
Leicester
LE1 5DR
Tel: 0116 265 4000
Fax: 0116 265 4008
DX 11900 Leicester (5)

6.13 Lytham
Birkenhead House
East Beach
Lytham St Annes
FY8 5AB
Tel: 01253 849849
Fax: 01253 840001
DX 14500 Lytham St Annes (3)

6.14 Nottingham (East)
Robins Wood Road
Nottingham
NG8 3RQ
Tel: 0115 906 5353
Fax: 0115 936 0036
DX 716126 Nottingham (26)

6.15 Nottingham (West)
Chalfont Drive
Nottingham
NG8 3RN
Tel: 0115 935 1166
Fax: 0115 935 0038
DX 10298 Nottingham (3)

6.16 Peterborough
Touthill Close
City Road
Peterborough
PE1 1XN

Tel: 01733 288288
Fax: 01733 280022
DX 12598 Peterborough (4)

5.17 Plymouth
Plumer House
Tailyour Road
Crownhill
Plymouth
PL6 5HY
Tel: 01752 636000
Fax: 01752 636161
DX 8299 Plymouth (4)

5.18 Portsmouth
St Andrew's Court
St Michael's Road
Portsmouth
PO1 2JH
Tel: 023 9276 8888
Fax: 023 9276 8768
DX 83550 Portsmouth (2)

5.19 Stevenage
Brickdale House
Swingate
Stevenage
Herts
SG1 1XC
Tel: 01438 788888
Fax: 01438 785460
DX 6099 Stevenage (2)

5.20 Swansea
Ty Bryn Clas
High Street
Swansea
SA1 1PW

Tel: 01792458877
Fax: 01792 473236
DX 33700 Swansea (2)

6.21 Telford
Parkside Court
Hall Park Way
Telford
TF3 4LR
Tel: 01952 290355
Fax: 01952 290356
DX 28100 Telford (2)

6.22 Tunbridge Wells
Forest Court
Forest Road
Tunbridge Wells
Kent
TN2 5AQ
Tel: 01892510015
Fax: 01892 510032
DX 3999 Tunbridge Wells (2)

6.23 Wales
Ty Cwm Tawe
Phoenix Way
Llansamlet
Swansea
SA7 9FQ
Tel: 01792 355000
Fax: 01792 355055
DX 82800 Swansea (2)

6.24 Weymouth
Melcombe Court
1 Cumberland Drive
Weymouth
Dorset

DT4 9TT
Tel: 01305 363636
Fax: 01305 363646
DX 8799 Weymouth (2)

5.25 **York**
James House
James Street
York
YO10 3YZ
Tel: 01904 450000
Fax: 01904 450086
DX 61599 York (2)